365 DAYS OF grace

EXPERIENCING GOD'S GRACE
FROM GENESIS TO REVELATION

MARCIA FURROW

WESTBOW
PRESS
A DIVISION OF THOMAS NELSON
& ZONDERVAN

Unless otherwise indicated, all Scripture quotations are taken from the
Holy Bible, New Living Translation, copyright © 1996, 2004, 2007
by Tyndale House Foundation. Used by permission of Tyndale House
Publishers, Inc., Carol Stream, Illinois 60188. All rights reserved.

WestBow Press books may be ordered through booksellers or by contacting:

WestBow Press
A Division of Thomas Nelson & Zondervan
1663 Liberty Drive
Bloomington, IN 47403
www.westbowpress.com
1 (866) 928-1240

Because of the dynamic nature of the Internet, any web addresses or
links contained in this book may have changed since publication and
may no longer be valid. The views expressed in this work are solely those
of the author and do not necessarily reflect the views of the publisher,
and the publisher hereby disclaims any responsibility for them.

Any people depicted in stock imagery provided by Thinkstock are models,
and such images are being used for illustrative purposes only.
Certain stock imagery © Thinkstock.

ISBN: 978-1-5127-6272-3 (sc)
ISBN: 978-1-5127-6274-7 (hc)
ISBN: 978-1-5127-6273-0 (e)

Library of Congress Control Number: 2016918491

Print information available on the last page.

WestBow Press rev. date: 11/15/2016

Dedicated to the
Glory of God

"Grace"

Divine love and protection bestowed freely upon mankind.
The state of being protected or sanctified by the favor of God.
An excellence or power granted by God.
An unmerited gift from God.

"My grace is sufficient for you, for my power
is made perfect in weakness."
2 Corinthians 12:9

ACKNOWLEDGMENTS

This project would not have come to fruition without several people who came alongside me with encouragement and love.

I would like to acknowledge Lynn Webb for her gracious insights, attention to detail, and her diligence in keeping my boots pointed in the direction in which I needed to walk. Thank you for the hours you spent reading and editing, even as you travelled around the world.

I would like to acknowledge Kacie Feeney who so generously created the graphics for the title and for the Monthly Headings. Thank you for sharing the creativity with which God has gifted you.

I would like to acknowledge the many prayer partners who have lifted this project before the Throne of Grace for years— Susan, Donna, Christa, Sue, Bev, Gayla, Barb, Karie, Kelli, Sandy, Maggy, Martha, Becky, Betty and so many others—you know who you are!

I would like to acknowledge my family: my husband, Brian and my sons and daughters-in-law: Dan, Nikki, Bob and Jen. Thank you for never wavering in your prayers and support. It means the world to me.

INTRODUCTION

How can we describe the indescribable God? To say that he is merciful, just, holy, awesome, and wise is insufficient. If we were to list all of his attributes the words on the page cannot do him justice. He describes himself as "I Am." And he is. He is beautifully, wholly, and majestically all that he is!

The more I study God, his Word, and his character the more convinced I am that all of God's attributes are woven together beautifully and it is quite impossible to separate them: God acts perfectly perfect in all of his attributes all of the time. Therefore, I believe, grace is always present along with every other attribute of God. Is it, therefore, possible to single out a single attribute? That is what this book attempts to do: This book highlights grace.

God's grace is truly overwhelming to me—as I think about it, every one of his actions toward humanity are actions of grace. God doesn't have to do anything for, with, to, or through us; but he does. He is not indebted to us, he is not our hostage, and he owes us nothing. We are his creation, he can do with us as he wants, or not do anything with us at all. In whatever way and in whenever time he interacts with or intervenes in our lives, it is always an act of his divine grace. God is a gracious God.

I have undertaken to write a daily devotional highlighting God's grace. For the most part, the devotional follows a chronological reading pattern through the Bible. As you read the suggested passage at the top of each page, by the end of the year (in about 15-20 minutes a day) you will have read the entire Bible. I have to confess, some of the passages are not truly chronological—for example, the perfect chronological order for the passages on November 5, would be: Mark 15:42–47; Matthew 27:57–61; Luke 23:50–56; John 19:38–42; Matthew 27:62–66; Mark 16:1–8; Matthew 28:1–7; Luke 24:1–12; Mark 16:9–13; John 20:1–18; Matthew 28:8–15. For reading ease (and hopefully to avoid the frustration of flipping back and forth), I have listed them this way: Matthew 27:57–28:15; Mark 15:42–16:11; Luke 23:50–24:12; John 20:1–18.

From each day's reading, my goal is to highlight one moment where God's act of grace is clearly seen. On some days, there will be obvious and plentiful displays of God's grace and I will choose only one. On other days, another of God's attributes might overshadow his grace, however, I have done my best to reflect the grace that is there, rather than imposing an idea of grace upon Scripture.

The format for this devotional is best described as: What it says, what it means, and finally, what it means for you and for me. Each day's reading consists of a concise synopsis of a portion of the passage: what it says. Then there will be a suggested way to see the same act of grace in our world today: what it means. Finally, there will be an application: what it means for me and for you. Each day concludes with a prayer, which could be a starting gate for your own personal time with God.

If you choose to use it as such, this devotional could be a springboard for your personal journal. While I have suggested questions to guide you in applying God's grace to your own life, it is highly possible that God will take you into an entirely different direction. Trust him and ask him to show you his sufficient grace for you each day. Ask God to show you daily where he has been gracious to you and to those you love, and how you might be a conduit of his grace.

In addition, for those of you who desire going a little deeper, I have added supporting Scripture verses in the text for further study.

On those days when life is so busy that you only have time to read one thing, please forego this devotional and read the Scripture. God's Word should always be our guide into his grace and he will speak to you with infinitely more power than my words ever will.

ABOUT THE AUTHOR

Having grown up in the beautiful Smoky Mountains of Western North Carolina, my siblings and I spent many evenings listening to our parents and grandparents tell stories of moonshiners, bootleggers, and preachers (all relatives), hard days in tobacco fields and apple orchards, lean years, and bountiful years. Oh yes, we have the cherished "Southern Story-Telling Gene" in our family.

Not everyone inherits the storytelling gene, but I believe that I have. With my many years of teaching the Bible—fourteen of which was as a Teaching Leader for Bible Study Fellowship, International (BSF)— I have done my best to develop my inheritance.

Telling Bible stories and relating the application of Bible principles to everyday life is something I love to do. As a daughter, sister, mother, wife, grandmother, and friend I have experienced many aspects of life from which to draw to lovingly and respectfully teach the Bible so that my listeners embrace its truths.

Writing this devotional was a special challenge and joy for me. After having read the Bible through for many years, I sensed the Lord calling me to do more; so I decided in January 2012 to outline the daily passages. Why not? Doesn't everyone outline the entire Bible? About a week in, I wondered if perhaps I had misheard the Lord. Had I bit off more than I could chew? However, the Holy Spirit encouraged me to keep at it, so I did.

Very early on November 30, 2012, as I was praying and praising God for the blessings of perseverance, I asked God what I should do with all the work I had completed. And then I had one of those thoughts that you never think yourself—I'm sure you know what I mean—a thought that I was convinced had come directly from God. I sensed him telling me to write a 365-day devotional.

What?! My heart started pounding, my breathing increased, and my hands started to shake. There was no way I could do something like that! And, I couldn't—apart from God I can do no good thing. However, I also sensed God saying to me, "I will carry you through." I couldn't possibly pass up this opportunity to see God at work in my life.

As I began the initial draft of this devotional in June, 2013, God took me on a walk down a path that led right smack through the Valley of the Shadow of Death: my precious dad moved into his Father's house in heaven. It seems odd that my favorite storyteller will not tell the story of how his daughter wrote a devotional.

So, that is the story of how this little devotional came to be. I hope that it will bless your life as you use it to lead you into the glory and majesty of Almighty God, the God who works miracles—this book is one of them.

And, for the more formal biographical information: In 1975, when I was a freshman at Judson College in Elgin, Illinois, I met the love of my life, Brian Furrow, and married him shortly after we graduated. Brian's various work assignments moved us from Illinois to Ohio, Minnesota, Wisconsin, Indiana, Missouri, and back to Illinois—which is where we lived until we decided to give Texas a try in 2014.

During our time in various communities I have held a number of jobs and roles. I've been a chair-side dental assistant, an advertising designer, a reading tutor, a room mom, PTA representative, teacher's assistant, substitute teacher K-12, and mentor to teen moms. As my dad would say, "I'm a jack of all trades, and master of none."

The most consistent role I've had over the years is as a BSF volunteer, I've served as a Children's Leader, Group Leader, Children's Supervisor, and Teaching Leader. I've also taught Sunday School and Vacation Bible School.

Recently I've enjoyed leading Christian women's events (retreats and conferences), and speaking at MOMS and MOPS meetings. Finally, I am currently serving as the Spiritual Advisor for Teen Mother Choices, International (TMCI).

Most importantly, Brian and I have two sons: Dan, who lives in England with his wife, Nikki, their three children, Jacob, Matthew, and Stella; and Bob, who lives in Texas with his wife, Jen and their son, Cal. Our lives are blessed beyond measure.

grace
JANUARY

JANUARY 1

Genesis 1:1–3:24

Toward evening they heard the LORD God walking about
in the garden, so they hid themselves among the trees.
The LORD God called to Adam, "Where are you?"
—Genesis 3:8–9

God created the world and everything in it and declared it good. Adam and Eve sin and use fig leaves to hide themselves and their shame from each other. God knows they are hiding from him. God still desires to be with them.

How gracious of God to give them an opportunity to come to him by asking, "Where are you?" Though they don't deserve his friendship, God still desires a relationship with them.

Only God can cover the guilt and shame of sin so that we might have a relationship with him. He does this through the blood of Jesus, which was shed for you and for me. In 1 John 1:9 we read that when we confess our sins, he is faithful to forgive our sins and cleanse us from all unrighteousness.

God graciously desires a personal relationship with us. He continually seeks us. He wants to uncover that which we are hiding. He is slow to anger, forgiving every sin and rebellion.

It is said, "Man is not what he thinks he is; he is what he hides." Is there guilt or shame that you are trying to hide from God? Will you expose them to God? Will you make a specific list? Will you begin this year walking unashamedly with God?

> God, I am afraid so I hide. Remind me that you already know everything about me. Humble me to confess what you see and have brought to my attention. Cleanse me by your grace through the blood of Jesus so that I might stand without shame in your presence.

JANUARY 2

Genesis 4:1–6:22; 1 Chronicles 1:1–4

"Why are you so angry?" the LORD asked him. "Why do you look
so dejected? You will be accepted if you respond in the right way."
—Genesis 4:6–7a

Both Cain and Abel bring offerings to God. God accepts Abel's
offering but rejects Cain's. God explains to Cain that a right heart
attitude is necessary in order to be accepted by God. God warns
Cain that sin is waiting to destroy him! Cain murders Abel.

How gracious of God to teach Cain that God is more concerned
with the status of the heart than the type of offerings laid before him.

Offerings are not about trying to please God or earn his favor.
Offerings are gifts of gratitude for what God has already done and
are brought before God with a heart that is humble and contrite;
these God will not despise (Psalm 51:16–17). Sin causes us to think
that we are sufficient in ourselves and that any gift we bring must
be accepted by God.

Sin is waiting to devour us. It is waiting to corrupt our hearts
in an ongoing battle. We can never fully subdue sin in our lives, but
isn't it wonderful to know that Jesus's death on the cross has broken
the power of sin in us?

Will you ask God to reveal the attitude of your heart as you
bring all your gifts to him each day?

> God, I thank you for saving me and breaking the hold that
> sin has over me. Thank you that when I repent of all my sins
> you purify my heart and I can give you the gifts that you
> deserve. Help me to fight sin and self-sufficiency in my life
> through the power of the resurrected Jesus.

JANUARY 3

Genesis 7–10, 1 Chronicles 1:5–23

The LORD said to Noah, "Go into the boat with
all your family ... One week from today I will
begin forty days and forty nights of rain."
—Genesis 7:1a, 4b

For one hundred and twenty years, Noah builds the ark and preaches that the Lord will destroy the earth. For one week, Noah and his family live in the ark with the animals while the door is open. People see the ark and hear Noah's message. The Lord shuts in Noah's family and the animals and shuts out everyone else.

Graciously, the Lord is long-suffering and patient. He waits to give everyone the opportunity to repent and come to him for salvation.

Anyone could have chosen to believe Noah and enter the ark until the Lord shut the doors and it was too late. The Lord knows when it is time to close the door.

Each one of us must make the decision to believe the truth. Are you living in the ark of God's salvation, or are you being swept along in the current of the culture? Who do you know that needs to hear the truth? Have you told them that Jesus is the only way to God (John 14:6)? The time is short. Today is the day of salvation! Only the Lord knows when the door will be closed.

> God, I want to live in the ark of your safety and salvation. I choose today to accept the truth that I cannot save myself. I know that apart from you, I will be destroyed in the flood of sinful living. I believe that the work Jesus accomplished on the cross when he died in my place is sufficient to save me, and I ask him to enter my being, take over my life, and save me from destruction.

JANUARY 4

Genesis 11–14; 1 Chronicles 1:24–27

The LORD scattered them all over the earth.
—Genesis 11:8a

The flood ends, and God commands the descendants of Noah to multiply and fill the earth. They migrate eastward and settle in Babylonia. They build a city with a high tower. The Tower of Babel is a monument to their greatness to bring themselves together and keep them from scattering all over the world.

How gracious of God to protect people from themselves. By confusing their language and scattering them over the earth, God accomplished the very action he had commanded them to do.

The inherent bent of humanity toward disobedience and self-promotion was not washed away in the flood; it lingers today. The Lord doesn't tolerate our sinful choices any more than he did in Noah's day. He sometimes acts to separate us from those who influence us toward disobedience while simultaneously giving us an opportunity to walk in obedience.

It may seem harsh to have to endure God's discipline, especially when it separates us from the familiar, but isn't it worth it if it prompts our obedience?

How is God acting to separate you from sin and sinful influences? Is he prompting you to move out of an area or situation that tempts you to focus on yourself and promote your greatness rather than focusing on obedience to him?

> God, it is so hard to stand up against the crowd, to swim against the cultural current. My focus is too often on what others say or what I think will make me look or feel great. I want to live for you and focus on your greatness. Teach me how to tune my ear to hear your command, and embolden me to act in obedience immediately.

JANUARY 5

Genesis 15–18

The angel of the LORD found Hagar beside a
desert spring along the road to Shur.
—Genesis 16:7

Sarai (Sarah) can't conceive a child, so she gives her maid, Hagar, to sleep with Abram (Abraham). Hagar conceives. Hagar treats Sarai with contempt. Sarai blames Abram. Abram tells Sarai to do with Hagar as she sees fit. Sarai treats Hagar so harshly that Hagar runs away. The angel of the Lord finds her alone and pregnant by a stream. God tells her to go back and submit to Sarai.

How gracious of God to come to Hagar in her hopelessness and despair. He always knew where she was. Life was not easy for Hagar, and returning to Sarai and submitting to her would be very difficult. Hagar's courage and humility to obediently return testify to her faith in God.

God knows our heartache, pain, despair, misery, and helplessness. He knows how difficult the circumstances of our lives can be. He knows how hard it is to endure humiliation, abuse, and shame. He knows because he endured it on the cross for us.

Do you believe that God sees you in your difficulty? Do you believe that he is with you in your lowest moments? Do you trust him to lead you? Are you willing to do whatever he tells you, even if it means humbling yourself before others?

> God, I believe that you see me in my hurt, shame, distress, fear, pride, and humility. God, sometimes I don't feel like I deserve what is happening to me and I want to run away. But I know that you allow my circumstances for my good and your glory. Cause me to trust your providential hand and submit to your instruction wherever you find me.

JANUARY 6

Genesis 18:1–21:7

"Yes, I know you are innocent," God replied. "That is why I
kept you from sinning against me; I did not let you touch her."
—Genesis 20:6

Abraham and Sarah, traveling in the Negev, stop in a place that
Abraham believes is godless. Fearing for his life, Abraham deceives
Abimelech and introduces Sarah as his sister. Abimelech sends
for Sarah. God warns Abimelech in a dream not to touch Sarah.
Abimelech professes his innocence.

How gracious of God to mercifully protect his people from sin.
Acting in fear, Abraham placed not only Sarah in danger but also
the soul of Abimelech. God graciously stopped Abimelech. God
graciously protected Sarah. Moreover, by protecting Sarah, God
graciously protected the undisputed paternity of the child she will
eventually bear.

God is never far from his people, even when they are far from
him. When we act in fear, we reveal how far from God we are. When
we let fear lead us, we endanger others and ourselves. We have no
way of knowing how many times God has intervened in our lives to
protect us from sinning and others from sinning against us.

Do you find it humbling to think of whom you would be today
or who you could become if God allowed you to do everything you
were capable of doing? How indebted to his grace and mercy are you?

> My Gracious Protector, thank you for saving me for yourself,
> for watching over me, and for keeping me from becoming
> the wicked person I would be apart from you. *Amazing
> Grace, how sweet the sound that saved a wretch like me.*

JANUARY 7

Genesis 21:8–23:20, 11:32; 24:1–67

Then Abraham looked up and saw a ram caught by its horns in a
bush ... Abraham named the place, "The LORD Will Provide."
—Genesis 22:13a, 14a

Testing Abraham's faith and obedience, God calls Abraham to
sacrifice his son, Isaac. God promised Abraham offspring through
the line of Isaac. Isaac has no children yet. Abraham believes God
and believes in God's promise. He knows that somehow God will
provide and that he and the boy will both return alive. Trusting God,
Abraham walks up the mountain, and Isaac lies down on the altar.

How gracious of God to provide a substitute. At the exact
moment of sacrifice, when Abraham had gone as far as God would
allow him to go, God provided a substitute: a ram in the thicket.
Abraham proved both his faith and his obedience. God proved to
be true to his word.

How gracious of God to provide a substitute for you and for me:
the Lord Jesus Christ, who died in your place and mine as the Lamb
of God who takes away the sin of the world (John 1:29). Christ: the
one who died that we might live; Christ who bore the punishment
for our sin.

What most precious thing has God called you to sacrifice, to
give up, for him? Are you willing to surrender all for Jesus? Is there
anything more precious to you than he? Is this your test of faith and
obedience?

> Father, help me to understand and accept the truth that
> Jesus, as my substitute, died in my place and endured your
> just wrath on my behalf. Cause me to trust your provision
> and to let go of anything that is more precious to me than
> you are.

JANUARY 8

Genesis 25:1–26; 1 Chronicles 1:28–34

Now Abraham married again.
—Genesis 25:1a

Abraham's beloved wife—his partner in life, the woman who leaves home with him not knowing where they are going, the one who follows him as he follows God, and the mother of his son Isaac—dies. Abraham marries again.

How gracious of God to give Abraham another opportunity to share his life, and his God, with a spouse.

There are many tools that God uses in our lives to refine us, to shave off the rough edges, to cause us to seek him, to burn away the pride and self-focus, and to make us holy—and one of these tools is marriage. Marriage is a tool, it is not a goal, but it's not a tool for everyone. For some God uses singleness. God knows which tool is best for each person.

Not everyone who loses a spouse by death or divorce will remarry. However, if you have, will you covenant with God to love this person as God loves you?

If you are married, do you see your spouse as a gift from God? Or do you see your spouse as the one who should make you happy? Do you believe your marriage is a tool that God is using to refine you? How is God using your marriage to affect your holiness?

If you are single, how is God using your singleness to affect your holiness? Will you embrace your singleness as a tool in God's hand for as long as he chooses to use it?

> God, please help me to embrace my marital status as your tool of refinement. Help me to embrace my spouse or my singleness as a gift of your grace for my eternal good.

JANUARY 9

Genesis 25:27–28:5

Now a severe famine struck the land. The LORD
appeared to [Isaac] there and said, "Do not go to Egypt.
Stay here in this land. I will be with you and bless
you … just as I solemnly promised Abraham."
—Genesis 26:1a, 2–3

As in Abraham's day, a famine strikes. Isaac, as his father before him
did, moves to Gerar. God appears telling him to stay where he is and
not go to Egypt. God restates the promise he made to Abraham then
promises Isaac that if he stays in the land, the promises will be his.

How gracious of God to have a unique plan for Isaac, and to
lead him with clarity.

The promises are the same, but the plan is different. Abraham
had to learn to follow God, so must Isaac. Isaac's relationship must
be with God directly, not as an appendage through Abraham. God
deals with each generation individually.

Each one of us must choose to come into a personal relationship
with God as individuals and when we do, he has a perfect and
unique plan for us. What we see God doing in the life of someone
else is probably not what he will do in ours. And his direction and
guidance in our past may be different in our future.

In your current set of circumstances, do you try to follow or
perhaps mimic what others have done that makes sense or that
brought them success? Or do you directly seek God's insights and
direction for yourself?

God Almighty, cause me to seek your will and your way every
day. Keep me from choosing paths that lead me out of your
will. Teach me to trust you to direct my path with clarity.

JANUARY 10

Genesis 28:6–30:24

At the top of the stairway stood the LORD, and he
said, "I am the LORD. What's more, I will be with
you, and I will protect you wherever you go."
—Genesis 28:13a. 15a

Jacob believes God. He believes there is a birthright. He believes the promises given to Abraham and Isaac. He believes the promises are worth obtaining. Yet, he schemes and deceives to appropriate the promises. Esau wants to kill Jacob. Jacob leaves home to save his life.

How gracious of God to use imperfect people to accomplish his perfect plan.

The Almighty Holy God assures Jacob, a runaway and deceiving fugitive, that Jacob is not now nor will he ever be alone. In addition, God confirms that he will give Jacob the birthright and promise that Jacob desired and used deception to obtain.

Amazingly, despite the thick fog of our failures, the mist of our misconceived ideas, the stench of our schemes, and the darkness of our deceptions God still finds us useful.

God uses people who believe that he breaks the power of sin's grasp. God uses people who trust that he has provided a way for all sin to be cast into the depth of the sea (Micah 7:19). God uses people who trust that Jesus bore every sin on the cross (Colossians 1:20).

Have you believed the lie that God can never use you because of the sins of your past? Are you willing to let God perfectly use imperfect you today? He is with you. He will never leave you (Joshua 1:5).

> Lord, God of Abraham and God of Isaac, surely you are in this place! I ask you to use me today, in spite of all my imperfections to accomplish your perfect plan in, for, and through me.

JANUARY 11

You had little indeed before I came, and your wealth has
increased enormously. In fact, except for the grace of God,
you would have sent me off without a penny to my name.
But God has seen your cruelty and my hard work.

—Genesis 30:30a; 31:42a

Jacob works for Laban for twenty years, and Laban grows very
wealthy. Now God commands Jacob to return home. Jacob leaves
without telling Laban because he knows Laban won't let him go
with what rightfully belongs to him. When Laban hears that Jacob
has left, Laban rushes after Jacob. God appears to Laban and warns
him to leave Jacob alone.

How gracious of God to vindicate Jacob's work before Laban,
Jacob's father-in-law and employer.

It has been said that it is amazing how much we can do if we
don't care who gets the credit. However, it is often difficult when
our hard work is not noticed. It's difficult to be taken advantage of.
It's most difficult to trust God to vindicate us.

God tells us that whatever we do if we work at it with all our
heart as working for the Lord, not for human employers, then the
Lord will reward us (Colossians 3:23). When we keep our focus on
the Lord and trust that there is a great reward in store for us, then
the recognition or reward from other people becomes less important.

Who are you working for? Is your motivation to receive due
credit? Is it sufficient to know that God sees everything and he will
both vindicate and reward you appropriately?

> God, help me to keep my focus on you every minute of
> every day in every job that I do no matter how big or how
> small. Please remind me that your rewards are more than
> sufficient for me.

JANUARY 12

Genesis 32:1–35:27

I am not worthy of all the faithfulness and unfailing
love you have shown to me, your servant.
—Genesis 32:10

Jacob journeys home. Angels of God meet him along the way. He sends messengers to Esau asking for his friendship. He is terrified when he hears that Esau is on his way with an army of 400 men. Jacob formulates a plan to protect his family and then he prays. Jacob knows that he is unworthy of all God has done to bless him thus far. Jacob asks God to protect him from Esau.

How gracious of God to answer Jacob's prayer. Even though angels of God camp nearby, Jacob lives in fear. It is in desperation that he turns to God in prayer and God answers his prayer; Esau's heart has changed—he no longer wants to kill his brother Jacob.

We may never have an army coming toward us. We may never have our lives threatened. Nevertheless, when our circumstances are overwhelmingly frightening, when it seems we are outnumbered by our foes and overwhelmed by our fears, God's Word promises us that we can cry out and he will listen and defend us. How comforting to know that the angel of the Lord is a guard, surrounding and defending all who fear him (Psalm 34:6–7).

How desperate do you need to be before you pray?

> God, I know that you surround me, that you guard me, and that you defend me. Oh Lord, when the circumstances of my life are frightening and it looks like things are stacked against me please help me to rest in the assurance that you are already working out my rescue.

JANUARY 13

Genesis 36; 1 Chronicles 1:35–2:2

Then Esau took his wives, children, household servants,
cattle, and flocks—all the wealth he had gained in the land
of Canaan—and moved away from his brother, Jacob.
—Genesis 36:6

Jacob and Esau bury their father Isaac. Their possessions increase
and the land cannot support them both. Esau moves away. Esau
grows into a nation as the Lord promised in Genesis 25:23. The
descendants of Esau are recorded.

How gracious of God to give Esau an inheritance that he did
not earn, nor did he deserve. Esau's children become leaders and
kings. There were kings in Edom (Esau's nation) before there were
kings in Israel.

Are you and I any different from Esau? We also have an
inheritance that we did not earn nor do we deserve. For those who
believe in Christ Jesus there is an inheritance that will never perish,
fade, or spoil. This inheritance is kept for us in heaven (1 Peter 1:4).
Our inheritance—eternal life—shall never perish (John 10:28).

How often have you despised the things of God, and yet God
never despises you? How often do you desire the wealth of the world,
the things that can spoil, perish, and fade away above the things of
God? Are you teaching your descendants to desire the things of God?

God, you've given me much and I deserve nothing. Your
abundance overwhelms me. Thank you for continuing to
pour out your blessings when I am so unworthy. Create
in me a desire for the things you have prepared for me in
heaven.

JANUARY 14

Genesis 37–39; 1 Chronicles 2:3–8

[Joseph] was purchased by Potiphar, a member
of the staff of Pharaoh, the king of Egypt.
—Genesis 39:1b

Joseph's brothers hate Joseph and cannot say a kind word to him. After throwing him into a pit and plotting his murder they sell him to Ishmaelite traders. Joseph is bound and forced to travel to Egypt where he is sold as a slave to Potiphar, the captain of the palace guard.

How gracious of God to bring Joseph to the attention of Potiphar. Joseph's life was in perilous hands along the road to Egypt. At any moment the Ishmaelite traders could have sold him to a harsh master who forced him to do extreme physical labor. Instead, God placed Joseph in a house where Joseph would learn the language, culture, household chores, bookkeeping duties, and responsibilities of an Egyptian official.

God knows the future and therefore knows that Joseph will eventually be leader all of Egypt. God knows Joseph will save the Israelites in a time of famine. God uses every experience to train and protect Joseph.

God knows our future. Sometimes our most difficult circumstances are God's training ground so that we might learn what we need to know for future service.

Are your circumstances difficult? Do you feel like you've been sold out, forgotten, or enslaved? We may not understand the activity of God, who does all things (Ecclesiastes 11:5) but we know we can trust him in all things (1 Peter 4:19).

> God, in my darkest hour, I trust that you are already shining your light of grace into my future. I trust that you are preparing me for the next thing. I commit to be faithful today so that I am prepared for tomorrow's responsibilities.

JANUARY 15

Genesis 40–41; 35:28–29

Then the king's cup-bearer spoke up. "Today I
have been reminded of my failure," he said.
—Genesis 41:9

Two years prior, Joseph interprets the dreams for the cup-bearer
and the baker. He asks only that when they get out of prison that
they might remember him. Once the cup-bearer is restored to duty,
he quickly forgets Joseph. Pharaoh has dreams that no one can
interpret. The cup-bearer remembers Joseph. Pharaoh sends for
Joseph. God gives Joseph the interpretation.

How gracious of God to give the cup-bearer timely recall. How
gracious of God, who is sovereign over all things people and time
(Psalm 103:19), to use all of these circumstances to bring Joseph into
the presence of the Pharaoh, with authority.

We know we let people down when we forget our promises or fail to
keep our word. We know the heartache of being let down or forgotten.

Has someone let you down? Have you let someone down? Do
you believe that God knows, and in his perfect timing is working
for your good (Esther 4:14)?

Will you trust that God never forgets about you; that he knows
where you are every moment? Will you trust that God knows what
he is doing and in his perfect timing he will act?

Does it encourage you to know that God is at work for good in
every moment of your life (Romans 8:28), including your failures?

Sovereign Lord, I believe that you are sovereign and have
the absolute right to do all things according to your good
pleasure. Remind me when I question your will and your
way, that you are perfect in all you do, and that your timing
is always accurate.

JANUARY 16

Genesis 42:1–45:15

"You can see for yourselves ... that I really am
Joseph!" Then Joseph kissed each of his brothers then
they began talking freely with him.
—Genesis 45:12, 15

Joseph's brothers travel to Egypt to buy grain. They bow before Joseph and Joseph recognizes them immediately; they don't recognize Joseph. Joseph accuses them of being spies. Joseph tests them by keeping one of them as a prisoner and sends the others home. The famine continues. The brothers return to Egypt with Benjamin, Joseph's younger brother. Joseph tests them again. Judah pleads their case. When he can stand it no longer, Joseph reveals his identity to the brothers. Amidst tears and kisses, the brothers begin talking freely with Joseph.

How gracious of God to reconcile families. It is a precious blessing when brothers and sisters—when families—live together in harmony (Psalm 133:1).

Joseph's brothers were fully responsible for their wickedness against Joseph. Joseph understood God's sovereignty and knew that while the Evil One was at work in the brothers' wickedness, God was at work for good (Genesis 50:20). Joseph chose to forgive them.

How wonderful it is to experience forgiveness. How precious it is to extend it. How sweet to live in a home where sins are confessed and quickly forgiven and forgotten; where love is freely given and received. How glorious to experience reconciliation.

How might you be an ambassador of reconciliation today?

God, please open my eyes to understand your sovereignty in the broken relationships in my home. Please humble me to extend forgiveness wherever necessary just as you have forgiven me. Help me to weed out bitterness and unforgiveness in my own heart before it can take root.

JANUARY 17

Genesis 45:16–47:27

So Jacob set out for Egypt ... During the night, God
spoke to him ... "Do not be afraid to go."
—Genesis 46:1a, 2a, 3b

Joseph's brothers return to their father Jacob and convince him
that Joseph is alive. Jacob's spirit revives and he prepares to leave
immediately. Jacob and his family reach the border of the Promised
Land; Jacob halts and worships God. God appears to Jacob in a
vision and tells Jacob that he will go with him to Egypt, and that
when Jacob dies in Egypt Joseph will be with him.

How gracious of God to appear to Jacob and reassure him
that God has a plan. God himself will go with Jacob, increase his
descendants into a great nation, and then bring them out again.

This was not the first time God appeared to Jacob, but it will
be the last.

We learn in Psalm 139 that God knows all things. He knows our
fears. He knows when we are unsure if we have heard him correctly. He
knows exactly how to reassure us, to lead us and, to guide us especially
when the path leads us out of the familiar and into the foreign.

Does it revive your spirit to know that you are always in God's
presence and that he is guiding you? Will you walk wherever God
leads you, abandoning your fear at the border of the familiar, and
courageously follow God?

> God, please open my eyes to see where you are leading me
> and tune my ears to hear your voice. Guide me each day so
> that I move forward—unafraid—toward the wonderful things
> and places you have prepared for me.

JANUARY 18

Genesis 47:28–50:26

Then Jacob called together all his sons and said,
"Gather around me, and I will tell you what is
going to happen to you in the days to come."
—Genesis 49:1

Jacob, near death, calls his sons together to pass the birthright and the blessings to them. Joseph receives the preeminent blessing. Jacob adopts Joseph's sons and they receive a special blessing. Then Jacob blesses his other sons.

How gracious of God to give Jacob an understanding of the future; a glimpse into his plan. Once again, the younger son receives the birthright.

If you could, would you want to know the future. Some desire so strongly to know what will happen that they turn to mediums or tarot cards hoping for a glimpse. But, do you really want to experience in advance the heartache, the suffering and the loss that the future holds? Of course, there will be wonderful and joyous moments, but there will also be suffering and death.

We do know the future. God's plan of salvation does away with death. Those who die in Christ don't stay dead but live eternally with God in heaven. Jesus defeated death when he rose to life on the third day, and one day Jesus will return, and when he does, he will bring all believers with him (Revelation 22:12).

Does it comfort you to know that God not only knows the future but controls it? Does it give you hope to know that the end of the story has been recorded in God's Word, and life wins?

> Eternal God, help me to remember that when people die, your great plan continues to live. As you fill me with your peace, may I be a source of comfort to those people around me who fear the future; who fear death.

JANUARY 19

Job 1–4

Satan replied to the LORD, "[Job] blesses
you only because you bless him."
"All right, do with him as you please," the
LORD said to Satan. "But spare his life."
—Job 2:4a, 6

God gives Satan permission to test Job who is a blameless man of complete integrity. The test begins. All of Job's animals are stolen and his farmhands killed. All of Job's sheep and shepherds die. All of Job's camels are stolen and his servants killed. All of Job's children die. Job does not sin by blaming God. God gives Satan permission to take Job's health. Boils cover Job from head to foot. His suffering is too great for words. Job does not curse God.

How gracious of God to allow tests in our lives.

Job didn't know he was being tested. I expect that most of the time neither do we. However, a faith that is not tested is never proved trustworthy. Faith chooses to believe God: that he is who he claims to be and that what he says is true (Hebrews 11:1–3). Faith fails when our faith is placed in anything other than God.

If you are in the midst of a test will you choose to trust in God; in his Word, his person, his trustworthiness, his sovereignty, his might, and his ability to save?

Sovereign Lord, thank you for allowing my faith to be tested. While I may not enjoy the test, I know that you are in control. Your Word tells me that I can turn to you for mercy and grace when I need it most (Hebrews 4:16). May I prove faithful, just as you continually prove your faithfulness. Help me to remember that in every test you are fully involved in my life.

JANUARY 20

Job 5–7

What are mere mortals, that you should make so much of us?
For you examine us every morning and test us every moment.
—Job 7:17–18

Job's friend, Eliphaz, tries to convince Job that God is chastening Job because of his sin. Job knows he has not denied the words of the Holy One. Job believes that God is his tormentor, but he doesn't know why.

How gracious of God to not abandon us in our suffering and ignorance. In spite of Job's friend's misguided attempt at comfort, Job's attention is not diverted away from God.

Like Job, we must remember who God is and what God does: he is just (Deuteronomy 32:4), right (Genesis 18:25), and good (Psalm 106:1) all the time, even in the most difficult times. We must also remember that suffering is the lot of humanity, both for the righteous and the unrighteous (Romans 8:18–22).

Unfortunately, like Job's friends, there may have been times when we jumped to wrong conclusions about another person's suffering. Might God have been testing a righteous person?

Is your suffering because of sin in your life? It could be. Or is God making much of you, refining you, and examining you. In your suffering will you focus your attention on the reality of who God is and what he is doing?

> Almighty God, I trust that you hear my prayers, prayers whispered through my suffering and tears. I also trust that you hear the prayers I have prayed in ignorance. Father, please humble me to recognize that I don't know all there is to know about you, and I surely don't know the details of another person's agony to make judgment calls that only you can make.

JANUARY 21

Job 8–11

Yes, I know this is all true in principle. But …
—Job 9:2a

Job's friends speak of what they know. Theirs is knowledge that has been passed down from generation to generation and it makes sense: God punishes the wicked. Therefore they reason, since Job is being treated harshly, Job must be wicked. Job agrees in principle. But Job wants an audience with God. Job tells his friends what he would say to God if God would listen: that he is innocent.

How gracious of God to be involved in, and understanding of, every detail of our lives. Job wanted an audience with God because only God could explain what was going on. However, God is not accountable to us. God is the one to whom we are accountable. (Hebrews 4:13)

There will be hard times in our lives. There may be times when the suffering is so intense that we question whether God is aware of what is happening to us. When we are convinced our pain is undeserved it is easy to slip into depression or self-pity.

Who will lift us out of the pit? Who will be our strength when we have none? Who will hear us when we cry out? God. Always God.

God hears when you cry out to him. Will you take refuge in him and rejoice? (Psalm 5).

> God, I confess that there are times when I feel so alone I wonder if you are near. There are times when I question what you are doing. There are times when I wonder why I was ever born. In those times, dear Lord, please help me to hold on to the knowledge that you hear me when I pray and you have surrounded me with your shield of love.

JANUARY 22

Job 12–14

> But true wisdom and power are with God; counsel
> and understanding are his. Yes, strength and wisdom
> are with him. He floods the darkness with light.
> —Job 12:13, 16a, 22a

Job speaks again insisting he is just and blameless. While Job's friends speak out of their own wisdom, Job speaks of the one who is truly wise and sovereign over all things. Job wants his friends to stop condemning him. He wants God to tell him what he has done wrong, to show him his rebellion and sin. Yet, Job does not lose hope.

How gracious of God to give Job a picture of the sovereignty of God.

There is hope for Job and there is hope for us. Our hope rests in the promises of God. There will be a day of judgment for all who have been wronged (Isaiah 42:3). There will be a day when we will see clearly (1 Corinthians 13:12). There will be a day when pain is gone (Revelation 21:4). A right understanding of God gives Job, and us, a right understanding of the circumstances which surround us.

God is sovereign over the circumstances of our lives today and even though there are times when he allows more than we can endure on our own we are never without hope for he is always with us. He is our hope.

How hard must life press in on you before you choose to rely on God (2 Corinthians 1:5–9)?

> God, please forgive me for putting you in too small a box.
> Thank you for your servant Job, who is teaching me that
> you alone are sufficient to rule the world. You alone have
> the wisdom, power, and majesty to govern all things, and
> to determine my lot.

JANUARY 23

Job 15–18

What miserable comforters you are! Won't
you stop your flow of foolish words?
—Job 16:2b–3a

Job's friends accuse and condemn Job even calling him a windbag.
They say he has no fear or reverence for God. Job speaks again. He
pleads with his friends to stop talking and put themselves in his
place. He pleads with God—his witness, his advocate. He cries out
for a mediator. His spirit is crushed. He cries out to God to defend
his innocence.

How gracious of God to provide a mediator, a High Priest—one
who understands our weaknesses (Hebrews 4:15).

Like Job, we need an advocate. Jesus is our advocate, our lawyer,
the one who pleads our case in the courtroom of the Most High
God. Like Job, we need a mediator. Jesus is our mediator, the one in
whom we can meet with God. Like Job we need a comforter, Jesus
knows our weakness, he leads and empowers us to endure.

Sometimes God may let us experience deep pain, loss, grief, and
despair, but he never abandons us to handle our suffering alone. God
is always with us. Jesus is always interceding for us. The Holy Spirit
is always within us to comfort and counsel us.

God forbid that we should comfort our friends who are in
distress the way Job's friends comfort Job.

Who do you know that is suffering? Will you comfort them
with God's comfort?

> God, sometimes I'm really not very good at comforting hurting
> people. Sometimes I'm afraid to say anything. Sometimes I say
> the wrong thing. Lord, please humble me to listen to them and
> to you. Please give me words that point to Jesus.

JANUARY 24

Job 19–21

Look at me and be stunned. Put your
hand over your mouth in shock.
—Job 21:5

Job is humiliated. He believes God has rejected him. His relatives turn against him. His presence repulses his wife. His family finds him loathsome. Young children despise him. He is emaciated. His friends torture him with incomplete theology. Job asks for a hearing; his complaint is with God not with people. Though appearances seem to contradict the principle, Job knows that God is the supreme and righteous Judge.

How gracious of God to work in all things for the good of his children (Romans 8:28). Job didn't know the back story; he didn't know he was in a test. He didn't know the greater event —that his life would be recorded by God as an example for generations to come, including ours.

Like Job, we see wicked people spared while the righteous endure one calamity after another and it doesn't seem fair. Our own circumstances sometimes seem unfair as we stumble in darkness, experience rejection, and undergo intense and unfair scrutiny. Nevertheless, God never leaves us; he is working for our good in every circumstance of our lives—the very good and the very bad (Romans 8:28–29).

It is not easy to see God at work in the details that drive us to despair, but he is. He is there, he is at work, he is at work for good; and he wants us to lean on him. Do you trust him? Will you humble yourself so that he might lift you up in due time? Will you cast all your anxieties on him. (1 Peter 5:6–7)

> Almighty God, in the trying times of my life please help me to remember that you are there and are working mightily for my good.

JANUARY 25

Job 22–25

If only I knew where to find God, I would go
to his throne and talk with him there.
—Job 23:2

Eliphaz restates his position: Job is wicked and guilty and God is punishing him. Job responds that he would lay out his case if only he knew where God was. If he could just be in God's presence he would listen to whatever God had to say. Job knows God would give him a fair hearing. He cannot find God. Thick, impenetrable darkness surrounds Job.

How gracious of God to be accessible even as Job fears that God is hidden from him.

When our lives are hidden in the thick darkness of doubt, anger, bitterness, betrayal, infidelity, debt, illness, upheaval, unemployment, depression, oppression, fear, bondage, addiction—or any number of things that seem to obscure God—we may fear that God simply cannot be found.

However, God is not hidden. He is on his throne, and we can come boldly before him there to receive his mercy, and find his grace to help us when we need it most (Hebrews 4:16).

Do you believe God is available to you? What holds you back? What keeps you from going to God in prayer? Will you set it aside, go to his throne and talk with him there, pouring out your deepest longings and questions to him?

> God, I know where you are, but sometimes I fearfully look
> at the darkness around me and I forget where to find you. As
> I kneel before you, please shine your light into the darkness
> of my circumstances so that I can see you. Open my heart
> and my mind to receive your grace and mercy so that I can
> walk through this dark valley in victory.

JANUARY 26

Job 26–29

And this is what he says to all humanity: "The fear of the Lord is true wisdom; to forsake evil is real understanding."
—Job 28:28

In his final speech, Job extols the character and attributes of God. God is all-powerful—he stretches the sky over empty space and hangs the earth on nothing. He created the world and the heavens. God is a just Judge—Job vows that he will speak no evil, no lies before God; he will maintain his innocence. God is wisdom—only God knows where wisdom can be found.

How gracious of God to give wisdom whenever we ask for it (James 1:5). Job is wise, he fears God and he praises God for who God is. Job's friends have consistently terrorized and humiliated Job based on their limited understanding of God.

Aristotle says, "Knowing yourself is the beginning of all wisdom," and this appears to be the position from which Job's friends' theology flows. They indulge their personal wisdom more than God's wisdom. Sometimes that is the most comfortable chair in which to sit and the most difficult chair from which to leave.

Do Job's friends fear God? Or have they used their incomplete understanding of who God is to heap abuse on Job? What about you? Do you fear God? Whose wisdom do you seek and cherish? Whose reputation for wisdom is more important to you—yours or God's?

> Father, please humble my heart so that I fear disappointing you more than I desire to be right. Please humble my attitude so that I fear misrepresenting you more than I desire the spotlight. Please give me wisdom to praise you as you are, for when I see you as you are, I stand in awe of your majesty.

JANUARY 27

Job 30–31

Have I tried to hide my sins as people normally do, hiding
my guilt in a closet? Have I feared the crowd and its
contempt, so that I refused to acknowledge my sin ...?
—Job 31:33–34

Outcasts mock and taunt Job. Depression haunts his days and pain
fills his nights. Job insists in his innocence. He has covenanted with
God not to look with lust. He hasn't lied or deceived anyone. He
hasn't lusted for another man's wife. He acts fairly with his servants.
He cares for orphans, widows and the homeless. He never curses
anyone or turns away a stranger. Job knows that if God were to show
him where he is in the wrong, he would own the accusation.

How gracious of God to provide a way for sinners to walk
blamelessly before him. Job confesses that he's a sinner, but he insists
in his innocence.

God sees everything we do and every step we take (31:4). There
is no area of our lives hidden from God (Psalm 139:1–6). He knows
what we see, say, think, and feel. He knows whether we control our
lusts. He knows our work ethic, moral code, how we treat the less
fortunate, and the way we deal with anger. Can we say that we are
innocent?

Oh, to have as clean a conscience as Job! We can! God has
provided a way of cleansing. He promises that when we confess our
sins—because he is faithful and because he is just—he will forgive
them. Not only does he forgive the confessed sin, he cleanses us from
all unrighteousness (1 John 1:9). What sin is God uncovering in you?

> Gracious God, I confess and repent of this specific sin today.
> Please cleanse me from its wickedness and restore me to
> your holiness.

JANUARY 28

Job 32–34

Or God disciplines people with sickness and
pain, with ceaseless aching in their bones.
—Job 33:19

Job's three accusers are silent. Elihu, a younger man, speaks. Elihu is angry with Job's friends because of their inability to answer Job's arguments. He is angry with Job. He insists Job listen to what he has to say. He is adamant that Job is wrong about God. Elihu submits that God speaks through dreams and visions, he whispers terrifying warnings but people don't listen. Elihu says God disciplines people with sickness and pain to keep them from sinning.

How gracious of God to discipline his children. We know that Elihu is wrong about Job. However, like Elihu, we know from Hebrews 12:6 that God does discipline those he loves.

Job's friends believe Job's suffering is because he has sinned. Sometimes that's our reality: we bring unyielding pain and suffering upon ourselves as the consequences of sin; but not all suffering is the direct result of sin. Sometimes God allows suffering for other purposes. Sometimes our pain is to keep us from sinning. Sometimes God uses suffering to direct our path. God knows when pain is the best tool to shape us into the person he is making us to be.

When we are in the midst of suffering, whether it is a consequence of sin or not, our suffering will change us. Will you come through the fire bitter or humble? Will you emerge trusting God with a stronger faith, or will you deny him?

> Father, as you discipline me, or as I suffer the consequences of my sin, I want to work with you through my suffering. I want to pass through the flames and not be consumed by them. I want to be humbled and refined.

JANUARY 29

Job 35–37

Stop and consider the wonderful miracles of God!
—Job 37:14

Elihu's speech defends the majesty and character of God: God is just, he is mighty in power and understanding, he punishes the wicked, his eyes never leave the innocent, he reveals sin, he calls people away from evil, he blesses the obedient, he punishes the rebellious, he rescues the suffering, he leads away from danger, he gives freedom. Elihu extols God as all-powerful, exalted beyond what we can understand, eternal and transcendent. He exhorts Job to consider the wonderful miracles of God.

How gracious of God to use Elihu, in Elihu's limited wisdom, to remind Job and Job's friends of the majesty of the Almighty! Elihu was wrong about Job, but he was right about God.

We know from God's word that when trouble comes our way it should develop our endurance and mature our faith (James 1:2–4). We must not shrink from suffering, and we must not waste our suffering by failing to acknowledge the majesty of the God who is sovereign over our suffering. The same God who accomplishes a myriad of wonderful things every day throughout his creation is the same God who carries us in our suffering.

Knowing that God is at work in your suffering, will you try to imagine how? Will you choose to rest in the perfect character of God as your endurance is strengthened and your faith is matured?

God, your majesty overwhelms me and brings me to my knees. Thank you that you are not hidden from me and I am not hidden from you when I suffer. Thank you that your eyes are ever on me, and that you will accomplish your magnificent plan for me through my suffering.

JANUARY 30

Job 38–40:5

Then the LORD answered Job …"
—Job 38:1

God answers Job from the whirlwind. It is time for Job to brace himself. God has some questions and Job must answer them. Does Job question God's wisdom? Was Job there when God laid the foundations of the earth? Did Job define the sea's boundaries? Does he know from where light comes? Can he move the stars? Can he control the rain? Does he still want to argue with God?

Job confesses that he is nothing, that he has said too much and has nothing more to say.

How gracious of God to insist that we that live in the reality of who he is rather than who we think he is based on our experiences and our limited understanding of his Word.

In those moments, when we feel unjustly treated by God, it would do us well to remember who God is, who we are, and who we are not. We are not God. God is the Almighty and we are his creation (Isaiah 29:16). We are not his peer. God is fully aware of every detail of our lives every moment of our lives. Not only is he aware of the details, he has allowed them for our good and for his glory.

Challenging God's wisdom regarding our circumstances, or offering God a better plan is akin to saying to God, "I know better than you." Or worse yet, "I am your equal."

Will you consider God's response to Job in your circumstances today?

> Almighty God you are the God of all wisdom and knowledge, power and authority. Humble me to acknowledge who you are, and to recognize who I am before you, and who I am not.

JANUARY 31

Job 40:6–42:17

Go to my servant Job and offer a burnt offering for yourselves.
My servant Job will pray for you, and I will accept his prayer
on your behalf, I will not treat you as you deserve.
—Job 42:8b

Job repents—not from the sin his friends insist he is guilty of—
but of demanding from God an explanation for his suffering and
for questioning God. Job confesses his ignorance. He takes back
everything he has said. God rebukes the three friends. God tells
them they have not been right in what they said about him. God
affirms Job. God does not treat the friends as they deserve, rather,
he accepts Job's prayer on their behalf.

How gracious of God not to treat Job's friends as they deserved.
Job's friends maligned the Name of God and terrorized Job; they
deserved punishment. Instead, God accepted their sacrifice and Job's
prayer on their behalf.

God doesn't treat us as we deserve either. We deserve to die
in our sin (Romans 6:23), to bear the full wrath of God, and to
experience his punishment. However, God provides a substitute, the
Lord Jesus Christ who died in our place, who bore the full wrath
of God and who was punished for our wickedness. We don't have
to offer bulls and rams as Job's friends did, our perfect sacrifice was
offered on the cross, once for all (Hebrews 10:10).

Have you accepted God's acts of grace on your behalf? Who is
praying for you? Who are you praying for?

> Almighty God, it overwhelms me to think that Jesus took
> every bit of the punishment I deserve and endured your
> wrath, dying in my place so that I can live. Father help me
> to live blameless before you and everyone else.

grace
FEBRUARY

FEBRUARY 1

Exodus 1:1–4:17; 1 Chronicles 6:1–3a

Years passed … The Israelites groaned beneath their burden
of slavery. They cried out for help … God heard their
cries and remembered his promise to Abraham …
—Exodus 2:23a, 24a

The famine ends, Joseph dies, and the Israelites continue to live in
Egypt. Over the course of 400 years God multiplies the Israelites from a
clan of 70 into a nation of millions just as he promised. The Egyptians,
trying to control the population growth of the Israelites, enslave them.
Under their growing oppression the Israelites cry out for help.

How gracious of God to remember his promise. That God
remembers does not mean he has forgotten, it means it is time to
act—like remembering one's birthday with a celebration. It's time to
remember the covenant and bring the Israelites out of their bondage.

Waiting on God isn't easy, especially when our circumstances
are inescapable or uncontrollable. Sometimes we may feel like God
has forgotten us, isn't aware of our situation, or doesn't realize our
difficulty and we question why we must wait.

Sometimes it's hard for us to remember that God's timing is
always perfect. Waiting while God takes as much time as he needs,
and allows as much difficulty as is necessary for our sanctification
might stretch our faith to the breaking point, but never beyond (1
Corinthians 10:12–13). God always hears us when we cry out for
help.

Are you waiting for God to remember you?

God, I know you have plans for me that require waiting. I
choose to believe that you know exactly what you are doing
in me and for me as I wait on you. Please help me to stand
firm and trust you to remember me in your perfect time.

FEBRUARY 2

Exodus 4:18–7:13

Before Moses left Midian, the LORD said to him,
"Do not be afraid to return to Egypt, for all
those who wanted to kill you are dead."
—Exodus 4:19

God calls Moses, confirms that Moses is the one to bring the Israelites out of Egypt, and provides for his brother Aaron to be with him. Now it is time for Moses to go back to Egypt. Moses talks it over with his father-in-law and receives his blessing to go. God also reassures Moses that the circumstances surrounding his departure from Egypt have changed; those who want to kill him are dead.

How gracious of God to reassure Moses that he is aware of the details in Egypt. How gracious of God to provide Moses with everything he needs to return to Egypt in full confidence that he is walking in God's perfect plan.

We may not see a burning bush or hear God's audible voice, but God gives us many ways to know his will. God speaks to us through the Bible, he gives us inner peace—not necessarily absence of fear but a settled assurance of his will—and he guides us through confirming circumstances (Acts 16:6–9; 27). When all three: inner peace, God's Word, and our confirming circumstances align, then like Moses we can move confidently wherever God leads.

Does indecisiveness keep you from walking where God is leading? Do memories from the past or anxiety regarding the future keep your feet planted in disobedience? What reassurances are you discarding because of your fear?

> God, whenever my limited vision and inabilities paralyze me, please help me to trust in your limitless foresight and abilities so that my fear is removed. Humble me to look beyond myself and focus on you.

FEBRUARY 3

Exodus 7:14–9:35

… I will send a plague that will really speak to you … I will
prove to you that there is no other God like me in all the earth.
—Exodus 9:14

God announces and then sends one plague after another to convince
Pharaoh to let his people go. God makes a clear distinction between
Pharaoh's people and his people. God tells Pharaoh that he could
have killed them all by now. God lets them live so they will see his
power and so that his fame might speak throughout the earth. Some
of Pharaoh's officials believe the Lord. With each plague, Pharaoh
refuses to let the people go.

How gracious of God to prove that he alone is God. We know
from Exodus 12:12 that with every plague God was proving false
the gods of Egypt and proving that he is greater than all other gods.

God continually proves to us that he is the one true God. The
heavens declare the glory of God (Psalm 19:1) and his Word proves
that he alone is the one true God. There is nothing in all creation
that compares to the one who created all of it (Isaiah 40).

What difficult circumstance/plague is God using to defeat the
false gods in your life? How difficult must things be before you
acknowledge the power and authority of the one true God?

> God, I thank you for graciously showing me that you are
> the one true God. Oh Lord, search every corner of my heart
> and bring whatever plague is necessary to cause me to let go
> of every impotent idol and cling to you.

FEBRUARY 4

Exodus 10–12

> On that night I will pass through the land of Egypt and kill all the firstborn sons … The blood you have smeared on your door posts will serve as a sign. When I see the blood, I will pass over you.
> —Exodus 12:12a, 13a

The final plague commences. Israelite families kill their Passover lamb, paint the doorpost with its blood, and God spares the lives of their firstborn sons. The Lord strikes down the firstborn sons of all who haven't smeared the blood of the lamb on their doorposts

How gracious of God to tell everyone, Israelite and Egyptian, how to be saved! The directions were simple and available to all. Perhaps some Egyptians followed God's word. Perhaps many more wish that they had. It may have seemed odd—paint the doorpost with the blood of the lamb—but it was all that was needed and the only way to be saved.

The way to salvation is still simple and available to all: believe on the name of Jesus Christ, and be saved (Romans 10:9–10). Jesus is the Passover Lamb who was slain that we might live (John 1:29). When we appropriate his work on the cross for ourselves, choosing to believe he died in our place, then we are saved. It is as though we apply his blood to the doorpost of our heart. Jesus's blood, poured out at the cross, is all that is needed and the only way of salvation.

Like the Egyptians, do you believe this is too odd? Too out-of-the-ordinary? There is nothing to add. Jesus died, so that you might live (Romans 5:8).

> God, while your salvation is simple and freely available to me, help me to understand the cost to you: your one and only Son (John 3:16)!

FEBRUARY 5

Exodus 13–15

But Moses told the people, "Don't be afraid. Just stand
where you are and watch the LORD rescue you."
—Exodus 14:13

Leading the Israelites by a pillar of cloud by day and of fire by night, the Lord brings them to the Red Sea where they are trapped between the sea and the pursuing Egyptian army. The people panic, cry out to the Lord for help, and turn against Moses. Moses tells the people that God will fight for them. God commands the Israelites to get moving!

How gracious of God to assure Moses that he has a plan to rescue Israel from the Egyptians. God brought them out of Egypt and God has a plan for their future and for his glory

There are times when circumstances make us feel like we can't move forward and we can't go back. We need a rescuer with a plan. God has a plan for each of us; he tells us in Jeremiah 29:11 that his plan is for good and not disaster to give us a future and a hope. We may not know what the good or the future will look like, but we do know the hope; our hope is in Jesus (1 Timothy 4:10).

Are you stuck between a rock and a hard place? If God has brought you to this place do you trust his grace and mercy to bring you through? If your own actions have brought you here, do you trust God has a plan to bring you through? If God says, "Get moving," will you go, even if the way looks impassable?

> God, you are the God of impossible things! Please help me to remember that you go before me, and you hem me in. Help me to trust in your plan and to walk in steadfast obedience.

FEBRUARY 6

Exodus 16–19

Those who gathered a lot had nothing left over,
and those who gathered only a little had enough.
Each family had just what it needed.
—Exodus 16:18b

Moses leads the Israelites into the desert, and they continually complain about what they don't have. God provides his presence to guide them, Moses to lead them, and water to sustain them. When they grumble about food, God provides daily manna so that they will know that he is the Lord their God.

How gracious of God to meet each family's specific need. God knew exactly what they needed; their complaining did not bring it to his attention.

We may not be travelling in the desert but sometimes we may feel as if we are. The days may seem long, the needs of others overwhelm us, and we feel lost, alone, thirsty and hungry. When our desert days continue one after another and we fail to see all that God is providing we complain.

Jane Austen wrote "Those who do not complain are never pitied." Is that why we complain? Are we seeking God's pity? Or do we want God's help?

We know that God knows what we need before we ask him (Matthew 6:8). We also know that if we don't have it is because we haven't asked (James 4:2). Where is there room for complaining in the Christian's life?

> God, you know exactly what I need and when I need it. You know that I need to confess and repent of my selfish desire for pity. You know that I need to subdue my pride that pushes my trust in you and my love for you aside and leads me to think it is OK to complain about your provisions. Please forgive me, Lord.

FEBRUARY 7

Exodus 20:1–22:15

Then God instructed the people as follows …
—Exodus 20:1

Two months after the Israelites leave Egypt they camp at Sinai where God puts forth a dramatic and frightening display of his power. Moses goes up into the smoke and fire; the people stay behind the boundaries God specifies. They must not touch the mountain of God. Eventually Moses returns and gives the Israelites the Lord's words.

How gracious of God to provide a code of law by which the Israelites are to live. The Law wasn't a list of suggestions, but a firm and specific way to conduct life. The Law reveals God's righteousness. There is no excuse for breaking the law; but no one can keep it in its entirety. The Israelites need a Savior.

As we read the Ten Commandments, we see the plumb line of righteousness; we also see how far we are out of plumb (Isaiah 28:16–17). We may think our walls of self-righteousness lean only a little when in reality they are falling down. No one is righteous (Romans 3:10–18).

The law shows us what righteousness looks like, but it cannot make us righteous. We cannot prop up our crumbling walls with good behavior. Like the Israelites, we need a Savior.

Does God's holy and perfect law cause you to flee to Jesus for salvation? Only Jesus's righteousness, imputed to you, can make you stand aright.

God, your word protects me, your commands set a healthy boundary around me, and your law shows me how much I need a Savior. I flee to Jesus. I flee to the only One who can wash away my sin and cover me with his righteousness so that I can stand upright before you.

FEBRUARY 8

Exodus 22:16–24:18

Work for six days, and rest on the seventh. This will ...
allow the people of your household ... to be refreshed.
—Exodus 23:12

God gives the Israelites guidelines for holy living. He gives them rules for community relationships, justice, restitution, care of the poor, and for times of celebration. God commands a day of rest for the people and the animals. God promises to protect the Israelites if they do not worship other gods and serve only him.

How gracious of God to command rest. God rested after creating the world, and he created us to need rest. While this rest ultimately points to our spiritual rest which is fulfilled in Christ Jesus (Hebrews 4), it also tells us that God expects us to rest physically.

Rest is often too hard to find. Our phones are on 24/7. Work, texts, e-mail, social media notifications, and various updates continually bombard us. The television or the radio is on even when no one is paying attention and should we find a quiet place, our minds and spirits often remain restless.

Do you need rest? Can you imagine setting your screen time to zero for a few minutes each day? What will you miss if you are not on call every minute? Is God not powerful and wise enough to lead you and protect you as you seek to quietly worship only him?

> God, I recognize that I am as plugged in as I am because I don't trust you with the details of my life. Sometimes I leave my phone on in church just in case someone needs me. Humble me enough to embrace rest. Remind me each day that you are in control, and that when I rest I am showing that I trust you.

FEBRUARY 9

Exodus 25–28

I want the people of Israel to build me a sacred
residence where I can live among them.
—Exodus 25:8

God calls Moses and Joshua up the mountain together, then he calls
Moses to come further alone. God reveals to Moses that he wants the
people to build a residence for him where he can live among them.
God gives Moses the plans for the tabernacle and its furnishings.

How gracious of God to live in the midst of his people and to
give them visual and tangible evidence of his continual presence.

God's Word tells us that the heavens cannot contain him (1 Kings
8:27) and yet God tells his people that he will live in their midst. The
tabernacle was a visual reminder of God's presence and the Israelites
were God's visual to the world. Every person who happened upon the
Israelite camp would see that God lived among his people.

How blessed we are that God still condescends to live among
his people today. The Holy Spirit of God lives within each one of
us who have been saved by his grace and adopted into his family
(John 14:15–18). We are still God's visual to the world; everyone
who happens upon us should see God in us and through us. Our
bodies are a sacred tabernacle; a dwelling place for the living Lord
(1 Corinthians 6:19).

How beautifully do you reflect the majestic and holy God who
is living in you?

> Almighty God, the heavens can't contain you, and yet you
> have chosen to live in me! I am overwhelmed. I pray that I
> would choose to live in such a way today that every person
> who happens upon me would recognize you and be refreshed
> by your Holy Spirit.

FEBRUARY 10

Exodus 29–31

Look, I have chosen Bezalel … giving him skill in all kinds of
crafts … And, I have appointed Oholiab to be his assistant.
—Exodus 31:2a, 3b, 6a

God gives Moses the details of the tabernacle: the furniture, the
clothing for the priests, the anointing oil, and the incense. Every
detail must be completed perfectly. God gives Bezalel and Oholiab
skill in all kinds of crafts to complete the tasks with excellence.
God also gives special skills to all the naturally talented craftsmen
to make the things he has instructed Moses to make.

How gracious of God to equip those whom he calls and uses. It
has been said that God doesn't call the equipped; he equips the called.

God equipped Bezalel, Oholiab and the other craftsmen to
build a tabernacle. Throughout biblical history we see God calling
the most unlikely people and equipping them to do amazing things.
God has work for you and for me (Ephesians 2:10), and he will equip
us to do that work (Hebrews 13:20–21). He will provide others with
skills that we don't have, to work alongside us.

What work has God prepared for you? It will probably be in
line with your natural talents. Will you reflect on your experiences
to see how God has prepared you through education, work, things
you enjoy, and things that you are good at or for which you have a
passion, and then ask God what he would have you do?

> God, thank you for the talents and skills you have given me.
> Please give me wisdom to use them for your glory. Please
> keep me from thinking that I am not equipped to work for
> you and help me to remember that my first responsibility is
> simply to answer the call.

FEBRUARY 11

Exodus 32–34

"Now leave me alone so my anger can blaze
against them and destroy them all." ... But Moses
pleaded with the Lord his God not to do it.
—Exodus 32:10a, 11a

While Moses is with God, Aaron builds a golden calf for the people to worship. God's anger blazes. He tells Moses he will destroy them and make Moses into a great nation instead. Moses intercedes for the people. The Lord withdraws his threat. Moses continues to intercede as he meets with God in the Tent of Meeting. The people know when Moses meets with God because the cloud that leads them hovers over the tent while Moses is inside. Inside the tent, Moses and God speak as friends.

How gracious of God to allow the Israelites a mediator to intercede with him on their behalf.

God gives us the same gift: our mediator is the Lord Jesus Christ and it is in him that we meet with God (1 Timothy 2:5). Not only can we go to God with the burdens of our own hearts, but like Moses, we have the privilege of interceding on behalf of the people we love and lead.

Oswald Chambers says that we are most like Christ when we are interceding. It is our privilege to intercede for other people as the Lord intercedes for us. Who has God placed on your heart today? Will you intercede on that person's behalf as if no one else is praying for them?

God, thank you for the privilege of praying for the people I love and lead. Through your Holy Spirit, would you direct my prayer today so that my intercession is fully in alignment with your will? Please increase my passion to pray continually for the hurting and lost people in my life.

FEBRUARY 12

Exodus 35–36

"This is what the LORD has commanded. Everyone is invited
to bring these offerings to the LORD ..." So the people of
Israel ... who wanted to help in the work the LORD had given
them through Moses—brought their offerings to the LORD.
—Exodus 35:4a, 29

It is time to build the tabernacle and God gives Moses the list of
needed supplies. The Israelites, as they are willing, prepare their
offerings and present them to the Lord. The craftsmen begin their
work. They bring more gifts until the craftsmen tell Moses they have
more than enough materials on hand.

How gracious of God to provide everything that is needed for
the building and furnishing of the tabernacle, and to allow the
Israelites the privilege of offering it back to him.

We know from James 1:17 that everything we have comes from
the Lord. Whether it's the paycheck we receive, the car we drive, the
house we decorate, the education we utilize, the children we raise, or
the church we attend—everything is a gift from God (1 Corinthians
4:7). God doesn't need our offerings, he owns everything, and yet
God invites us to bring our gifts to him for his use.

What has God given you? What is he inviting you to give back
so that his work will be accomplished with excellence?

> God, how often I forget that you are the giver of all things.
> Please forgive the times when I hold tight to what I have
> because I am afraid to give back to you what I think I
> might need. Please teach me to hold tightly to you, and to
> let everything else slip from my hand.

FEBRUARY 13

Exodus 37:1–39:31

All this was done just as the LORD had commanded Moses.
—Exodus 39:7

Construction on the tabernacle commences. Bezalel is in charge, just as the Lord commanded Moses. The people bring gifts of silver, bronze and gold. The materials are inventoried and the craftsmen set to work. Every detail is completed with excellence just as the Lord tells Moses.

How gracious of God to give detailed instructions and provide skilled craftsmen so that Moses can carry out the work on earth just as the Lord commanded.

While Moses was the leader of the Israelites, and the recipient of God's instructions, Bezalel was in charge of the whole project and other craftsmen were responsible for making the clothing for the priests. We don't know much about the relationship between Bezalel and Moses but we can imagine it was marked by mutual respect, trust, and submission to God's instruction.

God has work for you and me (Ephesians 2:10); he also has workers that he brings alongside us and we must trust God's equipping of them just as we trust that he has equipped us.

Who has God brought alongside to work with you in your current ministry? Do you graciously give each person with whom you work the room to do their job as God commands?

> God, you are the God of Excellence. I know that there are tasks you've assigned to me and my hearts' desire is to complete them with excellence. I also know that I often feel unsure about the outcome when I have to rely on other people's work. Humble me to trust you and respect them. Help me to remember that you are instructing others just as you are instructing me.

FEBRUARY 14

Exodus 39:32–40:38; Numbers 9:15–23

Then the cloud covered the Tabernacle, and the
glorious presence of the Lord filled it.
—Exodus 40:34

The tabernacle is complete and Moses inspects the work. Moses sets up the tabernacle as the Lord commands. Once everything is set in its proper place, God's glorious presence fills the tabernacle such that Moses can no longer enter it.

How gracious of God to fill the tabernacle with his presence and never leave the Israelites throughout their desert years. His presence was always visible to them through the cloud by day and the fire by night.

Moses stated in Exodus 33:16 that if God didn't go with them, no one would know they were a separate and distinct people. God did go with them and he continually led them with his presence. What a gift to the Israelites to see God's glory fill the temple.

Today, every believer is the temple of God's Holy Spirit (2 Corinthians 6:19). The Holy Spirit is given to every believer, a onetime event, when he or she believes on the Lord Jesus Christ. The Holy Spirit will never leave us, he is the seal of our salvation, the guarantee of our inheritance (Ephesians 1:13–14). However, each day we must choose how much of our lives we will allow him to fill.

How much of your heart and life does God's Holy Spirit fill? How much access are you willing to give him? Is there any part of yourself that you have barricaded from God? Why?

Glorious God, please fill me to overflowing with your Holy Spirit today. Fill me until there is no room for selfishness or pride. Fill me so that I can confidently go wherever you lead.

FEBRUARY 15

Numbers 7

The LORD said to Moses, "Let each leader bring his gift
on a different day for the dedication of the altar."
—Numbers 7:11

With the tabernacle completed, and the Lord's presence filling it,
it is time for each tribal leader to bring their offerings. Each leader
brings the exact same thing. Each offering is individually recorded.
Each family is credited with their gift. They bring the items that the
Levites will need to do their work.

How gracious of God to record each individual gift that is
offered to him.

The Bible is the full written revelation of God and every word is
important and chosen wisely; yet here God records twelve identical lists
given by twelve different men. God records each man's name twice.
Through this list, we see that gifts and individuals are precious to God.

God knows you individually; he knows your name (John 10:3).
Your name is written in heaven (Luke 10:20) and in the Lamb's
book of life (Revelation 21:27). God knows every detail of your life;
he knows the number of hairs on your head (Matthew 10:30), and
he sees every offering you give (Matthew 6:4) no matter how large
or how small.

When God reviews the record of your life nothing will be
overlooked. Will you be pleased with the way you gave your love,
possessions, time, talents, and finances? Will you be satisfied with
all that you gave? Will you wish you had given more?

> God, thank you for showing me that I am precious to you
> and that you know the gifts I bring. Please help me resist
> comparing my gifts. Please prompt me to remember that what
> matters most to you is the condition of my heart as I give.

FEBRUARY 16

Numbers 8:1–9:14; Leviticus 1–3

The LORD also instructed Moses, "This is the rule the
Levites must follow: They must begin serving in the
Tabernacle at the age of twenty-five, and they must
retire at the age of fifty. After retirement, they may assist
their fellow Levites by performing guard duty…"
—Numbers 8:2–26a

The Lord sets apart the Levites for service in the tabernacle and
gives regulations regarding work and age limits. The physical work
requires butchering animals: sheep, cattle, goats and birds. The
Levites must also keep the fires burning continually.

How gracious of God to provide places of service for both the
older and the younger generation. There would always be a place of
service for the twenty-five year olds, because there would always be
a spot vacated by a fifty year old. The younger men would do the
more physical labor; the older men would guard the tabernacle and
watch over the house of God.

There is no age-limit in working for God. God knows our
limitations, our strengths, and our weaknesses and he has a job for
each one of us.

Do you ponder what life will be like when you retire? Do you
think of days spent on the golf course or the beach, or are you excited
to begin the next work that God has planned for you? How encouraged
are you to know that God has work for you beyond retirement?

Lord, sometimes I think of retirement with joy, and
sometimes with fear. Help me to see retirement from your
perspective. Please help me to lovingly prepare, mentor and
embrace the generation that will replace me in the work
force; and cause me to trust that you are preparing me, even
now, to step into the next responsibility you have for me.

FEBRUARY 17

Leviticus 4–6

Then the Lord said to Moses, "Give the Israelites the following
instructions for dealing with those who sin unintentionally …
When he becomes aware of his sin … he must bring an offering."
—Leviticus 4:2a, 23a

God tells Moses what to say to the Israelites so that they will
understand God's holiness, their sinfulness, and the need for
reconciliation. God gives the Israelites a means of appeasing his
holy wrath against sin and reconciling the sinner to himself: once the
sinner is aware of his sin, he must bring an animal to the tabernacle,
confess his sin upon the animal, then the animal is slain and the
blood is presented before the Lord. In this way the priest makes
atonement for the sin, and the sinner is forgiven.

How gracious of God to provide atonement and reconciliation
between himself and sinful humanity. Because God is holy and
cannot tolerate, abide or condone sin, sinners are separated from
God (Isaiah 6:3–5).

You and I don't bring bulls, goats, sheep, pigeons, or grain
offerings to atone for our sins; the Lord Jesus Christ died on the
cross as our substitute atoning for our sin. Jesus's death paid the
penalty for our sins making reconciliation possible (2 Corinthians
5:18–19). When we receive Jesus's work on our behalf, the cause of
our estrangement—sin—is removed.

Will you ask God to show you the sin in your life? Will you
confess that sin and accept the atoning work of Christ on your
behalf? Will you ask Jesus to reconcile you to God?

Thank you, God, for the cross where the atoning sacrifice
of the blood of Jesus washed away all my sin, settled your
holy and just wrath against sin, and reconciled me to you.

FEBRUARY 18

Leviticus 7–8

For both the sin offering and the guilt offering,
the meat of the sacrificed animal belongs to the
priest in charge of the atonement ceremony.
—Leviticus 7:7

God gives Moses the instructions for the ordination of Aaron, the High Priest, and his sons. Moses washes, clothes, and anoints them. The sacrifices are offered for Aaron's sins and the sins of his sons. Moses tells them to eat the specified portion of the meat. From now on a portion of the offerings will belong to the priests.

How gracious of God to meet the needs of his servants through the offerings he receives from his people.

The priests were entitled to their designated share of the offerings just as the pastors and leadership of our local congregations are. When we bring our tithes and offerings to the church, our deacons and elders distribute those offerings as they believe God would have them, including the support of our pastors and leaders.

Church business meetings are not always easy to attend; they may go on for hours, there may be disagreements over how the offerings are spent, and the discussions can get quite heated. However, if God discloses his income and allocations in the pages of his Holy Word, doesn't it stand to reason that we should be aware of our local congregation's offerings and distributions as well?

How familiar are you with the business side of your church's finances?

God, I confess that I don't always enjoy the business side of church. Please develop in me an appreciation for those who tend to the business of church and show me ways to support them.

FEBRUARY 19

Leviticus 9–11

Then Moses said to Aaron and his sons Eleazar and Ithamar,
"Do not mourn … your relatives may mourn … But you
are not to leave the entrance of the Tabernacle …"
—Leviticus 10:6a,c, 7a

Aaron's sons disobey the Lord's command. Fire blazes forth from the
Lord's presence and consumes them; they die. Aaron is silent. Aaron
and his two remaining sons are not allowed to leave the tabernacle.
They are not to show signs of mourning. Their relatives will mourn
the dead. Aaron, Eleazar and Ithamar must continue to work.

How gracious of God to meet Aaron, Eleazar, and Ithamar with
strength to endure their family's tragedy and to carry out their work.

Death is an unwelcome and devastating enemy for which we
can never prepare. The sudden and unexpected death of a loved one
shocks us deeply. Even an anticipated death can be paralyzing. For
some of us work enables us to continue living in the face of death.
Death brings its own work: we must plan services, write eulogies,
and tend to survivors.

While work may be good for one hurting soul it may negatively
affect another, becoming the coffin in which someone buries
themselves in order to escape death's aftermath of mourning and grief.

We know that God is sufficient (2 Corinthians 12:9) and that
he loves us and will pour his strength into us as we choose to get up
and put one foot in front of the other. Death does not negate this
truth. How have you experienced God's grace in mourning?

God, thank you that when the waves of grief overwhelm
me, my feet always land on solid ground when I turn my
thoughts to you and choose to place my trust in you.

FEBRUARY 20

Leviticus 12:1–14:32

When a woman gives birth … she will be ceremonially unclean.
—Leviticus 12:1

God continues giving Moses instructions for purification, including the ceremonial cleansing after the birth of a child.

How gracious of God to give new mothers an opportunity to rest for an extended period of time after giving birth.

The need for ritual purification does not mean that sex is defiling or that babies are dirty. Being unclean—ceremonially defiled, not morally defiled—meant there was limited contact with other people and that the mother could not prepare meals or clean house. It provided a period of time to rest and to heal. We don't know why the time of uncleanness was doubled for a daughter; perhaps to allow the new mother ample time to bond with her little girl who would be considered a second-class citizen in a patriarchal society.

Having a period of extended rest seems to have gotten lost over the centuries. Today, mommies and babies are discharged from the hospital very soon after delivery and while some parents have maternity or paternity leave, many parents must return to work within a few days. Single parents bear the burden alone and grandparents often live far away. Are we moving in the wrong direction?

Are there new parents in your sphere of influence who could use some help? How might you help them today? Are you the new parent who needs help? Will you call someone today?

God, please show me where, and how, you would use me to help the young families around me. Please open my eyes to see who needs my help. Please prompt me to offer my help before they have to ask for it.

FEBRUARY 21

Leviticus 14:33–16:34

The people ... must bring two male goats for a sin offering ...
[Aaron] is to cast sacred lots to determine which goat will be
sacrificed to the LORD and which one will be the scapegoat.
—Leviticus 16:5a, 8

God gives purification regulations for contaminated houses, skin
disease, and clothing, and then he turns to the heart. Moses warns
Aaron that he must not enter the Most Holy Place whenever he
chooses, but only as God specifies. Moses gives God's instructions
for making atonement for the people: there must be two goats, which
together is one sin offering. One goat is sacrificed to the Lord, and
the other is the scapegoat. The goat that escapes death is led into the
wilderness carrying upon its head the confessed sin of the people.

How gracious of God to illustrate the removal of sin from the
hearts of his people. When God removes sin, it is gone. It is cast into
the depth of the sea (Micah 7:19); it is removed as far as the east is from
the west (Psalm 103:12); it is forgiven and forgotten (Jeremiah 31:34).

Jesus bore the sin of all people on the cross. He was both the
sacrifice and the scapegoat, for he was killed for your sin and mine;
and he removed that sin from us for all eternity. Jesus is the perfect
sin offering.

What sin are you still carrying? Can you visualize placing that
sin upon the head of Jesus, your scapegoat who was nailed to the
cross? Will you leave it there? He died for that sin. He died as your
substitute for all the sins you have ever or will ever commit.

God, what a precious reality you have given to me: Jesus, my
scapegoat who died in my place that I might live.

FEBRUARY 22

Leviticus 17–19

The LORD also said to Moses, "Say to the entire community of Israel: You must be holy because I, the LORD your God, am holy."
—Leviticus 19:1–2

The Israelites are to represent God to the world. Before they move into the new land God reminds them that he is calling them to holiness. He gives them instructions for holy living. Their worship must be as God commands. They must be holy in their most intimate relationships; and they must respect each other with their words and their actions.

How gracious of God to call his children to holiness. Holiness is not simply choosing to be like God; holiness is a life set apart to God and for God. Holiness is possible only after we've been separated from sin by virtue of a new birth (John 17:17).

Our call to holiness is the same as the Israelites' call: because we belong to God we must live a lifestyle that represents our Holy God. Holiness begins within a regenerated heart because our words and deeds originate in the heart (Matthew 12:33–34).

We must be careful not to confuse holiness with holier-than-thouness: a self-righteous, judgmental, or condemning attitude toward others that is not holiness at all. Holy lives are lives wholly dedicated to God and set aside for his use and purpose.

Is there a specific area of your life where you struggle with holiness? What would holiness in that area look like? What is the cost of unholiness?

God, I thank you for saving me and calling me to holiness. Please show me today the areas of my life where I have neglected holiness. Please teach me what holiness looks like and humble me to choose holiness because you are holy.

FEBRUARY 23

Leviticus 20–22

Tell Aaron that in all future generations, his descendants who
have physical defects will not qualify to offer food to their
God. However, he may eat from the food offered to God,
including the holy offerings and the most holy offerings.
—Leviticus 21: 17, 22

God gives regulations for the men who will be priests: the ones
who lead God's people. When the Israelites bring sacrifices to the
tabernacle, the dwelling place of God, the sacrifices (and the men
who receive them) must be as close to perfect as possible.

How gracious of God to fully protect the unblemished status
and privileges of the priestly position even as he places limitations
on the work of those with physical defects. God commands that all
priests may eat from the food offered to God.

Because God is perfect, every nuance of the tabernacle, including
the priests, must represent and reflect the perfection of the coming
Great High Priest.

Whether it is a physical limitation, a learning disability, a health
disorder, or an emotional disorder no one is perfect. We are all
born into a fallen world, and our bodies bear the results of the fall.
However, our physical state does not determine our spiritual status.
As children of God we can participate fully in the things of God.

Are you taking full advantage of your status as a perfected child
of the King? (Hebrews 10:14) or do you allow the imperfections of
your life to prevent you from enjoying the full status of your salvation?

> God, I know you have plans for me that include my
> imperfections. Please help me to see myself as you do. Please
> help me not to dwell on my imperfections but to serve you
> as perfectly as I can.

FEBRUARY 24

Leviticus 23:1–25:23

The LORD said to Moses, "Give the Israelites instructions
regarding the LORD's appointed festivals ..."
—Leviticus 23:1

God gives the parameters for approaching and worshiping him.
He includes specific times of the week and the year for worship
festivals. The festivals order the calendar for the Israelites and provide
opportunities for them to set aside work, to fellowship and worship
together as they share meals, give thanks, join in sacred assembly,
and experience periods of humility and fasting. During the festivals
the Israelites recall all God has done for them.

How gracious of God to establish worship that includes
festivals—specific set-aside times of corporate worship.

We no longer have appointed specific festivals for worship, but there
is something very special about going to church and worshiping alongside
other believers on Christian holidays such as Easter and Christmas. We
set aside work, we fellowship, we share meals, give thanks, and recall all
that God has done for us during these precious times.

You and I have many opportunities to give to God our allegiance
and love in worship apart from holidays. Worshipping regularly with
other Christians enhances our love for God and for other people.
Worship should define our daily lives as well as our Holy Days.

Is God the focus of your holiday celebrations, your weekly
worship and your daily life?

> God, I thank you for being a God who desires and deserves
> worship and for calling me to worship you alongside other
> Christians. As I meditate on all that you are, all that you've
> done for me, and all that you will do, may my life be a daily
> outpouring of worship.

FEBRUARY 25

Leviticus 25:24–26:46

I will walk among you; I will be your God, and you will be
my people. I, the LORD, am your God, who brought you
from the land of Egypt so you would no longer be slaves.
—Leviticus 26:12–13a

God brings the Israelites out of Egypt, and parks them at Mt. Sinai
while he instructs them in the way they are to live and worship. God
reminds them that they have been set free. God tells them if they follow
his decrees and obey his commands he will bless them with rain, crops,
produce, harvest, and peace and he will look favorably upon them.

How gracious of God to redeem Israel and set the people free.

God reached into Egypt and with a mighty hand and pulled
Israel out of slavery and bondage. Then he dwelt among them in
the tabernacle. He gave them glorious freedom. And he promised
that this was only the beginning of the blessings if only they would
choose to follow him.

Like Israel, we have been redeemed: purchased out of bondage
to sin, and paid for with the blood of Christ (1 Peter 1:18–19). The
enemy no longer owns us; we belong to Christ. Because of that great
redemption we have freedom, purpose, hope, and dignity. These are
only the beginning of the blessings God will pour out on us if we
choose to follow him.

From what land of sin has God reached in with his mighty
hand and delivered you? Are you living in freedom? Are you living
in abundance?

> Oh, God, may I never forget the miracle of your mighty
> hand that rescued me from the prison of my sin and that
> my freedom was purchased by the precious blood of Jesus
> at a great cost to you.

FEBRUARY 26

Leviticus 27; Numbers 1

Take a census of the whole community of Israel ... List the names
of all the men twenty years old or older who are able to go to war.
—Numbers 1:2–3a

The Israelites camp at Sinai for a little over a year. God gives the law
and regulations for holy living and now it's almost time to pack up
and move toward the Promised Land. Before heading out, Moses
must count the men and organize them into an army.

How gracious of God to show the Israelites how well he has
prepared them for the tasks to come. They are not a rag tag little
group, they are a nation of millions, and they have an army of
603,550 men ready to fight as they move toward the Promised Land.

God is taking Israel into a land where they will need to fight.
The Israelites will be God's tool of judgment. The sin of the current
inhabitants, like a malignant cancer, has overflowed its cup (Genesis
15:16).

Only God knows what the measure of sin is. Only God knows
how to judge sin rightly. Only God knows the tool he will use to
exact judgment and sometimes that tool is war. War is tragic. It
leaves scars. But sometimes, like cancer surgery, it is necessary.

As you search your own heart, is there a sin that has overflowed
its measure? Are you prepared to fight against it? Have you learned
how to use the Sword of Truth (Hebrews 4:12)? God's Word is sharp.
It may hurt. It may leave a scar. Nevertheless, it is worth it.

> Almighty God, King of Heaven's Armies, train me to
> appropriately and rightly handle your Word of Truth to cut
> away every sin and defeat every enemy.

FEBRUARY 27

Numbers 2–3

Each tribe will be assigned its own area in the camp, and
the various groups will camp beneath their family banners.
The Tabernacle will be located at the center ..."
—Numbers 2:2

Moses counts the army and assigns each clan and family a place in
the campsite. God himself is at the center. Each family arranges their
tents just as the Lord instructs them.

How gracious of God to organize the Israelites. This order
enabled them to pick up camp quickly when the Lord's presence
moved and everyone knew where to camp when the Lord stopped.
It enabled them to live in security. It enabled them to keep their
eyes on God.

All of us have experienced the frustration of disorder. When areas
of our offices or homes are cluttered, piled up, unorganized, and
haphazard it's easy to lose things. When our lives are disorganized
it's easy to lose sight of God and we find ourselves lost, adrift, and
separated from God's community. Clutter affects our ability to
see God.

God gives us direction to order our lives as we meditate on his
Word (Psalm 119). When God is the center of our lives, as he was in
the center of Israel's camp, we know that we will not get lost. He will
guide us. He will direct us. He will encamp around us (Psalm 34:7).

How are you defeating clutter and chaos in your life? Where is
God located in your camp?

> God, please give me a heart that desires order as much as you
> do in every area of my life. Show me where I've lost sight of
> you because of the clutter and disarray. Please show me the
> things that are taking your place in the center of my camp.

FEBRUARY 28

Numbers 4–5

But if she has not defiled herself and is
pure, she will be unharmed ...
—Numbers 5:28

God, who is holy, is in the center of the camp. God gives Moses instructions regarding physical purity and heart purity. God tells Moses how to deal with jealousy in marital relationships.

How gracious of God to provide a public means of determining guilt or innocence on the part of a wife in a society that treated women as property. If a man suspected his wife of unfaithfulness, God provided a way for her to prove her innocence.

At first read-through, we might chafe at this jealousy offering or offering of inquiry. However, should we put ourselves in the woman's shoes, perhaps we will see this as a protection for the innocent; for if she is indeed innocent, she will be unharmed (Psalm 26).

Sometimes innocent people are misjudged, misunderstood, and unfairly punished. Sometimes it is Christian brothers and sisters who slander or malign us, misjudging our motives and our actions. Only God knows the heart and God will see to it that his children are vindicated in his time and in his way (Psalm 35).

Have you been misjudged, misunderstood or unfairly punished? Are you willing to do whatever God asks you to do, then trust and wait on God to vindicate you? Is there someone you have misjudged? Might God be vindicating them?

> God, I know that you are the only Judge that matters in my life, but I also know how difficult it is for me when other people have misjudged me and I want to vindicate myself. Help me to wait patiently and trust you to vindicate me in your way and your time.

grace
MARCH

MARCH 1

Numbers 6; 10

One day in midspring, during the second year after Israel's
departure from Egypt, the cloud lifted ... So the Israelites set out.
—Numbers 10:11a, 12a

God safely brings the Israelites out of Egypt. He consistently leads
them and protects them. He moves them toward the land that was
promised to Abraham. He leads them with his presence: a cloud by
day and fire by night.

How gracious of God to lead the Israelites every moment of
every day. God never left the Israelites to their own devices. He never
abandoned them. He never forgot them. He had a destination and
he led them to it despite their many pitfalls along the way.

God continues to lead his people, individually, toward the
destination he has planned for them. Ultimately, our destiny is to
become like Jesus (Romans 8:29–30) and to share in his glory. We
also have the promise that God will diligently lead us until we reach
that destination (Philippians 1:6) despite the tug and pull of the
culture to lead us in a different direction.

We don't need the pillar or the cloud as much as we think we
may want them. As we spend time in God's Word our minds are
transformed so that we can stand against culture (Romans 12:2) and
actually understand and follow God's good and perfect will. How
confident are you that you are following God's path for you? Will
you set out with him today?

> God, please transform my mind as I read and meditate on
> your Word so that the culture around me is not my compass.
> I want to walk in the path of everlasting righteousness for
> your Name's sake. Thank you for your Holy Spirit's presence
> to guide me every moment of every day.

MARCH 2

Numbers 11–13

They will bear the burden of the people along with
you, so you will not have to carry it alone.
—Numbers 11:17b

The foreign rabble travelling with the Israelites complain and the Israelites follow suit. God's daily provision of manna appears more mediocre than miraculous. Nothing God or Moses does is good enough to please the people. The burden of carrying the people becomes too much for Moses; he would rather die than be treated this way. God provides help for Moses by anointing seventy leaders to assist Moses in bearing the burden of leading the people.

How gracious of God to provide capable people to share the burden of leadership. The complaining rabble and the ungrateful, rebellious Israelites have become a burden too heavy for Moses to bear alone so God provides men to come alongside and help him.

Independence and inner strength are attributes that we admire and frequently seek in the world today. As Christians, we know we're supposed to come alongside other Christians and share each other's burdens (Galatians 6:2), but often we don't know how. We don't want to offend anyone by suggesting they need help. And when we are the one who needs help, we are often too proud to ask for it.

God commands Christians to work together. Are you a leader at your wits' end? Have you asked God for help? Will you graciously receive whomever God sends your way?

> Father, when my burden becomes too heavy to bear, please humble my heart to ask for help. Help me to see and accept the help you provide, or to be the helper you are providing for someone else. Keep me from being a rebellious, complaining burden to those who lead me.

MARCH 3

Well, I will bring them safely into the land, and
they will enjoy what you have despised.
—Numbers 14:31b

The Israelites arrive at the boundary of Canaan—the Promised Land—and Moses sends twelve Israelites to scout out the land. Ten explorers convince the Israelites they are too small to take possession of the land. Two scouts, Joshua and Caleb, argue that the Lord will give them the land. The Israelites fearfully refuse to move forward and instead plot their return to Egypt.

God's judges their rebellion. They will wander forty years in the desert while all of that rebellious generation dies outside the Promised Land. Their children will settle the land.

How gracious of God, in this moment of crisis, to promise that there will be Israelites who settle in the Promised Land. The Israelites who fail to trust God and take the land will die in the wilderness, but their children will go in. In great sorrow, there is still hope.

God is a God of hope who keeps his word (Psalm 42). Even though we fail God, God will never fail us.

Has there been a time when you failed to take the land because you were afraid? Are you living in the consequences of your decision? If God should take you back to that place of failure what have you since learned about God that would cause you to behave differently?

Faithful One, thank you for continuing to offer forgiveness, mercy, and grace even though I often let fear of the things I see keep me from following you. Help me to trust you despite the circumstances that surround me, so that I am not afraid to take the land you've prepared for me.

MARCH 4

Numbers 16–18

When he went into the Tabernacle of the Covenant
the next day, he found that Aaron's staff ... had
sprouted, blossomed, and produced almonds!
—Numbers 17:8

Though God has appointed Moses and Aaron to lead the nation, the Israelites rebel and challenge the authority and position of both men. God judges the Israelite rebellion. God sets forth a test to show the people that Moses and Aaron are not self-appointed leaders, but God's men with God's authority behind them. Each tribe is to bring a staff to the tabernacle. The next day, only Aaron's staff has budded.

How gracious of God to validate the authority of his appointed leaders. God called Moses, equipped him, and used him to lead the Israelites out of Egypt. Moses was God's man; he was not a self-appointed leader, and Aaron was God's appointed High Priest.

Today, as in Moses' day God is with every believer. We are a nation of priests (1 Peter 2:9), however, God appoints specific people as leaders whom we must accept and to whom we must submit. We must not allow a personality clash or a complicated spider web of emotion, jealousy, or past history keep us from giving the respect that is due our leaders (Hebrews 13:17). Nor must we covet a leadership role that God has not assigned to us.

How has God validated the leaders whom he has placed in authority over you? How might you show your gratitude this week to those who lead you?

> God, please help me to be supportive of your chosen leaders in my life, and in my church. Please give me ways to show my respect for, and submission to them this week. Please enable me to both lead and follow appropriately, as I ultimately submit to you.

MARCH 5

Numbers 19–21

The time has come for Aaron to join his ancestors in death …
Take Aaron and his son Eleazar up Mount Hor. There you will
remove Aaron's priestly garments and put them on Eleazar …
—Numbers 20:24a, 25–26a

God tells Aaron and Moses that the time of Aaron's death has come.
God gives them the plan to transfer the high priesthood to Eleazar,
Aaron's son.

How gracious of God to allow Aaron to witness Eleazar, his own
son, assume the office of high priest and wear the high priest's clothing.

It must have been a somber day for the Israelites as they prepare
to grieve the death of their high priest, Aaron. As Moses, Aaron,
and Eleazar walk up the mountain I wonder if it was silent because
everything had been said. I wonder if they talked continuously so
that nothing would be left unsaid.

No one can adequately prepare to face the impending death of a
loved one. Death is always brutal (John 11:33–36). We hate death.
It is not natural. We are not created to die. We are created to live
eternally and we will. The only question is: where? heaven or hell?

God's people die, but God's plan continues. Who are you
preparing to take over your role in your ministry, your home, or
your church?

As you contemplate the reality that your final day will eventually
come, have you said everything that needs to be said today? What
if you were to die tonight?

> Everlasting Father, thank you that when we die, we don't
> end, and neither does your plan. Help me to view my life
> as temporary, and your plan as eternal, so that I might
> faithfully train the next generation to serve you.

MARCH 6

Numbers 22–24

But how can I curse those whom God has not cursed? How
can I condemn those whom the LORD has not condemned?
—Numbers 23:8

God gives the Israelites victory after victory as they move closer to
the Promised Land. They are a force to be reckoned with because the
Almighty God is their God. Balek, king of Moab, is afraid that he is
next to fall to the Israelite army so he calls upon Balaam to curse Israel.
Balaam has knowledge of the one true God. While Balaam's motivation
is financial gain, he realizes that he cannot control the words of God.

How gracious of God to protect Israel from unknown
wickedness. The Israelites had no idea what was going on behind
the scenes between Balek and Balaam. However, God did. God
knows everything. God knew who Israel's enemies were. God knows
who our enemies are.

We must not forget that the powers we fight against are not of this
world: we fight against rulers, authorities, and powers of this dark world;
the spiritual forces of evil in the heavenly realms (Ephesians 6:12).

We may not know where the Evil One is prowling, or whom
he is waiting to devour (1 Peter 5:8), however we do know that
he cannot condemn or accuse those whom God has declared just
(Romans 8:1).

As you look back on your life, where can you now see the
invisible protection of a loving God? How comforted are you that
God is sovereign, even over evil?

> Almighty God, thank you for all the times you protect me;
> the times I am aware I need protection, and especially the
> times when I am not.

MARCH 7

So these are the census figures of the people of Israel …
Not one person that was counted in the census had been
among those counted in the previous census …
—Numbers 26:63a, 64a

Israel will soon enter the Promised Land and God directs Moses to count the men once again. None of the men counted in this census had been among those counted in the first census; and yet, the size of the potential army is almost exactly the same.

How gracious of God to keep his word. Throughout their forty years of wandering in the desert the entire generation of rebellious Israelites died, just as God said they would. God cut away the cancer of rebellion that could have overtaken and destroyed the entire nation.

Because God perfectly keeps his word in the past, we know that we can trust him to keep his word in the future. God promises to bring to completion the work that he began in us (Philippians 1:6) just as he brought the Israelites to the Promised Land. He will make us holy, he will keep us from stumbling, and he will present us before his glorious throne without fault and with great joy (Jude 1:24).

What rebellion needs cut away from your heart before it destroys you? What disbelief? What envy? What bitterness? Will you ask God to search your heart and cut away every cancer that keeps you from believing him and trusting him completely?

> Holy God, I know your word is true, because you are Truth. Help me to remember that when life seems harsh, you are at work for my good. I surrender to your holy scalpel, please cut away everything within me that keeps me from trusting you wholeheartedly.

MARCH 8

Numbers 27–29

Moses laid his hands on [Joshua] and
commissioned him to his responsibilities.
—Numbers 27:23a

Moses' leadership nears its end. He loves the Israelites. He knows
they need someone who is both a capable warrior and a gentle
shepherd to lead them. Moses asks God to appoint a new leader and
the Lord tells Moses to take Joshua and commission him. Moses
obeys and transfers his authority to Joshua.

How gracious of God to prepare Joshua through a mentoring
relationship with Moses.

Moses mentored Joshua for forty years. Joshua was by Moses'
side when he first went up Mount Sinai to meet with God. Joshua
fought battles as Moses prayed. Joshua was with Moses when he
went into the Tent of Meeting in the desert. Joshua learned how to
lead by staying close to his leader, Moses.

We must be diligent to mentor the next generation of leaders
even as we lead them today. There will come a time to pass the baton
and it is up to this generation to hand it off cleanly to the next. If
we have not prepared the next leaders to take the baton, it will fall.
If it falls, who will pick it up?

If you are older, who are you mentoring? Are you preparing them
for your departure? If not, how will the work continue after you have
gone? If you are younger, who is mentoring you? What are you doing
to prepare yourself to receive the baton, and then pass it on?

God, you know the future, you know what kind of leader
your people need. Will you show me who you would have
me mentor, or be mentored by, so that the baton will not
be dropped.

MARCH 9

A man who makes a vow to the LORD or makes a
pledge under oath must never break it. He must
do exactly what he said he would do.
—Numbers 30:2

The Israelites are about to enter and establish themselves in the
Promised Land so God prepares them for the responsibility of
representing him in yet another aspect: their word. They must be
trustworthy as God is trustworthy; they must keep their word.

How gracious of God to draw our attention to the power of
spoken words. As Warren Wiersbe has said "We expect the Lord
to keep his promises, and he expects us to keep ours. Truth is the
cement that holds society together." Words matter.

The fundamental issue for the Israelites was telling the truth and
it is no less important today. If we say something, we must mean it,
and we must follow through. Our yes must mean yes and our no
must mean no (Matthew 5:37). This is true in the business world
and in the family. If we can't be counted on to keep our word, how
can we expect anyone to believe us when we tell them that our God
always keeps his word?

There is a multitude of ways in which we break our word, not the
least of which is to lie. Yet, God, in his amazing grace always keeps
his word and he promises that when we confess our sin, including
our broken vows, he will always forgive and cleanse us (1 John 1:9).
When did you last fail to keep your word?

God, thank you for your unbroken word and for forgiving
me. Cause me to recognize the importance you place on
my words so that I will always speak truthfully and keep
every vow.

MARCH 10

Numbers 32–33

At the LORD's direction, Moses kept a
written record of their progress.
—Numbers 33:2

The Israelites camp near the Jordan River with the Promised Land in sight. Moses records the stages of their march recalling their forty years in the desert. From the Lord's defeat of the gods of Egypt through their entire desert journey, Moses records everything.

How gracious of God to direct Moses to write down a record of their progress. Through Moses and many other men, God recorded his story on the pages of the Bible. People will die, memories will grow dim, but God's Word will never fail (Luke 21:33). God's Word will never change (Isaiah 40:6–7).

Sometimes we rewrite or edit our history so that it reflects our perspective. If we were to ask our siblings to describe a specific event in our shared history, each one of us would probably have a different recollection. As we recall our personal histories, there may even be times when we forget God's hand in our past and our stories become self-focused instead of God-focused.

As you look back on your life, where do you see God's mighty hand at work? What gods has he defeated in your life? What strongholds has he broken down? How has God fed you? Where has God led you? How does recalling all that God has done for you encourage you to walk boldly into tomorrow—that new job, the next phase of life, a new community, a new church—wherever God might lead you?

Thank you, God, for breathing your unchanging and perfect revelation of history into Scripture. Thank you for your Word that reminds me of all you are and all you've done which enables me to face the future fearlessly because you are already there.

MARCH 11

Numbers 34–36

Six of the towns you give the Levites will be cities of refuge, where
a person who has accidentally killed someone can flee for safety.
—Numbers 35:6

The Israelites are a nation of campers travelling and living close
together. In preparation for their entering and spreading throughout
the Promised Land God appoints men to oversee the division of the
land. He also allots land to be set aside specifically for the Levites
and for cities of refuge.

How gracious of God to provide for every need for his people,
including protection from one another. God knows that there will
be Israelites who succumb to vigilante justice, and therefore he acts
to protect those who might be wrongly accused.

There are times when our innocence may be brought into
question, our motives misjudged, or our actions misunderstood.
We may not be able to flee to a city for refuge—though we may
want to run and hide—but we can flee to God (Psalm 46:1). He is
our wall of protection.

Have you ever been wrongly accused? God is your refuge; he
will avenge you in his time. Have you ever jumped to a wrong
conclusion about someone else? Have you ever murdered another
person's reputation by misrepresenting them or misstating facts
about them? What should you do to set things right?

> God, you alone know all the details of life; please keep me
> from hurting others in my ignorance. Please show me where
> I need to ask for forgiveness, and where I need to extend it
> so that I am not a source of pain, but of protection.

MARCH 12

Deuteronomy 1:1–3:20

So Moses addressed the people …
—Deuteronomy 1:5

Before he dies, and before the Israelites enter the Promised Land, Moses reminds them of all God has done for them. He recalls Sinai, the appointment of the judges, the exploration of the land, and their rebellion. Moses reminds the Israelites of the people who died during the forty years, and of the victories in battle that God gave them. Throughout all, Moses reminds the Israelites that it is God who has given them everything.

How gracious of God to provide a leader who did not take the credit for leading his people, but gave all the glory to God.

We know that apart from God we can do nothing. (John 15:5). We know that we can do all things through Christ who strengthens us (Philippians 4:13). We also know that it is tremendously tempting, even as leaders for the cause of Christ, to take credit for a lecture, a sermon, a word of encouragement, a blog post, or even what we learn in our Bible studies. It's possible to put such a high value on being important, having great accomplishments, and making a name for one's self that proclaiming the Name of Jesus can become secondary.

As you prepare and teach your Sunday school class, as you wash dishes and clean your house, as you entertain your friends, or when you chat at the bus stop do you lift up the name of Jesus? Do your friends and neighbors know who enables you? Who receives the glory for the successes in your life?

> Almighty God, I know that you will not share your glory with anyone else and I confess the times when I have tried to do just that. To you alone be the glory!

MARCH 13

Deuteronomy 3:21–5:33

Search all history from the time God created people on
the earth until now. Has any nation ever heard the voice of
God speaking from fire—as you did—and survived?
—Deuteronomy 4:32a, 33

Moses recalls all that God has done and reminds the Israelites how
unique they are. Never, in all of history, has God spoken to a nation
as God speaks to them. Never. God did this, not because of how
great the Israelites are, but because of his great love.

How gracious of God to make himself known to his children
as the one true God

Only God is the one true God. As God he is the source of all
our hopes, dreams and pleasures. Every good gift comes from him
(James 1:17). His pedestal is unreachable (Isaiah 55:8) yet he is not
hidden; he reveals himself to everyone who wants to find him (1
Chronicles 28:9).

God still speaks to his children and he has much to say; our
job is to listen to his voice (John 10:24–27). When God speaks,
he speaks in the language of "Bible", are you listening as you read?

Other gods—idols—are those things or people to which we
assign the responsibility of our hopes, our dreams, and our pleasures.
When we exalt our idols we set them up on pedestals fabricated out
of false ideals. Idols are not gods, they are lies.

Have you established idols in your life? To whom do you turn
to find fulfillment, purpose, approval or happiness?

> Almighty God, I do believe that you are the one true God
> and it amazes and humbles me that you would choose me,
> speak to me, and love me. You are my God! And I will
> always love you!

MARCH 14

Deuteronomy 6–9

The LORD did not choose you and lavish his love on you
because you were larger or greater than other nations ...
it was simply because the LORD loves you ...
—Deuteronomy 7:7a, 8a

Moses continues to remind the Israelites of God's love and protection
and he reminds them that they did not earn God's affection because
of how wonderful they are. Nor did they merit God's choice because
of how large they are. God did not choose Israel because of anything
Israel did or didn't do, or because of anything Israel was or wasn't.
God chose Israel simply because he is God and it pleases him to
choose and love them.

How gracious of God to make his choice of Israel based on his love.

God chose you and me before the foundation of the world
(Ephesians 1:4–5). Thankfully, it is not because of anything inherent
in us: our winning nature, looks, intelligence, height, age, pedigree,
or any other thing that draws attention and praise from people.
God chose us simply because he loves us and it pleased him to do
so (Ephesians 1:5–9). If God's choice were based on anything else,
then if we should lose the criteria for being chosen, we'd lose God.

Have you chosen to accept God's choice of you (John 15:16;
Romans 10:13)? Do you believe God chose you simply because
he loves you? God's love is unconditional love, you cannot earn it
nor can you merit it. Have you accepted God's unconditional love
of you?

God, your love overwhelms me! Thank you for choosing me
while I was dead in the pit of my sin, loving me when I was
unlovely, and drawing me into your heart.

MARCH 15

Deuteronomy 10–12

> At that time the LORD said to me, "Prepare two stone
> tablets like the first ones … and I will write … the
> same words that were on the ones you smashed."
> —Deuteronomy 10:1a, 2a

Moses carefully records the history of the Israelites in the desert,
including his own weaknesses and failures. Moses writes so that all
future generations will know the character of God. Moses records
that when he destroyed the original tablets on which God had
written the Ten Commandments, God replaced them.

How gracious of God to prompt Moses to record the entire story.

If you or I were to write our life story, would we be tempted
to leave out the failures and errors that make us look foolish, less
attractive or far from perfect? Who wants their embarrassing
moments brought up if the retelling makes us appear less than what
we want others to think of us? Who wants to talk about the times
we failed God, ourselves, or others?

But, when we gloss over those events, do we remove the ability
to share God's forgiveness, provision, restoration, love, grace, justice
and mercy with others who might need to hear and experience it?
Do we remove the fact that God is a God of second chances? Heaven
forbid we clean up our history at the expense of God's reputation!

Whose reputation is more important to you? Who needs to hear
that God has given you second and even third chances? How is God's
reputation enhanced when others hear of his mercy and grace to you?

God, your reputation is more important than mine is or
ever could be. I realize that apart from you, and your grace,
I am nothing. Thank you for all the times you've let me
begin again.

MARCH 16

Deuteronomy 13:1–16:17

The purpose of tithing is to teach you
always to fear the Lord your God.
—Deuteronomy 14:23

Moses reminds the Israelites that true and sincere worship of God includes giving a tithe of the crops, grain, wine, olive oil, and the firstborn of all their flocks and herds. Then Moses tells them the purpose for the tithe: Giving the prescribed gift teaches the giver to fear God.

How gracious of God to provide a practical tool to teach his children to fear him. Tithing is an act of worship and worship flows from a heart that cherishes the worthiness of God.

When we worship God we are giving him his due. We recognize that apart from God we are nothing and have nothing. Bringing an offering says that we trust God to continue to provide for us because we know that we cannot provide for ourselves alone and to think that we can is spiritual arrogance (Malachi 3:6–15). When we give our financial gifts, whether a tithe, or whatever the amount that we have decided in our hearts to give, it must be done cheerfully and freely (2 Corinthians 9:7).

Our giving should flow from a heart of gratitude and thanksgiving and it should be a sufficient amount to reveal our dependence on God.

Why do you bring a financial offering before God? Is it an act of worship for you? Is it a way to say thank you? Does the amount you are currently giving increase your awesome respect for and holy fear of God?

Almighty God, I know that all I have you have given me. Teach me to love, respect and fear you more than I love having the financial gifts you have given me.

MARCH 17

Deuteronomy 16:18–21:9

When he sits on the throne as king, he must copy
these laws … He must always keep this copy with
him and read it daily as long as he lives.
—Deuteronomy 17:18a, 19a

In preparing the Israelites to move into the Promised Land, Moses
addresses their possible future desire for a king. Moses gives them
God's guidelines for selecting a king, and God's responsibilities for
that king. God lists much the king shouldn't do, but there is only
one requirement that he must do: he is to copy the law, keep it with
him, and read it every day.

How gracious of God to require that any future king must know
and lead by God's law.

We need godly leaders. Every person who sits in authority was
placed there by God and no one has any authority that God has not
established (Romans 13:1). However, for a multitude of reasons, not
all people in places of authority submit to God or his Word. That
does not mean God is not sovereign over them.

How different the world would be if every leader recognized the
true authority behind their position and studied God's law daily.

Do you recognize that your authority comes from God? As you
read God's Word, what difference have you observed in the way you
respect and administer your authority?

> God, my desire is to lead those you've placed under me in
> the same way you lead me. As I study your Word, teach me
> what I need to learn to be a godly leader. Humble me to
> remember that I have no authority that you have not given
> to me and cause me to be a leader who uses that authority
> in a way that honors you.

MARCH 18

Deuteronomy 21:10–25:19

True justice must be given to foreigners living among you
and to orphans … Always remember that you were slaves
in Egypt and that the LORD your God redeemed you from
your slavery. That is why I have given you this command.
—Deuteronomy 24:17a, 18

Moses continues his words of instruction before Israel possesses the
Promised Land. Moses gives regulations to protect relationships
within the family and the community.

How gracious of God to remind the Israelites that righteousness
in relationships is required, and possible, because they have been
redeemed out of slavery.

The Israelites are on the verge of possessing the Promised Land
and they must not forget from where they came. We must never
forget from where we have come either. Before we were redeemed—
purchased by the blood of Christ—we were spiritually dead
(Ephesians 2:5–7). We were unable to understand spiritual things
(1 Corinthians 2:14). We lived an empty way of life (1 Peter 1:18).
And we had no righteousness of our own (Romans 3:10).

As we meditate on all that we have, and are, because of our great
salvation we will loathe the sinner we used to be and our hearts will
grow tender toward the people we know and love who have not yet
believed on Christ.

Who do you know who needs to hear of the saving grace that is
available in Christ Jesus?

> Almighty God, I thank you for purchasing me out of the
> marketplace of sin. Keep me from behaving as though I still
> live there. Please open my eyes to see where I am denying
> your love and justice to anyone who is still lost in sin. Open
> my heart to love them. Open my mouth to share with them
> the glorious truth of salvation.

MARCH 19

Deuteronomy 26:1–29:1

Today you have become the people of the LORD
your God. So obey the LORD your God by
keeping all these commands and laws...
—Deuteronomy 27:9b, 10a

The time has come. Israel is soon to enter the Promised Land and
Moses reminds them they are God's people. Moses gives instruction
to hold a public ceremony when they enter the land: they will stand
on opposite mountains calling blessings for obedience and curses for
disobedience back and forth across the valley. They will carve God's
law on stone pillars as a public reminder of God and his protection
over them in the desert.

How gracious of God to make his people known to all the nations.

The Israelites were God's people and they would not slip into
the land unnoticed. There would be a public ceremony with pillars
erected so that everyone would know who these people are and the
God to whom they belong.

God has public ceremonies for his children today. When we
come to faith in him we must publicly declare our faith and be
baptized (Acts 2:41; 8:12).We must live our faith boldly as salt and
light in the world (Matthew 5:13–16). We must stand confidently for
the Lord Jesus Christ (Mark 8:38). In addition, we must recognize
and pray for our brothers and sisters who must practice their faith
in secret at the risk of their lives.

How are you proclaiming the God to whom you belong? How
does God make known to the people in your sphere of influence
that you belong to him?

God, please cause me to live boldly for you. Make me a blessing
to each person I meet. Please remove my insecurities and fears
and teach me how to publicly proclaim that you are my God.

MARCH 20

Deuteronomy 29:2–31:29

Though you are at the ends of the earth, the LORD your
God will go and find you and bring you back again.
—Deuteronomy 30:4

Moses summons the Israelites—men, women and children—and reiterates all that God has done for them. He calls them to promise to obey God so that they will prosper. Moses tells them to repent when they are disobedient. He promises that whenever they call on the name of the Lord, God will go to the ends of the earth to find them and bring them back.

How gracious of God to promise that he will go to any lengths to bring his repentant children back to him. There is no place of disobedience that is beyond the reach of Almighty God when his children confess their sin, repent, and turn wholeheartedly to him (1 John 1:9).

This promise of God is still true today. God lays before every person the choice of life through obedience or death through disobedience. The choice for life means choosing to live in Christ, to accept the atoning work Jesus accomplished on the cross for our salvation.

Where have you chosen the temporary pleasures of disobedience at the cost of a rift in your fellowship with God? Do you believe that he will go to the ends of the earth to bring you back into fellowship with him? Do you know someone who needs to hear this truth?

> God, you created the universe for your glory, and it humbles and amazes me that when I confessed my sin and sought your forgiveness you reached across the vast chasm of sin to bring me into your fold. Thank you.

MARCH 21

Deuteronomy 31:30–32:52; Psalm 90

So Moses recited this entire song to the assembly of Israel.
—Deuteronomy 31:30

On this day, Moses recites a song to the Israelites encapsulating their history and proclaiming the name of the Lord, their glorious God. He tells all the people to memorize the song and teach it to their children. When Moses finishes God tells Moses to go up the mountain and look out over the land. God tells Moses again that he will not enter the land. Moses sees the land from a distance.

How gracious of God to give every generation knowledge of his holy character. The Israelites passed along the knowledge of God orally from generation to generation; everyone memorized and sang the song Moses wrote.

Moses' song includes everything: famine, snakes, and terrors and also the glorious faithfulness, justice, mercy, and discipline of a God who loves his people without end.

We have a myriad of means for passing along knowledge today from the internet to Bible apps, television shows, radio programs, and printed pages. Nevertheless, how complete is the knowledge we are passing to the next generation? Do we teach the entire counsel of Scripture?

Are there parts of the Bible that you omit, overlook, disregard, or fail to read and study? Why? Who will pass to the next generation things which you have failed to learn?

> God, please help me to embrace the entire counsel of Scripture and enable me to transfer it to those whom I am responsible to teach. Please give me age-appropriate words when I teach children and settle my heart to know that you will bring about understanding as it is needed.

MARCH 22

Deuteronomy 33–34; Joshua 1–2

This is the land I promised ... I have now allowed you to see it.
—Deuteronomy 34:4

Moses, 120 years old, blesses the Israelites, climbs a mountain, hears the voice of God, and looks out over the Promised Land. Then on that mountaintop, Moses dies.

How gracious of God to allow Moses to see the land with his own eyes before he dies.

God doesn't owe Moses anything. Moses lived a long life. The first forty years he lived in Egypt in Pharaoh's palace and was educated in the things of the world. The second forty years he lived in the desert as a shepherd and God educated him in the things he needed to know in order to lead God's people and form them into a nation. The final forty years, Moses walked with the Israelites and with God, wrote the first five books of the Bible, and was used as God's tool to establish the true worship of God.

Moses led the Israelites out of Egypt, through the desert, and to the border of the Promised Land but he would not physically walk into the Promised Land with them. Unfair? No. Moses knew this was a consequence of his sin. Moses did receive the blessing of seeing the land with his own eyes.

God lets us make our choices, and God wisely allows specific consequences (1 Thessalonians 5:16–18). We, like Moses, must walk in the consequences of our choices.

What consequence of your sin has God allowed in your life? What blessing is he showing you along the way.

God, please give me eyes to see all of your blessings even as I walk in the consequences of my sin.

MARCH 23

Joshua 3–6

The LORD told Joshua, "Today I will begin to make
you great in the eyes of all the Israelites. Now they will
know that I am with you, just as I was with Moses."
—Joshua 3:7

Before Moses died he commissioned Joshua to lead the Israelites. God promises Joshua he will be with him and commands him to be strong and courageous. God promises to make Joshua great in the eyes of the Israelites so they will know God is with him.

How gracious of God to reassure Joshua that he is God's chosen leader; and that God will make it clear to everyone that it is God who leads Joshua even as Joshua leads them.

God's program will always continue with God's appointed leaders at the helm. God has his leaders in ministries throughout the world. Some lead in mega-churches where thousands worship each Sunday and some lead tiny flocks of toddlers. Leaders however, don't stay in the same place forever. When it's time for a change of guard, it can be difficult for those they lead.

Our responsibility as Christians is to be committed to God and in that commitment we pray for our leaders, embrace whomever God calls to lead us, submit to their authority, and do all that we can to make their time of leadership joyful (Hebrews 13:17).

When a new leader is set over us, we must pray for and embrace God's choice. This is easiest when our commitment is to God rather than the program or the leadership. To whom or what have you committed? Will you trust God to validate your leaders, and you as a leader?

God, I thank you for the leaders you have placed over me
and that you are the ultimate leader over all your programs.

MARCH 24

The Israelites were paralyzed with fear and their courage
melted away. But the LORD said to Joshua, "Get up!"
—Joshua 7:5b, 10a

The Israelites soundly defeat Jericho then march into Canaan
only to suffer an abysmal defeat by a small and insignificant army.
Confused, Joshua tears his clothes and the leaders bow before the
Lord. God tells Joshua they were defeated because Israel has sinned.
The defeat causes the Israelites to renew their covenant with God.

How gracious of God to allow humiliating defeats. God could
have given one victory after another to the Israelites but this campaign
was not just about conquering land; it was about establishing God's
holy nation in the Promised Land. It was about the just exercise of
God's holy wrath against wicked people who had reached the full
measure of their sin (Genesis 15:16). God's tool, Israel, needed to be
holy because God is holy.

When there is sin in our camp, when we go forth without God,
when we haven't humbled ourselves before God, and for many other
reasons God allows defeat (Numbers 23; Psalm 127:1). Our defeats
are often the impetus that leads to God's triumph in our hearts.

How have you handled the defeats in your life? Do you recognize
God's hand in the defeat? Is there hidden sin that God is prompting
you to confess? Will you ask God to reveal the sin you need to
acknowledge? Will you confess that sin, repent and regroup with God?

> Sovereign God, I thank you for the defeats in my life. I know
> that in the defeat, you are working. Help me to embrace
> your good character, your sovereignty, your perfect plan
> and your intervention in my life so that my failures become
> your triumphs.

MARCH 25

Joshua 10:1–12:6

"Do not be afraid of them," the LORD said to Joshua,
"for I will give you victory over them …"
—Joshua 10:8a

After Joshua falls for the Gibeonite deception and signs a treaty with them, Gibeon is attacked. Gibeon calls upon Joshua for protection. The Lord promises Joshua victory. One battle follows another during years of heartache, bloodshed, slaughter, and destruction. Joshua subdues the whole region. Finally, there is rest from war.

How gracious of God to use our blunders to accomplish his good plan.

God is not limited by our humanness and shortcomings. God is not limited by the mistakes we make when we act in self-confidence. God is not limited by the size of the enemy's army. God uses Joshua's mistake (making a treaty with Gibeon without consulting God) to bring Israel's enemies out into the open. War is declared and battles are fought. God is the victor.

Sometimes our mistakes bring our enemies up against us. We make foolish decisions without consulting God and everything comes crashing down. Our errors don't catch God off guard, he never slumbers, he never sleeps, he doesn't need to catch up (Psalm 121).

What errors in judgment have you made because you didn't consult God? Have you made treaties with the enemy? How are the consequences playing out? Will you trust that God is in the battle and he is bringing a victory?

> Almighty God, please show me the foolish mistakes and treaties I have made. Help me to understand how you are at work in my life for your glory and my good, bringing victory out of my weaknesses.

MARCH 26

Joshua 12:7–15:19

The LORD has kept me alive and well … Today I
am eighty-five years old. I am as strong now as I
was when Moses sent me on that journey …
—Joshua 14:1, 11a

Caleb wholeheartedly follows God throughout his life. Joshua
allocates the land, giving an inheritance to each tribe. Caleb, who
explored the land with Joshua forty-five years prior, tells Joshua that
Moses promised him a specific portion. Now at eighty-five, Caleb,
still strong, asks for the land. Joshua gives Caleb his inheritance.

How gracious of God to reward faith; rewarding Caleb's faith
with the gift of the land.

God promises many rewards to his children, not the least of which is
reward for keeping his commands (Psalm 19:10–11), for acts of kindness
(Proverbs 19:17), for right conduct (Jeremiah 17:10), and for our labor on
his behalf (I Corinthians 3:8–9). God rewards all faith (Hebrews 11:6).

Sometimes we will enjoy our rewards in this life, sometimes
we will not. We can rest assured that an eternal reward awaits us;
a reward that will last forever (1 Corinthians 9:25). The greatest
reward will be the privilege of laying our crowns before the throne
of Jesus (Revelation 4:10).

In light of eternity, no matter what your chronological age, you
are still quite young. You are still strong enough to fight the battles
that God would have you fight and receive the land, the rewards,
that God has promised to you.

God, I thank you for life and spiritual strength. I will not
shrink back from the work you have for me because I desire
every reward you have planned for me. I will focus on living
wholeheartedly for you despite my weaknesses, my aches,
and my pains all the days of my life.

MARCH 27

Zelophehad ... had five daughters ... So Joshua gave them an inheritance along with their uncles, as the LORD had commanded.
—Joshua 17:3, 4b

Zelophehad has five daughters and no sons. In their earlier appeal to Moses and Eleazar, God directs Moses to allot to them their father's inheritance; Joshua gives the women the land.

How gracious of God to have an inheritance for all his children.

God has an inheritance for you and for me! We become God's children when we receive Christ as our Savior, and as God's children we are co-heirs with Christ. When we believed God blessed us with every spiritual blessing in Christ Jesus (Ephesians 1:3) and we received the promises and the guarantee of eternal life with him.

God does not withhold anything because of gender, race, nationality or ethnicity. There is neither male nor female in Christ; we are not the same, but we are all spiritually equal (Galatians 3:28–29). We all are given the same salvation and the same destination; God does not have favorites among his children (Romans 2:11).

Are you a child of God through rebirth and regeneration by the Holy Spirit? There is no other legal ground upon which to stake your claim for an eternal inheritance. Are you living as a spiritual pauper or in the richness of your inheritance as a child of the One True King?

> Gracious God, I thank you for adopting me and marking me as your child. Thank you for allowing me to come into your presence and call you Father. Thank you for my eternal inheritance that enables me to live today in the riches that are mine in Christ Jesus.

MARCH 28

Joshua cast sacred lots in the presence of the LORD to
determine which tribe should have each section.
—Joshua 18:10

The Israelites are in the land and yet there are tribes that have yet to
take the land God gave them. Joshua asks them how long they are
going to wait. Joshua sends them to map the land and then he casts
sacred lots to determine the allotment. Joshua knows the people need
to take possession of what God has given them.

How gracious of God to spur the Israelites out of complacency
and into action. To claim the land that God had already given to
them, the Israelites needed to physically take it. They must prove
their faith in God's word by their actions (James 2:18, 26).

God gives many things to every believer, and yet in our careers,
our homes, our neighborhoods, and our churches, we forfeit many
gifts because of what is required to claim them: faith. When we fail
to take possession of what is ours we inadvertently surrender ground
to the enemy.

Faith believes God and acts on his word. Have you taken
possession of the land that the Lord, the God of your ancestors, has
given you? If not, how long will you wait? What does your delay
reveal about your faith?

> God, I know that you have allotted land for me: a place to
> lead for you, a place to take a stand for you, a place to grow
> in wisdom and knowledge, a place of safety and rest, a place
> that I should possess. I know that you have defeated my
> enemies and yet I live as if they are too strong to displace.
> Please forgive my delay and my lack of obedience to claim
> what you have given me.

MARCH 29

Joshua 19:49–21:45; 1 Chronicles 6:54–81

So the LORD gave to Israel all the land he had sworn to
give their ancestors, and they conquered it and settled
there. And the LORD gave them rest on every side.
—Joshua 21:43–44a

God does what he said he would do. He brings the Israelites out of
Egypt, through the desert, and into the Promised Land. He gives
them victory after victory as they move into the land and then the
Lord gives them rest. For now, there is no more war.

How gracious of God to provide rest. Now it is time to live in
the land.

The Promised Land for you and me is salvation. We don't have
to fight to earn it because Jesus Christ earned it for us. We rest in his
completed work. When Jesus declared on the cross, "It is finished!"
it was because the work of reconciling a sinful people to a holy God
was complete. There is nothing to add. There is no more fight. God
has provided rest.

We know that our salvation is complete and no one can snatch us
out of the Father's hand because God's Word says so (John 10:27–30).
God promises the Holy Spirit as our guarantee of eternal life (Ephesians
1:13–14). God promises that no one can separate us from his love
(Romans 8:38–39). When we are in Christ Jesus, we are at rest.

Are you resting in the completed work of Jesus? Are you trusting
that Jesus defeated death and fully won your salvation? If not,
why not?

> God, I thank you for sending your one and only Son; my
> Savior Jesus Christ, in whose completed work on the cross I
> trust for my salvation both now and for all eternity. Thank
> you for the gift of rest.

MARCH 30

Joshua 22–24

Choose today whom you will serve.
—Joshua 24:15b

Joshua leads the people into the Promised Land and settles the Israelites there. Before he dies he desires to settle their hearts on the Lord. Joshua recounts their history with God and promises them that if they hold fast to God he will fight for them; but if not, they will perish. Joshua reminds them of the gods their ancestors worshiped in Egypt and then Joshua asks them whom will they serve. Today, he tells them, they must choose.

How gracious of God to give everyone a choice of whom he or she will serve. After everything they had been through with God the people continued to worship idols. Joshua knew it was time to call the people to choose.

As Christians, we have chosen God. However, throughout each day you and I face the recurring choice of obedience or disobedience to him. We experience opportunities to hold fast to God or grasp at straws. We must choose daily whom we will serve in each situation: our idols or the Lord. God doesn't force allegiance upon us, it is our choice.

If you have not yet chosen God in saving faith will you choose today whom you will serve? If you are a Christian, after all you have been through with God, what idol(s) competes for your service and allegiance? Will you definitively choose today whom you will serve?

> Oh God, please forgive me for all of the days that I have chosen to serve myself and my idols instead of you. Open my eyes to see where I have allowed idols to draw my allegiance away from you. Today, and every day that remains of my life, I choose you.

MARCH 31

Judges 1:1–3:30

Then the LORD raised up judges to rescue
the Israelites from their enemies.
—Judges 2:16

Under Joshua's leadership, the Israelites publicly and wholeheartedly choose to serve the Lord. Joshua dies, the Israelites fail to take the land, and then they worship the idols of the land. They anger the Lord. They abandon the Lord and the Lord fights against them. In their distress they call on the Lord and he raises a judge to lead them. The judge dies and the Israelites return to their corrupt ways. The Lord raises another judge. In these days each person does as he sees fit.

How gracious of God not to abandon his people in their sin. We know that God is holy and cannot abide sin; nor will he allow sin to go unpunished (Exodus 32:34). Nevertheless, God always hears his children when they cry out to him (Psalm 18:6).

When you or I do as we see fit we will eventually, if not immediately, suffer heartache and distress (Ephesians 4:17–32). During those times, God may even fight against us. However, the moment that we repent, turning from our sin and turning to Jesus, we are immediately forgiven and restored (1 John 1:9).

In what area of your life have you have turned away from God to chase after other gods? Could God be fighting against you? Could your suffering be the result of your simply doing as you see fit. Is it time to cry out to God for rescue?

> God, I am sorry for the times when I have foolishly chased after other gods and chosen to walk my own way. Thank you for not abandoning me in my rebellion. Thank you for calling me back to a closer walk with you.

grace
APRIL

APRIL 1

Judges 3:31–6:40

Get ready! ... For the LORD is marching ahead of you.
—Judges 4:14

The Israelites do what is evil in the Lord's sight and they suffer under ruthless oppression. The Israelites cry out to the Lord for help. The Lord raises up Deborah, a respected and godly woman in Israel to lead them into victory. Her military leaders insist she accompany them in battle. Deborah proclaims that it is the Lord who leads them.

How gracious of God to use ordinary men and women to lead his people in victory.

No leader leads alone; every victory is from God and godly leaders will always give God the glory for they know it is the Lord who gives them the victory.

How easily we may forget that God is the source of every victory. Sometimes the greatest battle for victorious leaders is the battle within: the fight not to claim the glory and adulation that we know belongs to God.

Over what do you need a victory? Who has God raised up to lead you? Has God raised you to a place of leadership? Are you ready to go into battle as God leads? Are you insistent that God alone receive the glory for your victory?

> God of Heaven's Army, sometimes the enemy seems too big, too powerful, and too crafty and I just want to run and hide. There are times when I stand firm but then I lose the ultimate battle because I accept the praise that is due only to you. Please humble me to recognize that you are always with me, fighting for me, and that every victory is yours.

APRIL 2

Judges 7:1–9:21

The LORD said to Gideon, "You have too many warriors with
you. If I let all of you fight the Midianites, the Israelites will
boast to me that they saved themselves by their own strength."
—Judges 7:2

Gideon prepares for battle with an army of 32,000 fighting men.
God pares Gideon's army to three hundred. At God's command
Gideon keeps only the small contingent and he sends home all the
others. As God leads, Gideon marches into battle. God gives Gideon
the victory.

How gracious of God to reveal himself as a wise warrior. God is
the only warrior Gideon truly needed.

We must remember that when we are on God's side the enemies we
battle against have already been defeated. There is no power on earth,
or under the earth, that can stand against the power of the resurrected
Lord Jesus (Philippians 2:10). The power of the resurrection is in each
believer through the presence of the Holy Spirit (Ephesians 1:19–20).
God is our sufficient army against any and every enemy.

Is there an enemy that outnumbers you: an enemy that seems
bigger, stronger, wiser, and more resourceful than you are? Are you
afraid of the battle? Are you amassing warriors and weapons to fight
on your side? Are you on God's side in the battle? If you are, do you
believe God is bigger, stronger, wiser, and infinitely more resourceful
than your enemy is?

God, I realize that no matter how resourceful I think I need
to be that there is no victory apart from you. Teach me to
abandon any battle plan that does not begin and end with
you. Please show me the resources that you would have me
use to fight the battles that you have for me.

APRIL 3

Judges 9:22–11:28

Then the Israelites put aside their foreign gods and
served the Lord. And he was grieved by their misery.
—Judges 10:16

The Israelites continue the cycle of rebellion, prostituting themselves
before idols, abandoning God and then, under oppression, crying
out to the one true God. The Lord tells them that he will not rescue
them anymore; they should go and cry out to their foreign gods. The
Israelites turn from their gods and plead with God. God grieves and
cannot bear their misery any longer.

How gracious of God to show mercy and rescue perpetually
sinful and rebellious people.

God could have abandoned the Israelites. He could have turned
aside and walked away. However, God is a merciful and gracious God;
when his children cry out to him, he comes to their rescue (Psalm 9).

God is merciful; he withholds the punishment and wrath that
we rightly deserve. Our sin calls for death (Romans 6:23) and yet
God gives us life and forgives our sin when we cry out to him in
confession and repentance. Because God is merciful, he rescues us
from the false idols that claim the thrones of our hearts. Because
God is faithful, he always forgives confessed sin (Micah 7:18).

Do you believe your sin and idolatry grieve God? Are you like the
Israelites: on a vicious cycle of walking away from God and then back
again? Do your actions grieve you? What gods must you turn from
in order to turn toward the Living God in wholehearted abandon?

> God, please search my heart and show me the foreign gods
> that I rely on—the things that offend you—and then, O
> Righteous One, break my heart over the things that break
> yours.

APRIL 4

Judges 11:29–15:20

At that time the Spirit of the LORD came upon Jephthah…
—Judges 11:29a

God prepares Jephthah, an outcast from his family, to lead Israel. Jephthah is a mighty warrior and the Spirit of the Lord is upon him. Before leading his men into battle, Jephthah vows that if the Lord gives him victory, he will sacrifice to the Lord the first thing that comes from his house to greet him. There is victory. His only daughter runs out to meet him.

How gracious of God to anoint Jephthah with the Holy Spirit. God puts his Spirit upon or within anyone whom he chooses at any time of his choosing.

Unfortunately, the presence of the Holy Spirit does not insure that we make wise decisions. In a time when everyone did as he saw fit, Jephthah made a rash vow that affected the rest of his and his daughter's lives.

You and I are not immune to the folly of making decisions based on emotion, adrenalin, or impulse. The Holy Spirit leads, guides, comforts, and counsels us in God's way; but the Holy Spirit is not the Holy Puppeteer. God allows us to exercise our free will however we desire. However, there are times when the consequences of our choices bring pain to others and to us.

Have you made rash vows or promises that have had negative impact? If so, would you ask God to lead you through his Holy Spirit to set things right?

God, I desire to follow your lead as a warrior for you, but sometimes I irrationally act or speak before I think. Teach me to pause and allow you to guide me. Please help me overcome the impulsiveness of my character.

APRIL 5

Judges 16–18

But before long his hair began to grow back.
—Judges 16:22

God chooses Samson to lead Israel. Samson falls in love with Delilah. Attempting to discover the secret to Samson's strength, the Philistines bribe Delilah. Persuaded by Delilah, Samson reveals the secret: his uncut hair. Delilah betrays him and cuts his hair. Powerless, Samson is captured, blinded, bound with chains, and imprisoned. In prison, Samson's hair grows back. With a final feat of strength, Samson destroys the pagan temple of God's enemies.

How gracious of God to restore Samson to service. Samson made poor choices but God was not finished with him. Samson destroyed more enemies of God and God's people with his death than he did throughout his entire lifetime.

Failure is not the end for us either. We must not allow our humiliations or defeats to become the enemy's victory. Our failures reveal that we need a Savior, and we must let them propel us to flee to God and beg for forgiveness. God is bigger than any embarrassment or mistake in our lives and he waits at the bottom of every pedestal to catch us when we fall.

Has God allowed a fall, humiliation, or mistake in your life so that he might re-grow you into the person he can use for an even greater victory? Do you know someone who is suffering from the consequences of betrayal or poor choices? How might you show God's restoring love to that person and let them know they are still useful to God?

God, for all the times I've failed you and others, I am sorry. Thank you for your grace to forgive me and continue to use me for your glory.

APRIL 6

Judges 19–21

The LORD said, "Go! Tomorrow I will give you victory over them."
—Judges 20:28b

In the days when Israel has no king and the Israelites do whatever seems right in their own eyes, a Levite tries to save himself by handing his wife over to a group of men. The men rape the woman and she dies. The Israelites plan revenge and then seek the Lord's direction.

How gracious of God to be accessible.

The Israelites lived according to what was right in their own eyes and it took a horrible act of violence to cause them to seek the Lord's will. We don't have to live leaning on our own limited understanding (Proverbs 3:5–6). We have a God who is accessible and willing to give his wisdom and guidance whenever we ask. We must not wait until we are overwhelmed with disaster before we seek God's direction.

God promises he will never leave or forsake his people (Joshua 1:5). God tells us he is near us whenever we pray (Deuteronomy 4:7). God also tells us that he is the one who directs our paths (Proverbs 16:9).

Whose life is more important to you than your own? How far will you go to protect yourself and others from the evil that is in the world? What horror must you see before you turn to the always accessible God?

> God, you promise that when I seek your counsel your Word will be the light that guides my way. You promise that when I come to you for wisdom you will give it in abundance. Please forgive me for the times my cowardice has contributed to the horrors and wickedness around me. Please cause me to seek your guidance and courageously stand for what is right for your name's sake.

APRIL 7

Ruth 1:1–4:12

That man is one of our closest relatives,
one of our family redeemers.
—Ruth 2:20c

Ruth, a young Moabite widow, follows her Israelite mother-in-law, Naomi, into Judah. Needing to provide food for both of them, Ruth gathers grain behind the harvesters. The field belongs to one of Naomi's closest relatives, Boaz. Boaz, a godly man, arranges to redeem Naomi's property. With the purchase of land Boaz acquires Ruth as his wife.

How gracious of God to direct Ruth to a place of safety and protection.

Ruth was a pagan who left everything familiar to be with God's people and God protected her. God protects those who are loyal to him and who put their hope in him (Psalm 31:19–24). God's plan is not to harm us but to give us hope (Jeremiah 29:11).

Coincidence or Fate did not lead Ruth to Boaz's field. Coincidence or Fate has not led you to where you are. When you chose to identify yourself as a member of God's family, there were no guarantees that your life would always be easy. There is, however, a promise that God will place you where he can most use you to accomplish his plan for you; and that is in circumstances where you must learn to rely on him (2 Corinthians 1:8–9).

Do you believe God is in control of all your circumstances? Are you ready to step out and follow God wherever he leads, trusting that his plan for you is perfect?

God, when life is hard, I choose to believe that you have me
right where you want me for your glory and my eternal good.
Help me to embrace my difficulties as opportunities to trust
you as I stand on the solid foundation of hope in Christ.

APRIL 8

Ruth 4:13–22; 1 Samuel 1:1–8; 1 Chronicles 2:9–55; 4:1–23

So Boaz married Ruth … the LORD enabled her to
become pregnant, and she gave birth to a son.
—Ruth 4:13a, c

Ruth and Boaz marry, Ruth conceives, and they have a child.

How gracious of God to enable Ruth to conceive, carry, and
bear a child. This child is neither the beginning nor the end of God's
promises, but he is a great reminder that God is in control of all
things. This child's descendants include Israel's great king, David,
and greater King, the Lord Jesus Christ.

Every child has a place in God's plan for the world; there is no
random child. The Lord fearfully and wonderfully makes every
human being (Psalm 139:18) for his own purpose (Romans 9:20–
21). Before we are born the Lord ordains a place of service for each
one of us (Ephesians 2:10) and allows the circumstances of our lives
to shape us so that we perfectly fit that place of service.

As Christians, we are God's children; we are not random. We
are made exactly as we are to fit the plan and purpose God has for
us and for the world.

Have you ever wondered why you were born into your specific
family, circumstances, culture, country, race, or gender? Does it
comfort you to know that nothing is random; that God is sovereign
over all things? Does it comfort you to know that you are a very
important piece in God's perfect plan for the entire world?

God, I know you made me as I am. I know your plan for
me is perfect. Thank you that I can rest in your sovereignty
and trust that you never make mistakes.

APRIL 9

1 Samuel 1:9–4:11

Then Eli realized it was the LORD who was calling the boy.
—1 Samuel 3:8b

Samuel, a young boy, serves the Lord during a dark time in Israel when messages from the Lord are very rare and visions are uncommon. Samuel assists the priest, Eli. Late one night, alone, Samuel hears a voice calling. Thinking it is Eli, Samuel obediently runs to him only to hear that Eli didn't call him. Finally, after the third call, Eli realizes it is the Lord calling Samuel. Eli instructs Samuel how to respond so that Samuel might hear God's message.

How gracious of God to speak to his people.

God cares about his people and his leaders. God uses the current generation's leaders to train the next generation's leaders. Like Eli and Samuel, each generation is responsible for hearing the Word of God and passing along the truth to those whom they lead. Each generation must teach the next how to hear God. If one generation fails, who will teach the next?

We must train our ears to hear God's voice; a voice we recognize deep within our souls. All God's children hear and know the voice of their Shepherd (John 10:4).

If you are a leader, you are responsible to teach others to hear God; to listen to him and to recognize his voice. In order to do that you must listen, hear, and recognize his voice. Do you? Are you like Eli: rarely hearing from the Lord? Or are you like Samuel: a servant who is ready to listen and to obey?

God, in the cacophony of noises and voices that vie for my attention, tune my ear to hear your voice. Please quicken my heart to obey immediately despite the cost.

APRIL 10

1 Samuel 4:12–8:22

"Do as they say," the LORD replied, "for it
is me they are rejecting, not you."
—1 Samuel 8:7a

Samuel grows old and the Israelites want a king to lead them. They want to be like all the other nations around them with a king, not a priest, to lead them in battle. Samuel goes to the Lord for advice and the Lord tells Samuel to give the Israelites a king.

How gracious of God to console Samuel with the truth that the people are not rejecting Samuel; they are rejecting God.

God appoints leaders in every area of our lives: we have bosses at work, pastors at church, and even our homes have a divine hierarchy (Ephesians 5:21–6:9). When we rebel against those in authority over us, or decide we want someone new, we are effectively rebelling against God and rejecting him.

Sometimes there are legitimate biblical reasons to ask a leader to step aside, but when there are not, we have no authority to reject the leadership God has placed over us. To reject an appointed leader is to say we know more than God. To reject God's leaders is to say we don't trust God to lead us.

Do you trust God to lead you? Do you submit to the leadership he has placed over you? If not, from whom are you rebelling?

Perhaps others have rejected your God-appointed leadership. Will you, like Samuel, lay it before the Lord and continue to act in obedience to all God calls you to do?

God have I broken your heart by rejecting your chosen leaders? When others reject me because I represent you, please keep me from resentment. Please help me to stay focused solely on my own submission to the authority you have placed over me, and ultimately to you.

APRIL 11

1 Samuel 9–12

Saul was the most handsome man in Israel—head and
shoulders taller than anyone else in the land.
—1 Samuel 9:2

God gives the Israelites a king: the tall, handsome Saul who is
without equal in all Israel. At God's direction, Samuel anoints Saul
as the king and the Spirit of the Lord comes upon Saul. At his public
coronation the missing Saul is found hiding among the baggage.
Samuel presents Saul to the people, crowns him, and all the people
respond and shout, "Long live the king!"

How gracious of God to anoint a shy, fearful Saul to lead the
Israelites.

We know that God uses ordinary people to do extraordinary
things; we know because he uses us. We know that God uses
imperfect people to accomplish his perfect plan. God reveals his
strength through weak people and his wisdom through foolish people
(1 Corinthians 1:20–29). God uses you and me even though we may
not look or feel particularly suited to the role to which he assigns
us. God created the universe out of nothing and he can create in us
whatever we need to serve him with excellence and lead for his glory.

Have you refused a call to serve the Lord and his people because
you don't see yourself as God does? Would God call you to service if
he didn't see you as a useful servant? Do you believe God will equip
you and provide you with everything you need to do the work he
has called you to do?

God, though I am imperfect, weak, and often foolish I
believe that you are my perfection, my strength, and my
wisdom. Please help me to walk away from the baggage I
want to hide behind and lead fearlessly in you.

APRIL 12

1 Samuel 13–14; 1 Chronicles 9:35–39

Suddenly, panic broke out in the Philistine army. And just
then an earthquake struck, and everyone was terrified.
—1 Samuel 14:15a

King Saul and a remnant army of 600 men set out to meet the
Philistine army of well over 6,000. Relying upon the Lord for help,
Jonathan and his armor-bearer secretly head toward the Philistine
outpost. Jonathan knows that nothing can hinder the Lord. Jonathan
trusts that God can win any battle he desires despite the number of
warriors. Jonathan and his armor-bearer kill twenty men and the
Philistines panic. The Lord saves Israel that day.

How gracious of God to over-rule circumstances and bring
victory out of seeming defeat.

Jonathan was courageous because of his confidence in the truth
that nothing can thwart God's plan (Psalm 33:10–11). Saul panicked
when he stopped looking to God and looked at the size of the enemy.
Now as then, when we focus on our overwhelming circumstances
we can feel defeated. However, as we focus on God, we know our
circumstances will be defeated.

We know that God is at work in all things (Romans 8:28;
Genesis 50:20), and that nothing can hinder the Lord. However, like
Saul, when we take our eyes off the Lord and look at the growing
army of opposition, or the difficulty of our circumstances, then our
confidence in God wavers. It is nearly impossible to trust God to
bring victory when we already feel defeated.

Do you most identify with Jonathan or Saul? Why? Do you
believe God can, and will, act within your circumstances to bring
victory? If not, why not?

God, help me to remember that you are the Victor in my
life, and that in you I can overcome every obstacle.

APRIL 13

1 Samuel 15:1–17:31

And the Lord said, "This is the one; anoint him." ... And, the Spirit of the LORD came mightily upon him from that day on.
—1 Samuel 16:12b, 13b

Saul rejects the Lord's command to destroy God's enemy. The Lord rejects Saul as king. Samuel mourns for Saul until the Lord tells him it is time for the mourning to end. God gives Samuel a task: go to Bethlehem and find Jesse—one of his sons will be the next king. Samuel obeys. The Lord passes over Jesse's seven oldest sons then Samuel anoints David, the youngest, the shepherd, to be the next king.

How gracious of God to empower the people he chooses for the work he assigns.

Samuel, deep in mourning because he understands the vast failure of Saul, is given a task for the present. David, a shepherd boy, the youngest and smallest in his family is anointed for a role that will not come to fruition for many years.

The Lord has a specific work for each individual that belongs to him (Ephesians 2:10). Often, our work today is the tool God uses to prepare us for tomorrow's tasks. David must wait to be king, and until then God will use every experience to prepare him. Apart from God we can do nothing; with God, we can do all things (Philippians 4:11–13). It behooves us to wait while God prepares us.

As you work today and as you prepare for tomorrow will you diligently remain in an intimate and close relationship with Jesus (John 15:5)?

> God, I am humbled that you chose me, an insignificant, fallen human being to be a part of your plan for the world. Thank you for all you do to prepare me and train me for service.

APRIL 14

1 Samuel 17:32–19:24; Psalm 59

You come to me with sword, spear, and javelin, but I
come to you in the name of the LORD Almighty ...
—1 Samuel 17:45b

David, a shepherd boy, steps up to fight the Philistine giant, Goliath.
David knows how to fight vicious enemies. He protects his lambs
from bears and lions; he will protect God's flock from the Philistine.
David knows he is not alone; the Lord has saved him before and will
save him again this day. David goes forth armed with weapons that
are familiar: a sling and stones. David fights so that the whole world
will know that there is a God in Israel.

How gracious of God to open David's eyes to see God as the
conqueror in every battle.

David had a high view of God. He knew God had protected him
in the past and he knew God would protect him in the future. David
relied on God, his refuge; on God who shows him unfailing love.

We face giants everyday: debt, infidelity, illness, busyness,
diapers, bosses, temptations to sin and disobedience—the things
that keep us from trusting God. However, like David, we are not
alone (Deuteronomy 1:30), and we do not fight alone (Deuteronomy
20:4; Nehemiah 4:20).

What is your response to the giants in your life? Like the
Israelites, do you cower in fear? Or do you trust God to fight your
battles with you and for you? Will you fight so that everyone will
know there is a God in your life?

Almighty God, please keep me from fearing the giants that
are out to destroy me. Help me to stand so that everyone
will see that you are the God who fights for me.

APRIL 15

1 Samuel 20–21; Psalm 34

And Jonathan made David reaffirm his vow of friendship
again, for Jonathan loved David as much as he loved himself.
—Samuel 20:17

Jonathan finally accepts that his father, Saul, wants David dead.
Jonathan is heartbroken. Jonathan realizes that David must leave.
Knowing they will never see each other again, David and Jonathan
tearfully embrace. They make a pact that extends to their descendants
forever and then they say good-bye.

How gracious of God to give David a friend who loves him deeply.

Jonathan and David share a valuable gift: unconditional love
and friendship. Today, when friends are little more than a click on
social media, the blessing of one close friend is a treasure.

It has been said that if you want a friend, you must be a friend.
If we want a friendship like Jonathan and David had, we must be
that kind of friend.

Do you want a friend who has your back no matter what? Do
you want a friend who will stand by you through thick and thin and
never let you down (Proverbs 18:24)? Jesus is that friend. (Romans
8:39). He loves you deeply and he will never let you down! (1 John
3:16, John 15:13).

Are you friends with Jesus? He desires to be your friend! Will you
come to Jesus today and invite him to be your friend by accepting
the work he did for you on the cross? Who do you know that needs
Jesus as their friend?

Jesus, I thank you for being a friend of sinners and for loving
me enough to lay down your own life. Thank you for never
letting me down. Thank you for the promise that ours is an
eternal friendship.

APRIL 16

1 Samuel 22:1–23:12; 1 Chronicles 12:8–18;
Psalm 52, 57, 142

> We are yours, David! We are on your side …
> for your God is the one who helps you.
> —1 Chronicles 12:18

Saul wants to kill David, but God has plans for David. Alone, David escapes Saul. God soon brings relatives, discontented men, and warriors to come alongside David. They see that God is with David. God builds David's army and kingdom. God's Spirit comes upon one of the men and the man proclaims for all to hear that God is the one who helps David.

How gracious of God to reveal to David's men that David is God's man. David knew his purpose: he was to be king, and yet he was an outcast. David fully trusted God to make him king in God's own time.

When we are doing God's work, in God's way, God causes things to happen that we could never imagine. Where God is at work, the work will stand for all eternity. Conversely, when we attempt to do God's work in our way, we labor in vain (Psalm 127:1). Like David, our confidence must be in the Lord; at any cost we must choose to wait on the Lord.

What are you building for the Lord? Are you content to wait on him to bring the help you need? Will you wait upon the Lord for your validation?

> God, teach me to rely fully on you. Teach me to be content as I wait on those whom you are bringing. Help others to see and know that you are the one who helps me. Cause me to remember that the people who work alongside me were brought by you and are working for you.

APRIL 17

1 Samuel 23:13–25:44; Psalm 54

> But then David's conscience began bothering
> him because he had cut Saul's robe.
> —1 Samuel 24: 5

Saul, with an army of three thousand Special Forces, continues to hunt David. When nature calls, the king separates himself from his men and seeks privacy. Saul enters the cave where David and David's men are hiding. David's men see an opportunity for David to exact revenge and become the king. David creeps forward and cuts off a piece of Saul's robe. Immediately, David knows he has done wrong. David doesn't let his men kill Saul.

How gracious of God to immediately convict David's conscience of guilt. David knew it was the Lord convicting him; he repented and he rebuked his men.

We train our ears to hear God when we immediately heed the Holy Spirit's conviction (Romans 14:23) and choose to repent and obey. God has written his word in our hearts (Romans 2:15), and therefore our conscience bears witness to the truth. When we do something wrong, if we are attuned to God, we know it immediately. When you or I refuse to heed the Holy Spirit's conviction, we train ourselves to ignore God and it gets more difficult to hear him at all.

Do you recognize when God is convicting you of sin? How quickly do you respond in repentance? Are your actions training your ears and heart to hear God, or to ignore him?

> God, thank you for training me to see sin as you see it. Humble me until I heed your conviction. Discipline me so that I grow as your child. Soften my conscience so that I can more clearly hear your voice. Tune my ears to listen. Tune my heart to obey.

APRIL 18

1 Samuel 26–29; 1 Chronicles 12:1–7, 19; Psalm 56

You keep track of all my sorrows. You have collected all my
tears in your bottle. You have recorded each one in your book.
—Psalm 56:8

Saul's pursuit of David continues. Yet, when David has another
opportunity to kill Saul, he refuses. David knows that Saul is God's
anointed and David will not kill him. David hides from Saul.
David writes about God's mercy and his own fear. He writes of his
deliberate choice to trust in God's ability to rescue him. David walks
in God's presence.

How gracious of God to reassure David that he is aware of every
one of David's sorrows and every tear that he sheds.

God knows your sorrows and mine. He knows when we suffer
because we have trusted him. He knows when, and why, we cry in
secret. He knows when we feel hunted. He reassures us that he is
keeping a record and there will be a day when all wrongs are made
right (Isaiah 42:3). Until then, though we will have sorrow in the
world, our comfort is in knowing that Jesus has overcome the world
(John 16:33).

When you are afraid, do you put your trust in God? When
slanderers hound or attack you, does it comfort you to know that
God keeps a record? When people twist what you say or plot to harm
you, will you rest in the knowledge that God is on your side?

> Almighty God, your care and concern for me overwhelms
> me! Who am I that you should notice my tears? Who am
> I that you should rescue me? Who am I? I am yours! And
> you are mine!

APRIL 19

1 Samuel 30–31; 2 Samuel 1; 4:4;
1 Chronicles 9:40–10:14; 12:20–22

David was now in serious trouble ... But David
found strength in the LORD his God.
—1 Samuel 30:6

David and his six hundred men return home to find that everything is burned to the ground and their families are missing. The men hold David responsible; they want to kill him. David finds strength in the Lord. David seeks the Lord and the Lord tells him to go after those who are responsible for the carnage. The Lord assures David that he will recover everything.

How gracious of God to be strength for his people.

Homes and villages are destroyed today by addiction, infidelity, economics, moral decay, depravity, war and terrorism. We live in a world where evil people crucify, burn, gas, or behead men, women, and children, and where human beings are trafficked as merchandise.

In the midst of a world that seems to have gone awry, we can rest in the assurance that God has a plan and nothing can thwart God's plan: one day Jesus will return with judgment and completely restore the earth (2 Timothy 4:1; 1 Peter 5:10). That is our hope. Until then, our strength is in him.

Where do you find strength? Will you trust God for the strength to accomplish his plan?

God, you are my strong tower, I run to you for my strength. When the day is hard and destruction is all I see, my strength comes from the reality of who you are. You are the Sovereign God who reigns over this world. Though it seems chaotic and filled with destruction and carnage, I know that nothing can thwart your perfect plan.

APRIL 20

2 Samuel 2:1–3:5; 23:8–39; 1 Chronicles 3:1–4a; 11:10–47

Then Judah's leaders came to David and crowned
him king over the tribe of Judah.
—2 Samuel 2:4a

When David hears that Saul and his sons have died in battle he mourns deeply. David seeks the Lord and asks if he should move back to Judah. The Lord says "Yes." David moves to Judah and the leaders crown him king over Judah. Meanwhile, Abner, the commander of Saul's army pronounces Ishbosheth, Saul's son, as king over Israel. There is war between Israel and Judah.

How gracious of God to guide David in times of mourning, victory, and war. David was obediently in the center of God's will, and yet there was rejection and war.

When God calls us to a work for him and we accept that call, we are in the center of his will. However, being in the center of God's will does not mean our lives will be dramatically easier and it doesn't mean there won't be any battles (Acts 27). Though people may not follow us, if we know we are where God would have us be, and doing what he would have us do, we are on the right path (Romans 12:2). God is more than capable of bringing his plan for us to fruition despite opposition.

Have you thought about abandoning God's call to service because the fight has become too much? What affirmation do you need from God to know that you should continue moving forward? Will you ask for the affirmation? Will you look for the affirmation?

God, you are the Victor, the fight has been fought and won. Embolden me to follow you whenever and wherever you would have me go.

APRIL 21

2 Samuel 3:6–4:12

Then Abner sent messengers to David, saying,
"Let's make an agreement, and I will help turn
the entire nation of Israel over to you."
—2 Samuel 3:12

Ishbosheth accuses Abner of sleeping with one of Saul's concubines:
a grave disrespect. Furious, Abner switches loyalty from Ishbosheth
to David. Abner communicates with David and the leaders of
Israel. Now, Abner declares, it is time to make David king over all
Israel. David agrees to see Abner and hear him out. Joab, David's
commander, wrongly assumes Abner is a spy and rushes to David.
Without David's knowledge, Joab murders Abner. David declares
his innocence and Joab's guilt. David mourns for Abner. Everyone
in Judah and Israel is pleased with David's innocence.

How gracious of God to sovereignly rule over confusing
circumstances.

It's easy to think like Joab and assume the worst when an
enemy presents himself. However, we must remember that God
directs the hearts of men. He uses the circumstances of life and the
consequences of choices to direct the hearts of the kings and the
hearts of his children (Proverbs 21:1). There is no one whose heart
is beyond the reach of God.

How is God directing your heart? How is he using the confusing
consequences of your choices and your circumstances to direct you
in the way you should go (Isaiah 30:21; John 10:3)? Is there an area
where you need to pause and seek God's insights before you rush
headlong into error?

God, open my eyes to see where I am fighting battles that you
never intended I fight. Open my mind to understand where
I am fighting against you. Direct my heart and align it with
your plan so that your purpose will be accomplished in me.

APRIL 22

2 Samuel 5:1–6:11;
1 Chronicles 3:4b; 11:1–9; 12:23–14:2, 8–17

They anointed him king of Israel, just as the LORD had promised.
—1 Chronicles 11:3b

David's future as a shepherd forever changes when Samuel, at God's direction, anoints him to be king of Israel. Many years and battles, tears, and scars later David is anointed king of Israel just as the Lord had promised. There is great joy throughout Israel.

How gracious of God to have a perfect plan for each of his children and to accomplish his plan despite the follies and failures of his children.

The years while David waited to be Israel's king were not wasted. God used those years to teach and mature David's faith. Life as king will not be easy for David: there will be great failures, but David's failures will not defeat him because he loves and believes in a God who never fails (Hebrews 13:5). Knowing God's character enabled David to trust God as he awaited the fulfillment of God's promises.

We know that God is sovereign and purposefully controls all of history, bringing it to a magnificent culmination when the King of Kings, the Lord Jesus Christ, returns. And while we await the return of the King, we can trust that God is never off in his timing regarding the plans he has for us. He never has to scrounge for a plan B, and he never fails to accomplish his purposes.

Do you trust your life and your future to God, even in times of waiting? Do you believe he can accomplish his plan for you, despite your failures (Jude 1:24)?

God, you are the Solid Rock upon which I choose to stand today and upon which my future rests.

APRIL 23

2 Samuel 6:12–23; 1 Chronicles 15–16

So all Israel brought up the Ark of the LORD's
covenant to Jerusalem with shouts of joy.
—I Chronicles 15:28a

David captures the city of Jerusalem and plans to bring the Ark
there. The first attempt is unsuccessful and ends in death. David
consults with the priests and Levites and charges them to follow
the instructions for transporting the Ark that the Lord gave Moses.
When the Ark is transported as the Lord had instructed Moses, the
Lord helps them and there is great joy in Jerusalem.

How gracious of God to use circumstances to draw us into
obedience.

David thought he was doing the right thing, but he did it the
wrong way. The means are not always justified by the end. God will
never ask us to do anything that contradicts his character. Our work
for the Lord must never be separated from our walk with the Lord.
We must remember that if we want to do great things for God, we
must spend great time with God in order to understand how to do
things God's way.

What about you? Are there days when you are so busy working
for God that you have no time for him?

Have you embarked on a program for God's glory that seems
right from every perspective, but it is failing? Is it time to ask "Why"?

> Almighty God, thank you for failures that teach me that I
> am incapable of accomplishing work for you apart from you.
> Lord, please draw me back to obedience every time I forge
> ahead on my own. Please cause me to seek your direction
> for every step of every project with which I am involved.

APRIL 24

2 Samuel 7:1–8:14; 1 Chronicles 17:1–18:13; Psalm 60

How great you are, O Sovereign LORD! … For
when you grant a blessing to your servant, O
Sovereign LORD, it is an eternal blessing!
—2 Samuel 7:22a, 29b

God brings peace to the land and David settles into his palace. David desires to build a suitable temple for the Ark of God, however, God declares that he, God, will build a house for David: a dynasty of kings. God promises David that he will establish David's throne forever. David sits before God and humbly prays, acknowledging that he does not deserve what God is doing. He confesses that it is God who has brought him this far even though God knows what David is really like.

How gracious of God to establish David's kingdom eternally.

Throughout the rest of biblical history, we see God fulfill this promise to David through one king after another until it appears David's throne has ended when the Israelites are exiled to Babylon. However, like a tree that is cut down, the stump of David's kingdom remains. From the stump, a shoot grows. Jesus is the shoot. Jesus, the king of the Jews, the king of all people, is the rightful heir to David's throne (Isaiah 6:13; 11:1). God's amazing promise to you and to me is eternal life through the salvation that is available in our king, Jesus (Acts 4:23).

Are you, like David, amazed that God loves you as unworthy as you are, and has offered you eternal life? Will you receive that life today?

O Sovereign God, there is none like you. Your words are truth and you have promised good things to me, even though you know what I am really like. Thank you for your amazing grace.

APRIL 25

2 Samuel 8:15–10:19;
1 Chronicles 6:16–48, 50–53; 18:14–19:19

And Mephibosheth, who was crippled in both feet,
moved to Jerusalem to live at the palace."
—2 Samuel 9:13

David recalls the promise he made to his deceased and beloved
friend, Jonathan: to remember Jonathan's family with kindness once
he became king. David asks Ziba, who had been one of Saul's
servants, if there is anyone still alive from Saul's family. Ziba tells
David that Jonathan's son, Mephibosheth, is alive. David summons
Mephibosheth to the palace.

How gracious of God to take promises seriously and hold his
children to account for every word spoken (Matthew 12:36).

If we thought about all the hearts that have been broken because
of all the promises we have not kept, perhaps we would take our
promises, and our responsibility to keep them, a bit more seriously.
God takes them quite seriously, just as he takes his own promises
seriously. God keeps every promise and assures us that every promise
God has made is "yes" in Christ Jesus (2 Corinthians 1:20). There
are no broken hearts in heaven.

Is God bringing to mind a promise you've forgotten? Has a
broken promise broken your heart? Is there a promise upon which
God is prompting you to act? Is there forgiveness that you need to
seek or extend?

God, I thank you, that though you forget my sins, you
remember and fulfill every promise you make. Please cause
me to be a person of my word who takes every promise and
vow as seriously as you do. Please bring to mind the promises
I have made, to you and others, so that I can keep them.

APRIL 26

2 Samuel 5:14–16; 11:1–12:25;
1 Chronicles 3:5–9; 14:3–7; 20:1; Psalm 51

Then Nathan said to David, "You are that man!"
—2 Samuel 12:7

In spring, the time when kings to go war, David remains at home on his rooftop. He sees Bathsheba taking a bath. David sends for her, sleeps with her, and she becomes pregnant. David tries to hide the sin, but when his plan fails he arranges for the murder of Bathsheba's husband, Uriah. David marries Bathsheba and a child is born. The Lord knows David's secret sin and sends Nathan the prophet to confront David.

How gracious of God to provide opportunity for confession, repentance, and reconciliation through conviction of sin.

David thought he had covered the tracks of his sin, but God was not fooled then, and he will not be now. We may try to hide our sin behind innocuous words like mistake, youthful indiscretion, misjudgment, error of our way, an accident or even thoughtlessness, but attempts to cover our sin never removes it. We may try to balance sin with compensating acts of contrition, but sin will always weigh heavily on our hearts and souls. Removing sin requires confession, repentance, and forgiveness (Psalm 51:7; Hebrews 9:22; 1 John 1:9).

The Lord knows your secret sin; there is nothing you can do to cover it or hide it from him. He knows every detail of your life and he waits for you to come and be reconciled to him.

> Holy God, I confess I have sinned against you. Have mercy on me, O God, because of your unfailing love. Blot out the stain of my sins. Wash me clean from my guilt. Thank you for your amazing grace. I rejoice in your forgiveness.

APRIL 27

2 Samuel 12:26–14:33; 1 Chronicles 20:2–3

That is why God tries to bring us back when we have
been separated from him. He does not sweep away the
lives of those he cares about—and neither should you!
—2 Samuel 14:14b

Amnon, David's son, rapes his half-sister, Tamar. Absalom, Tamar's
brother, kills Amnon. Absalom flees and stays away for three years.
David, reconciled to Amnon's death, longs for Absolom. A wise
woman reminds David of God's character—that God does not
sweep away the lives of those he cares about—and neither should
David. David insists that Absalom return to Jerusalem; but not to
the king's presence.

How gracious of God to use an ordinary person to speak wisdom
to David.

It is easy for us on the outside looking in to stand in judgment
of David's failure to parent his children. However, when God speaks
wisdom to David, David listens. It is not easy being called on the
carpet, especially when you are the king.

When God speaks wisdom to us through ordinary people,
people we might not look up to, it can be a hard pill to swallow.
It might also be the first domino to fall in a long line that leads to
complete restoration and reconciliation (2 Corinthians 5:18–21).

Is there a past decision or action that you regret? As a child? As
a parent? Have you swept away someone because you, or they, acted
hastily? Is it time to seek restoration and reconciliation?

God, I thank you for the ways you bring wisdom to me.
Please give me an open heart and mind to embrace your
wisdom; and courage to act on that wisdom to right the
wrongs of my past.

APRIL 28

2 Samuel 15:1–17:14

"We are with you," his advisers replied.
"Do what you think is best."
—2 Samuel 15:15

In rebellion, David sins against God. God tells David that he, the Lord, will cause David's own household to rebel against David. The rebellion comes to fruition when Absalom conspires to take the throne of David. David leaves Jerusalem. David is not alone; his loyal friends and advisors are with him.

How gracious of God to walk alongside his children as they experience the consequences of their sin. David trusts God to do what is best for him even as God disciplines him.

This was a low point in the life of David; sin has a way of humbling us. Even though we confess and repent of our sin we must endure the consequences of that sin, and sometimes the consequences of our sin will touch lives that we never imagined in ways we never expected. The consequences for each individual person are unique and different: some will be brief and easy, and some will be harder to endure and last a lifetime.

God knows what is best (1 John 3:20). God is with the repentant believer and he will not abandon them to walk alone through the valley of sin's consequences.

How is God comforting you with his presence in the midst of your discipline? Are there Christians whom God has brought alongside you to strengthen you and remind you that you are not alone?

> God, you promise you will never leave me nor forsake me. Thank you that you are always with me, even as I experience the difficult consequences of my forgiven sin. Thank you that you are fighting for me. Thank you that your plan for me includes victory in you!

APRIL 29

2 Samuel 17:15–19:30; Psalms 3, 63

But you, O LORD, are a shield around me ... I lay down and
slept. I woke up in safety, for the LORD was watching over me.
—Psalm 3:3a, 5

David flees Jerusalem. Absalom sets himself up as king, but it is
God who is in control. David arrives at Mahanaim and is met by
compassionate men who bring sleeping mats and cheese. David
writes that he sleeps because he knows that God is his shield and
his glory: the one who lifts his head high. David is not afraid of the
enemies who surround him because he knows that God is in control.

How gracious of God to provide food for the hungry, rest for
the weary, and sound sleep for those who trust in his sovereignty
and protection.

David wrote this Psalm, but the words are God's (2 Timothy
3:16). God is a shield around us. He is the one who lifts our heads
high. When we cry out, he answers us.

Whatever battles God has for us, God always has our back.
Nothing happens to God's child that has not sifted through the
hand of God; we are not victims. Every circumstance in our lives will
be used by God for our eternal good and his eternal glory (Romans
8:28–29).

What battle keeps you awake at night? Is your battlefield at
work, home, church, or school? Is it in the dark or the silence?
Will you sleep tonight, resting in the knowledge that God watches
over you?

> O God, when I lie awake at night, I will meditate on you.
> I will think of how much you have helped me. I will sing
> for joy in the shadow of your protecting wings. And, I will
> trust you as I fall asleep.

APRIL 30

2 Samuel 19:31–21:22; 1 Chronicles 20:4–8; Psalm 7

So all the people crossed the Jordan with the king.
—2 Samuel 19:39a

Absalom dies in battle and David returns to Jerusalem as the rightful king. Immediately a group of Israelites revolt and David's men put down the rebellion. David writes of God's protection and justice.

How gracious of God to lead the king, as the king leads the people. Not only did David follow God physically back into Jerusalem, but he followed God's character granting amnesty to the men who had opposed him and rewarding those who had been faithful to him. (1 Samuel 26:23)

Following God is not easy. When we know that people are following us our responsibility is to lead them as God leads us. We must follow God's Word and God's character. We must do what God says is right. We must not rely on impulse or emotion but calmly lead as we follow closely to God (Psalm 119:105–106).

We can only lead as far as we have gone, therefore, we must go far with God. We must follow him as he leads us along paths of suffering, learning, training, and growing. We must follow wherever his light illumines our path.

Do those whom you lead see God leading you? Do they see you following God? Do they see God in your actions, words, and decisions? Are you willing to go further with God so that you might lead others further? Are you training those you lead to follow you, or to follow God?

> O God, please illumine the paths you would have me walk, so that I can follow you wherever you lead, going further than I ever imagined. I will follow in your footsteps and your character so that I lead others to you.

MAY 1

2 Samuel 22; Psalm 18

He led me to a place of safety; he rescued
me because he delights in me.
—2 Samuel 22:20

The Lord rescues David from Saul, Absalom, and all his enemies. David sings a song to the Lord. David sings to God who is his rock, his shield, and his savior. He sings of God's rescue and of God's delight in him. He exalts the Lord, the rock of his salvation, and praises God for his unfailing love. David credits God for every victory.

How gracious of God to condescend to love and delight in his children. David understood who he was apart from God and how blessed his life was because of God.

When our vision of God is small, our God is small; why would we ever want a small God? David saw God as gloriously high and lofty! Read David's words again; this should be the vision of God that we carry with us throughout every day. God, who reaches down from heaven to rescue us! God, who causes the earth to quake and tremble! God, who shakes the foundations of the heavens when he is angry! God, mounted on a mighty angel and soaring on the wings of the wind to our defense! God, our place of refuge!

Are you amazed that God would stoop low to love you, a sinner? Today, if you hear his voice, it is because he delights to save you (Hebrews 3:7–8).

If you have received God's salvation, how will you praise him? How will you thank him? Will you sing with David?

> O God, thank you for reaching down from heaven and rescuing me. Thank you for drawing me out of the deep water of sin, and setting my feet on the Solid Rock.

MAY 2

2 Samuel 24; 1 Chronicles 21–22

But just as the angel was preparing to destroy [Jerusalem], the
LORD relented and said to the death angel, "Stop! That is enough!"
—1 Chronicles 21:15

The Lord's anger burns against Israel. Satan rises up against Israel and
causes David to take a census. Almost immediately, David's conscience
begins to bother him. David confesses his sin before the Lord, and the
Lord gives David a choice of consequences. David chooses to fall into
the hands of the merciful Lord rather than the hands of men. The
Lord sends a plague and seventy thousand people die.

How gracious of God to limit the destructive consequences of
sin. God is just (Deuteronomy 32:4), he is not arbitrary; his just
anger rightly burned against Israel. Israel's sin was very great and in
the unfathomable wisdom of God, David's sin and Israel's sin were
punished together.

We do not know the details that God chooses not to share, but
we do know God's character: in his justice, perfection, and holiness,
he always does what is right.

We do know that no one sins in a vacuum. All of our sin affects
the people around us, including the innocent. What innocent people
have suffered because of your sin?

We also know that God forgives confessed sin (1 John 1:9), and
knows exactly when to halt the destruction that accompanies sin. Is
there sin that God would have you confess today?

> God, my heart is breaking. I know others have suffered
> because of my sin. Please be merciful as you determine and
> bring to pass the consequences of my sins. Thank you for
> not acting arbitrarily in your decisions and for faithfully
> doing what is just and right.

MAY 3

For David said, "The LORD, the God of Israel, has
given us peace, and he will always live in Jerusalem.
Now the Levites will no longer need to carry the
Tabernacle and its utensils from place to place."
—1 Chronicles 23:25

David appoints Solomon as king over Israel and holds a coronation
ceremony. David registers and assigns tasks to the Levites for their
service in the temple, listing all of the duties according to the
procedures established by their ancestor Aaron.

How gracious of God to establish a permanent place and pattern
for worship.

In ancient days Israelites came to Jerusalem to worship God and
bring their offerings. Though God exists everywhere all the time
(Psalm 139:7–10), he ordained that his people should offer worship
formally and corporately in Jerusalem.

Today, God lives within believers (John 14:17), and our lives
are to be our worship. We have the privilege and the blessing of
worshiping God wherever we are, all day, every day. This doesn't
mean that we should forsake corporate worship (Hebrews 10:25).
As we meet with other Christians and worship God together our
worship is enhanced and our lives are blessed.

What responsibility has God assigned to you in your place of
worship? Is God prompting you to change, add, or drop something
so that your entire life is an offering of worship to him?

> God, I thank you for the privilege of worshiping you. The
> depth of my joys increase and the weight of my sorrows
> decrease when I worship you. Every experience of my life
> is incomplete until I share them with you. Worshiping you
> brings a clearer perspective of whatever I am going through
> because it enables me to see you guiding, leading, and
> orchestrating every bit of my life.

MAY 4

> The Lord has chosen you. Be strong, and do the
> work. Don't be afraid or discouraged by the size of the
> task. [God] will not fail you or forsake you. He will
> see to it that all the work is finished correctly.
> —1 Chronicles 28:10b,c, 20b

David prepares to build the temple, but he will not be the one to build it; God chooses Solomon as the builder. David charges Solomon to obey the Lord, to get to know him, and to worship and serve him wholeheartedly. David gives Solomon the plans for the temple. David assures Solomon that the Lord is with him and will see to his success.

How gracious of God to reassure Solomon that he is with him and will see to it that the task is finished correctly.

God often calls ordinary people, people like you and me, to do big things for him. God's plan and his call always align. When we obediently embrace God's call we have no need for scheming or scrounging to pull a plan together, we need only follow God's plan. Sometimes we are the builder and sometimes our preparations are for others. Always we must simply do our part (1 Corinthians 3:7–8).

Has God called you to a task that is overwhelmingly big, far exceeding your comfort zone? Are you afraid? How has he prepared you? Will you trust God's plan and commit to do things his way? Will you rest in the knowledge that he is with you?

> God, when the task you have given me seems overwhelming and fear creeps in, will you please remind me that you are with me and will be with me every step of the way. Please teach me that when you are in the work the outcome will always be successful.

MAY 5

1 Chronicles 29:1–22; 1 Kings 1

Everything we have has come from you, and we
give only what you have already given us!
—1 Chronicles 29:14

David charges Solomon with building the temple. David tells the people all he has done to provide the materials for the building, and challenges them to follow his example. The people rejoice and give to the Lord freely and wholeheartedly. King David, filled with joy, praises the Lord in the presence of the whole assembly for the Lord's greatness, power, glory, and victory. David declares that everything in the heavens and on the earth is the Lord's.

How gracious of God to provide abundantly for his children so that they might give abundantly back to him.

As David said, everything is the Lord's (James 1:17). Everything you and I have belongs to God (Psalm 24:1); we are caretakers, or stewards, of God's resources. Because our lives are brief and we know we can't take anything with us when we leave this life to go to live with the Lord in heaven, we must hold things with open hands. Hearses don't pull trailers.

When God examines your heart as you give your offerings, is he rejoicing in your integrity? Does he celebrate your good motives? Will he observe willing and joyful giving? What are you doing to ensure that your love for the things God provides never overtakes your love for God?

O Lord, God, please open my eyes to the wealth you have bestowed on me. May I be a grateful and generous person, holding the things you have given me in an open hand as I hold onto you with clenched fists.

MAY 6

2 Samuel 23:1–7; 1 Kings 2:1–12;
1 Chronicles 29:26–30; Psalms 4–6; 8–9; 11

> When I look at the night sky and see the work of
> your fingers—the moon and the stars you have set
> in place—what are mortals that you should think of
> us, mere humans that you should care for us?
> —Psalm 8:3–4

David's death approaches and he glorifies God with his final recorded words. David leaves behind the Psalms he has written proclaiming the blessings God has poured out on him. David's Psalms tell of his understanding of God's unfailing love. He thanks God for the marvelous things God has done and sings the praises of the Most High.

How gracious of God to care for mere mortals, to even think of us. God does care for us; he made us in his image (Genesis 1:27) and he condescends to love us (1 John 4:10).

David presents a magnificent and majestic vision of God, reminding us that everything God does for us is an act of his grace. Every time God intervenes in our lives we experience his unmerited favor.

How high is your view of God? Do your words as you praise him and pray to him prompt you to adore and worship him as he rules in majesty?

How often do you praise God simply for being the amazing God that he is? Would you spend time today, pouring out the love in your heart for a God who chooses to love you?

O God, my King, forgive me for making you small, for thinking that you are indebted to me in any way. Cause me to develop a higher view of you than I currently have. Open my eyes to see the majesty of your name that fills the earth!

MAY 7

Psalms 12–17; 19–21

The heavens tell of the glory of God. The skies display his marvelous craftsmanship. Day after day they continue to speak; night after night they make him known. They speak without a sound or a word; their voice is silent in the skies; yet their message has gone out to all the earth, and their words to all the world.

—Psalm 19:1

Through his Psalms, David declares the majesty of God. His poetry and songs state that there is nowhere on earth that God's presence cannot be felt and his person cannot be known. David writes that the heavens declare the glory of God day after day and night after night.

How gracious of God to reveal himself to the entire world (Romans 1:20).

Many of us believe in God as David did: that God shaped the world and everyone in it with precision and foresight. However many people refuse to accept this truth and instead worship the heavens that proclaim the glory of God. Yet, God promises that anyone who looks at the heavens and sincerely desires to know God will find him (1 Chronicles 28:9).

Do you wonder if there really is one true God? Are you sincerely seeking the truth? If you are, God will reveal himself to you, he promises this, but you must choose to believe (Hebrews 11:6).

If you do believe in the God of the Bible as the one true God, will you declare his majesty today?

> God, I cling to your promise. I sincerely sought you and you revealed yourself to me; how can I praise you sufficiently? I see the majesty of your hands and I bow before you. Please cause the words of my mouth and the meditation of my heart to be pleasing to you.

MAY 8

Psalms 22–26

The LORD is my shepherd; I have everything I need.
—Psalm 23:1

In the Psalms David proclaims God's sufficiency. He writes of his ancestors' trust in God and God's rescue of them. Of how they place their trust in God and are never disappointed. He calls God his rescuer and his strength. He praises God, the one who comes quickly to his aid and the one who does not ignore the suffering of the needy. David writes that God is the shepherd who provides blessing, goodness, and unfailing love. David sings of God: the King of glory, strong and mighty, invincible in battle.

How gracious of God to provide for every need of his people.

God created the world and everything in it; there is nothing that we need that God cannot provide. When we lay before him our list of wants, we know that he may choose to say "No." However, he promises that when we seek first his kingdom and righteousness that he will meet all our needs (Matthew 6:33).

What do you need? Do you need rest? He leads you beside peaceful streams and renews your strength. Do you need direction? He guides you along right paths. Are you afraid? Even though you walk through the dark valley of death he is close beside you, comforting you. Do you need love? His goodness and unfailing love pursue you all the days of your life.

> God, why do I turn to my own strength and wisdom trying to meet my own needs? Why do I think I can handle life apart from you? Please humble me and teach me that when I trust in you I will never be dismayed, that you are indeed sufficient to meet my every need.

MAY 9

Psalms 27–32

The LORD is my light and my salvation—so
why should I be afraid? The LORD protects me
from danger—so why should I tremble?
—Psalm 27:1

David's God is his protector and his salvation. When trouble comes, God conceals him and hides him out of reach. God holds him close; the Lord is his strength and his shield, the one who carries David in his arms forever. The Lord blesses his people with strength and peace. The Lord rescues, restores, and keeps his people from falling. The Lord blesses David publicly and keeps him safe from those who conspire against him. David praises God for forgiving his sin, removing his guilt, advising and watching over him, and surrounding him with unfailing love.

How gracious of God to intimately involve himself in the lives of his children. He is light in the darkness, strength for the weak, and protection in the storms and battlefields of life.

God is the same yesterday, today, and tomorrow. Our God, David's God, never changes (Malachi 3:6), he is and will always be the God who alone is capable of sustaining his people throughout their lives.

Have you embraced the reality of God? Do you allow him to overpower the darkness, fears, and worries that come against you? Will you sing, with David, a song that rejoices in the power and majesty of Almighty God?

God, my heart sings with joy because I know that you are the never-changing God who loves me. You hold me secure in the palm of your hand, and I know that you will bring me unblemished into your presence.

MAY 10

Psalms 35–38

I will be glad because he rescues me.
—Psalm 35:9b

David's Psalms continue. David praises God as the one who rescues him from people who oppose and attack him. David turns to the Lord for salvation from his enemies and from his sin. David waits on the Lord even when it seems the Lord is silent, for he knows God will not abandon him. David publicly proclaims the justice and goodness of God. David writes that though sin whispers and plots evil in the hearts of those who do not fear God, God's love and faithfulness, righteousness, and justice will never fail.

How gracious of God to record David's praise and worship of God, his rescuer.

David knew that his was a rescued life; and so our ours (Psalm 18). When guilt overwhelms us, and the burden of our sin is too heavy to bear, when we fall into the trap the enemy has set for us, when physical, spiritual or emotional pain is overwhelming, when loneliness, despair or depression is oppressive, in every circumstance God is always there to rescue us (Deuteronomy 33:26–27a). When we confess our sins, and cry out to God, he runs to rescue us.

From what do you need rescue? Will you call upon on God? Are you waiting on God? Have you been waiting? God knows the exact moment to hasten to your rescue; he will not delay a moment too long, nor rescue you a moment too soon.

God, I know that you alone can rescue me. I will wait for your rescue. I know that when the delay seems long, you are doing a work in me as I wait. I praise you for your perfectly timed and executed rescue.

MAY 11

Psalms 39–41; 53; 55; 58

I have not kept this good news hidden in my heart; I have talked
about your faithfulness and saving power. I have told everyone
in the great assembly of your unfailing love and faithfulness.

—Psalm 40:10

Throughout David's life God faithfully protects him and David
publicly praises God for his protection and success. David knows it
is God who lifts him out of the pit of despair. David praises God for
teaching him that obedience is more important than burnt offerings.
David writes of God, who nurses the sick and eases their pain. David
sings of God who hears the prayers of his children and responds to
their cries for help. David declares that God bears the burdens of the
godly and does not permit them to slip and fall.

How gracious of God to provide us with voices, platforms and
opportunities to proclaim and praise his character and attributes.

Every one of us has a platform from which to proclaim and
praise God. Our platform may be a stage in a stadium filled with
tens of thousands of hurting and lost people, a rocking chair in a
nursery, a bedside in a nursing home, or a neighbor's front porch.
Any place is a platform for praise (Psalm 51:5; 63:3–5).

What platform has God given you to proclaim his goodness?
Are you making the most of your opportunity? To whom will you
speak of God's unfailing love and faithfulness today?

> God, please forgive me for thinking that I have nothing to
> say about you to the person next to me at any given moment.
> Remind me that whether it is beside a child's bed at night,
> across the table from a friend, or from a pulpit, that everyone
> hungers to hear about you!

MAY 12

Psalms 61–62; 64–67

If I had not confessed the sin in my heart, my LORD would
not have listened. But God did listen! He paid attention
to my prayer. Praise God, who did not ignore my prayer
and did not withdraw his unfailing love from me.
—Psalm 66:18–20

David understands the barrier of unconfessed sin that separates God
from believers. David knows that God listens to his prayers. He
knows God forgives every confessed sin, and answers prayers with
awesome deeds. David praises God for listening to his prayers after
he confessed the sin in his heart. David rests in God.

How gracious of God to attend to, listen to, and respond to the
prayers of his people with unfailing love.

Unconfessed sin is like being on a restrictive diet: The only food
that sounds satisfying is that which we cannot have. When there is
unconfessed sin, that which we cannot have is intimacy with God.
However, the moment we confess our sins God hears our prayer and
he forgives (1 John 1:9). Though sin may separate us from intimacy,
we can rest in the knowledge that we are never separated from God's
love (Romans 8:38–39).

Is there a cleansing fire burning in your heart prompting you
to confess your sins and restore the intimacy with God that you
crave? Are you ready to experience God's forgiveness, cleansing and
restoration?

> O God, when I carry my sin my heart feels like a barren
> and dry land. When I confess, you are there immediately
> forgiving me and quenching my parched soul with living
> water. Thank you for vigilantly waiting for me to pray and
> for lavishing your forgiveness upon me.

MAY 13

Psalms 68–70; 86; 101

Nowhere among the pagan gods is there a god like you, O Lord.
For you are great and perform great miracles. You alone are God.
—Psalm 86:8a, 10

In a time when people worship multiple gods, David writes of the one
true God: the Father to the fatherless and the defender of widows;
the one who leads the people out of Egypt, into the Promised Land,
and who lives among them. He is the Almighty who scatters kings.
God: who saves and rescues from death. God: the source of life.
David worships God, the Sovereign Lord Almighty.

How gracious of God to reveal himself as the one true God.

How blessed we are to know David's God: the God of the Bible
who is the one true God (Isaiah 44:6–8). We can know, as David
did, his unfailing love and sure salvation. We can trust that he hears
our cries and does not despise us. We know that he is the God who
answers us in our troubles, who performs great miracles, and who
can rescue us from the depths of death. This God is our hope and
solid foundation

Do you know this God? No other god loves as he loves. No other
god can save as he saves. No other god has eternal life. Today, if you
hear his voice, will you respond and receive him as the one true God
(Hebrews 3:7–15)?

> Sovereign Lord Almighty, none can compare with you. You
> rescue the weak and you protect the poor and needy. You
> rescued me from the deception of sin and idolatry in my
> heart. I surrender my entire being to you. *Love so amazing
> so divine, demands my life, my soul, my all.*

MAY 14

Psalms 103; 108–110; 122; 124

He forgives all my sins and heals all my diseases. He ransoms
me from death and surrounds me with love and tender mercies.
—Psalm 103:3–4

In Psalm 103, David's heart overflows with praise to God for all the
things the Lord has done. David praises God's character: merciful,
gracious, slow to anger and full of unfailing love. He praises God
for not dealing with him as he deserves, but rather removing his
rebellious acts away from him as far as the east is from the west.
David praises God's salvation and exalts God above the heavens.
David calls on everything that God has created to praise the Lord.

How gracious of God to pour blessings upon his people and
treat them with the love, protection, mercy and patience that no
one deserves.

Like David, we have been ransomed (1 Peter 1:18–19)! Jesus paid
the price to free us from the bondage of sin and death. We deserve
punishment for the many transgressions and rebellions that burst
forth from our hearts and minds, but we have been rescued—we
have been saved from that punishment, which Jesus endured on our
behalf and in our place.

We do not deserve God's love and tender mercies. We do not
deserve forgiveness. We do not deserve to have our spirits regenerated
from death to new life. Yet, while we were yet sinners, Christ died
for us (Romans 5:8).

How will you praise God for saving you today? Will you choose
today to live every moment in gratitude to God for his grace and
mercy in ransoming you from death?

God, I stand in awe of your grace. I am overwhelmed by
your love. I too, will praise the Lord! Praise to the King!

MAY 15

Psalms 131; 133; 138–141; 143

Teach me to do your will, for you are my God. May your
gracious Spirit lead me forward on a firm footing.
—Psalm 143:10

David puts his hope in God, choosing not to concern himself with
matters he knows are too great for him. David does not worry
because God backs his promises by all the honor of his name.
David's relationship begins and ends with God. David knows that
God is continually working out his will in David's life and knows
everything about David. David wants God to point out the things
that God finds offensive.

How gracious of God to communicate with believers. David knew
what pleased God because God communicated those things to David.
Therefore, David had no fear to lay his heart bare before the Lord.

Like David, we know God's will for us: to love him with all
our heart, soul and mind; and as a direct result of that love, to obey
(Romans 12:1–2). We know that when we obey, God is pleased; God
has not withheld that communication from us.

Like David, we know what displeases God, we know what we
try to get away with, and we know what we try to hide. Will you ask
God to search your heart and show you the things that offend him?
When he does, will you own those things, remove them, and be free?

> Father, I know you communicate with your children; you
> communicate with me. Thank you for calming my heart
> and encouraging me with the understanding that you want
> to guide me into your will. Please search my heart; show me
> the offensive things that have taken root, and I will, with
> your help, uproot them and throw them into the fire.

MAY 16

The LORD is close to all who call on him,
yes, to all who call on him sincerely.
—Psalm 145:18

David's final Psalms celebrate the faithfulness of God: his rock, his loving ally, his fortress, his strong tower, his deliverer. David praises God's name and faithfulness to all generations.

Ethan's Psalm speaks of the tender mercies of the Lord, and declares the Lord's faithfulness. He praises God and calls on the angels to praise God.

Heman's Psalm cries out for help and rescue. He recognizes God's salvation, his faithfulness, righteousness and unfailing love. However, Heman's Psalm does not end with praise for rescue.

How gracious of God to hold his people close in the days of joy, and in the days of pain, illness, death, and despair.

The writer of the book of Hebrews assures us that we can boldly come before the throne of grace to find grace and receive mercy in our time of need (Hebrews 4:16), but it is always up to God to determine what that grace and mercy will be. We know that there are times when God's rescue doesn't come in this life. Because of God's character and his great love for us we can accept that God always knows what is best and that his purpose and plan for our lives is perfect.

For what are you asking God today? Do you believe that he continues to hold you close even if he chooses to withhold that which you seek? How does that comfort you today?

God, you are faithful and you are doing what is best for the people that I love, and for me. You proved your love at the cross. Because you hold me close, I will trust your perfect plan.

MAY 17

Then I realized how bitter I had become. I was so foolish and
ignorant. Yet I still belong to you; you are holding my right hand.
—Psalm 73:21a, 23

Asaph, David's musician, writes of God's goodness to Israel and to
those whose hearts are pure. He writes of the time when his own
foot almost slipped because he envied the proud. Asaph questions
God's awareness of injustice, then confesses that when he thinks
about things from God's perspective, he realizes that though the
prosperous look blessed they are on a slippery slope into destruction.
Asaph confesses the bitterness in his own heart. With a cleansed
heart Asaph holds tight to God, who is his strength.

How gracious of God to correct wrong thinking in his people.

It is easy to envy the wicked because of their prosperity and
wonder if God is aware of what seems to be inequality and unfairness
in our struggle as opposed to the apparent ease of the wicked.

It is self-focus that causes us to doubt God's goodness.
Questioning God's goodness should be a warning bell to pause, as
Asaph did, and focus on the attributes and character of God (Psalm
37:4–11). Meditating on the majesty, holiness, glory, and worthiness
of God, enables us to have a right perspective of our circumstances.

Is there anything on earth you desire more than God? Has that
desirable thing distracted you from worshipping God?

> Sovereign Lord, when I think of you, sitting on your
> majestic throne, speaking in claps of thunder, and radiating
> glory then I am reminded of how foolish and ignorant it is
> to desire material things. You are my wealth. You are my
> glorious destiny. You are all I need.

MAY 18

You have redeemed your people by your strength.
—Psalm 77:15a

In his Psalm, Asaph cries out to God in trouble. He writes of his search for the Lord as he prays all night long. He writes of his distress. Asaph longs for the good old days, when his heart was full of joyful songs. He questions if the Lord has rejected him forever. Then Asaph recalls all that God has done. He remembers God's wonderful deeds. Asaph ends with praises to the mighty God who performs miracles and wonders.

How gracious of God to remind his people of who he is: The unchanging God who redeems his people by his own strength.

Life can be difficult and overwhelming. When our circumstances seem insurmountable we must choose to remember the character of God. When we focus on God, the one who saves us and protects us, the Mighty One who never abandons his people (Zephaniah 3:17), the Sovereign God who controls all things on earth, it is then that *the things of earth will grow strangely dim in the light of his glory and grace.*

Oh, soul, are you weary and troubled, no light in the darkness you see? There's light for a look at the Savior, and life more abundant and free. Is darkness enveloping you? Will you pause and write down the attributes of God? Will you list the blessings of your redemption? Will you allow God to turn your thoughts from despair to praise?

> O Lord, Most High, I am redeemed and I belong to you. I lift my eyes up to you, and my feet find solid ground. You are the Almighty God who rescues me with your strength. I know that nothing is too difficult for you.

MAY 19

Psalms 79–82

Turn us again to yourself, O God. Make your face
shine down upon us. Only then will we be saved.
—Psalm 80:3

In Psalm 80 Asaph calls upon God to display his glory and rescue his
people. They have become the scorn of nations. They are treated as
a joke; however, Asaph knows God hasn't abandoned them. Asaph
asks God to strengthen them, revive them, turn them back to God
and make his face to shine down upon them. Only then will they
be saved.

How gracious of God to discipline the ones he loves.

God is the perfect Father, and in his perfect wisdom, he knows
the exact tool to use to discipline his children. (Hebrews 12:6–7).

We discipline our toddlers with a "Time Out" chair. We ground
our adolescents and send them to their rooms. We remove privileges
from our teens; taking away the keys and turning off the electronics.
We discipline our children in the way that best fits each child and
so does God, only God does it perfectly in each situation for each
one of his children.

In our rebellion, God allows and uses the sorrow, heartache and
rejection—every consequence of our sin—to turn us back to him.
We must endure the hardship, but it is our choice whether it softens
us toward repentance or hardens us into further rebellion.

Is there an area of your life where you've turned away from God?
Are consequences of your sin prompting you to cry out to God for
rescue? Or run away from him in arrogance?

Please listen, O Shepherd of Israel, and come and rescue me.
I repent of rebellion and submit to your mercy and grace as
you discipline me.

MAY 20

1 Kings 2:13–3:15; 1 Chronicles 29:23–25;
2 Chronicles 1:1–13; Psalm 83

Solomon, the son of King David, now took firm
control of the kingdom, for the LORD his God was
with him and made him very powerful.
—2 Chronicles 1:1

Solomon succeeds David as king. Solomon puts down his half-brother Adonijah's challenge to the throne, and then has Adonijah executed. Solomon executes Joab, the military defector. Solomon executes Shimei, the man who cursed David when David fled from Absalom. God exalts Solomon and establishes the kingdom in his hand.

How gracious of God to be with Solomon as Solomon takes firm control of the kingdom. In a day when the threat of enemies could prevent Solomon from taking control of the kingdom which God had called him to rule, death was the political and physical solution.

You and I may never be called to rule a kingdom, however, we have been given a realm of influence. In whatever arena God has placed us it is our responsibility to fight against every force that tries to prevent us from being an influence for the Lord (2 Corinthians 10:3–5).

Are you prepared to step up and take firm control of the realm God has given you? What challenges must you overcome from without, and from within your own heart, so that you lead with God's authority? Are there spiritual or emotional enemies that you need to overcome in order to firmly grasp the responsibility that is yours?

Lord God, please help me to establish the realm you have assigned to me. Please give me wisdom to take firm control, and the humility to know that only in you do I have any authority. Help me to overcome every threat that challenges my ability to obey you.

MAY 21

1 Kings 3:16–28; 5–6; 2 Chronicles 2:1–3:14

*...the people were awed as they realized the great wisdom
God had given him to render decisions with justice.*
—1 Kings 3:28b

When God appears to Solomon and asks Solomon what he wants
from God, God is prepared to give him whatever he wants. Solomon
asks for wisdom and knowledge to rule. Solomon's wisdom is tested
when the two prostitutes each lay claim to one living child. Solomon's
decision—to cut the baby in half—reveals the true mother and
leaves the people in awe. Solomon acts wisely as he builds the temple,
enlisting laborers, stone cutters, and foremen.

How gracious of God to give his leaders wisdom as they ask for
it. God is the source of wisdom and he promises that if we desire
wisdom, we are to ask him and he will give generously (James 1:5).
Solomon asked and God gave generously.

James also tells us that the wisdom that comes from heaven is
pure, peace-loving, considerate, submissive, merciful, impartial and
sincere (James 3:17). This is the only wisdom that we should be
dispensing. Does it describe the wisdom you give out?

Where is God on your list of resources for wisdom? How
frequently do you call friends, consult vast libraries, search the
internet, or turn to science before you go to God? Will you seek
God's wisdom as you work through the difficult situation that you
are facing today?

God of Wisdom, please forgive me for the times when I turn
everywhere but to you for wisdom. Please give me wisdom
to lead, to govern, and to make the difficult decisions that
you have laid before me.

MAY 22

1 Kings 7; 2 Chronicles 3:15–4:22

So Solomon made all the furnishings of the Temple of the Lord.
—1 Kings 7:48

Solomon builds the temple. Huram, a skilled craftsman from Tyre, is recruited for the bronze work. He completes everything Solomon assigns him to do. There is so much bronze work it cannot be measured. Solomon brings all the gifts his father David had dedicated. It takes skilled craftsmen seven years to complete the temple with precise attention to detail.

How gracious of God to provide everything that is necessary to worship him as he ordains. In Solomon's day worship required a temple and blood sacrifices.

Solomon's temple must have been glorious. It was the dwelling place of God. Today, God dwells within each believer (Revelation 3:20, 1 Corinthians 6:19); and every temple is glorious because God has made us in his image.

Not only does God provide the temple, he also provides the sacrifice. We know that we cannot march willy nilly into the presence of the Almighty; we must come to the Father through the Son (John 14:6). In order to worship God, we must appropriate the sacrifice Jesus paid on the cross for us individually. When we accept Jesus's sacrifice on our behalf, we can boldly come into God's presence through Jesus's precious blood (Hebrews 4:14–16).

Attempting to worship God any other way is futile. Will you come before the throne today, as God ordains, through the blood of Jesus, the sacrifice that God himself provided?

> God, worthy is the Lamb that was slain to receive all glory, honor, majesty and power! What a privilege to worship you! What a gloriously gracious God you are. I humbly bow before you and repent of the flippancy with which I have approached you in the past.

MAY 23

1 Kings 8:1–53; 2 Chronicles 5–6

At that moment a cloud filled the Temple of the LORD.
The priests could not continue their work because the
glorious presence of the LORD filled the Temple of God.
—2 Chronicles 5:13d, 14

Solomon finishes the temple, brings the gifts King David had dedicated, summons the leaders of Israel, makes numerous sacrifices, and then moves the Ark into the Most Holy Place. When the people and priests join to worship God with songs and music, praising and giving thanks to the Lord, the glorious presence of the Lord fills the temple. Solomon thanks God, then lifts his hands toward heaven and prays. He asks God to watch over the temple. Solomon asks that God would hear the prayers of his people and forgive them when they call upon his name.

How gracious of God to fill the temple with his glorious presence.

Solomon knew, as do we, that a brick and mortar structure can never contain God, nor can the highest heavens (1 Kings 8:27). Yet, have we tried to confine him to the brick and mortar churches that we visit on Sunday? Or worse yet to the internet or television churches we listen to every now and then? God forbid!

As Christians, our bodies are the holy temple of the living God, and his glorious Holy Spirit fills us (Acts 9:17). Our lives should be a continual worship service because he is here!

Does God's Spirit dwell in you (Romans 8:9)? Does he fill every bit of your temple?

> God, will you please fill me with your Holy Spirit so fully that there is no room for pride or ego to flourish? Please dwell in me so completely that I continually reflect your glorious presence.

MAY 24

1 Kings 8:54–9:14; 2 Chronicles 7

> Then if my people who are called by my name will
> humble themselves and pray and seek my face and
> turn from their wicked ways, I will hear from heaven
> and will forgive their sins and heal their land.
> —2 Chronicles 7:14

After the temple dedication, Solomon sends the people home, and the Lord appears to Solomon. God assures Solomon that he will always watch over the temple and care for it. God tells Solomon that when God's people abandon and disobey him, he will make them an object of ridicule and the temple an appalling sight for all. God tells Solomon there will be times when God will bring drought, plagues, and locusts to cause his people to turn to him in repentance; and when they repent he will act on their behalf.

How gracious of God to forgive and restore humble repentant sinners.

Oswald Chambers says, "The great miracle of the grace of God is that he forgives sin." The Bible tells us that we can approach God's throne of grace with confidence, because of the work of our Great High Priest, Jesus (Hebrews 4:16). When we go before God and confess our sin, he removes the guilt (Psalm 32:5) and heals us.

Are you experiencing a drought of peace or a plague of remorse? God is waiting for you to come to him, humbly seek his face, and confess your sin so that he might act on your behalf. God is waiting and he is ready to act.

> God, I am sorry to have kept you waiting. Thank you for the conviction in my heart that turns me back to you in repentance, for it is against you, you only, that I have sinned.

MAY 25

1 Kings 9:15–10:29; 2 Chronicles 1:14–17; 8:1–9:28

So Solomon became richer and wiser ... People from every nation came to visit him and to hear the wisdom God had given him.
—1 Kings 10: 23a, 24

Solomon's wealth, wisdom, influence, and reputation grow. The Queen of Sheba comes for a visit and is amazed at everything she sees. The Queen praises God for placing Solomon on Israel's throne. As he promised, God provides Solomon with wisdom and riches. Kings from every nation visit Solomon to hear the wisdom God has given him.

How gracious of God to delight in Solomon, to place him on the throne and give him great wisdom to lead God's people. God kept every promise he made to Solomon.

How precious to think that the Lord might delight in you and in me just as he delighted in Solomon. Yet, he does! The Lord delights in those who fear him, who place their hope in his unfailing love (Psalm 147:11).

As he kept every promise he made to Solomon, he fulfills every promise he makes to us. His word tells us and our lives bear witness that every promise is "Yes" in Christ Jesus (2 Corinthians 1:20). God is steadfastly faithful and his word is true; what he says he will do.

Do you live in the poverty of doubt and fear or in the spiritual wealth of God's promises?

> Almighty God, my trust is in you and your faithfulness. I will read your Word and learn your promises so that I can claim them and live in the spiritual wealth that you have planned for me. Forbid it Lord, that I should forfeit the riches of your grace by living in doubt and fear.

MAY 26

1 Kings 4; Psalms 72; 127

Unless the LORD builds a house, the work of the builders is useless.
—Psalm 127:1

Solomon has a huge military force including 1,400 chariots and 12,000 horses. He has eleven high officials, twelve district governors, and one governor over the land of Judah. He rules over a people as numerous as the sand on the seashore. Throughout Solomon's lifetime, all of Judah and Israel lives in peace and safety. From Dan to Beersheba, each family has its own home and garden. Solomon acknowledges it is the Lord God, the God of Israel, who alone does such wonderful things.

How gracious of God to build Solomon's house. God promised King David, Solomon's father, that he would establish an eternal house for David; it begins with Solomon (2 Samuel 7). Solomon understood that his success was entirely of God.

We work hard to build our houses, our lives, and to make our homes a sanctuary from the world. However, all of our work is in vain if the Lord is not the builder. No matter how much time or energy we spend working, if we work apart from God then our accomplishments have no spiritual value and will bear no eternal fruit (1 Corinthians 3:10–15). What we build will exist only for the moment. It is what it is, and then it will be no more.

What is God building in your life? What are you attempting to build apart from him?

God of Israel, you do such wonderful things when I step back and allow you to be the contractor of my life. Please humble me and search my heart; show me where I am wasting my energy by working hard to accomplish temporary success when I could be working with you for eternal successes.

Proverbs 1–4

Through these proverbs, people will receive instruction in discipline, good conduct, and doing what is right, just, and fair.
—Proverbs 1:3

Solomon records the wisdom God gives him. Solomon knows that wisdom begins with the fear of the Lord. He knows that wisdom is to be valued and it is to be applied. Solomon entreats the reader, his children, to listen to his instruction, pay attention, and grow wise.

How gracious of God to impart his applicable wisdom that we might grow wise, experience transformation, and live lives that will bring glory to him.

God cares about how we live, and he gives instruction for our lives so that when we apply it we will stand apart from the culture in which we live (Matthew 5:13–16). When we live lives of selflessness and love other people will see and know to whom we belong (John 13:35). Our desire must be to represent God attractively through our decisions, words, and actions. The way we live should be a radiant beacon that points people to God and brings him glory.

God imparts wisdom to us through the Bible, godly teachers, pastors, and friends. When we hear God's wisdom, we must learn it and apply it to our lives, hearts, and minds. Wisdom that is not applied cannot be tested; and wisdom that is not tested, cannot be trusted.

How is God transforming your life as you apply his wisdom (Romans 12:1–2)?

> Lord, I don't want to be puffed up with wisdom that I can only preach. I want to apply everything I learn so that my life looks pleasantly different from the world. Please teach me to handle and apply your Word correctly so that I reflect you and your wisdom beautifully.

MAY 28

Proverbs 5–7

Her feet go down to death; her steps lead straight to the
grave. And she doesn't even realize where it leads.
—Proverbs 5:5–6b

Solomon warns against sexual sin, calling it the path that leads
straight to the grave. He teaches to run from sexual sin; don't go
near it. Solomon compares lust to scooping hot fire into one's lap;
you will be burned. Sexual sin brings with it wounds and constant
disgrace and it will be punished. Sexual sin is subtle; little do its
victims know it can cost their very lives.

How gracious of God to define the destructive path of sexual
sin for his people.

Solomon knew the danger of sexual sin and he also understood
sexual purity. Sexual purity protects our hearts, our bodies, our
souls, and our spirits. God's way is the way of protection.

The world paints a picture of sexual sin as sexual freedom. The
world tells us that sex is a simply a means of expressing ourselves,
of discovering who we are, or of sharing ourselves with another
person. Sexual images bombard us every day from advertising to
entertainment. Every manner of pornography is no more than a
computer click away. This is the path to destruction.

Are you carrying the wounds and disgrace of sexual sin? Perhaps
you were the one who sinned. Perhaps you were the target of someone
else's sin. There is healing and restoration in Christ Jesus for both
(Jeremiah 17:14; Isaiah 53:5; Acts 10:38).

God you see me clearly, and you know the path I am on.
Please open my eyes to the subtle ways that sexual sin might
be drawing me away from you. Please lead me onto the path
of sexual purity.

MAY 29

Proverbs 8–10

> Listen as Wisdom calls out ... "Listen to me! ... For
> everything I say is right, for I speak the truth ... My advice
> is wholesome and good. ... My words are plain to anyone
> with understanding, clear to those who want to learn."
> —Proverbs 8:1a, 6a,c, 9

When he could have asked for anything, Solomon asks for wisdom. Solomon knows that God's wisdom is understandable, wholesome, good, and of greatest value. Wisdom is available to everyone, and useful to all who choose to learn. Wisdom begins with the fear of the Lord.

How gracious of God to impart wisdom in clear and plain ways so that even the simplest person can learn and understand.

The world tells us that the Bible, God's Word, is too difficult to understand, however, God tells us that he makes his words plain to anyone with understanding (Romans 1:19). It is clear to those who want to learn. Do we want to learn? Or do we want to surrender to the world's discouragement?

Bible studies abound and yet so few people attend. There are a multitude of books and plans to help us read through the Bible and we begin with good intentions, but rarely finish. However, we do find that the more we read the more we understand.

Will you trust that the more you read the Bible, the clearer it will become? Will you prove that God's words are clear to those who want to learn?

God, I confess that there are days when I want to set your Word aside. I also confess that the more I read the more I understand and the closer I feel to you. Please create in me an insatiable hunger for daily spiritual bread—for your Holy Word.

MAY 30

The life of the godly is full of light and joy,
  but the sinners light is snuffed out.
    —Proverbs 13:9

Solomon records many proverbs—short, pithy sayings that express well-known truths—for the benefit of his people so that they might know how to live godly lives.

How gracious of God to record boundaries and guidelines through the proverbs that enable a Christian to live a life full of light and joy.

It is God who inspired Solomon to record his proverbs and it is God who protects his written Word through all generations.

Some of Solomon's proverbs have made their way into the language of the day and when we read through the Proverbs it is easy to find one or two that we want to embrace as divine promises of God, for example: "Truth stands the test of time; lies are soon exposed." (12:19) However, we know that sometimes lies are not exposed for years, if ever.

We must be careful that we don't make any proverb into something it is not, but study and heed the principles God gives us. We are called to be as salt and light in the world (Matthew 5:13–16) and applying the spiritual principles of these proverbs helps us obey this command.

How does your life and your knowledge of God's proverbs bring light into another person's darkness? How do these proverbs enable you to maintain your saltiness?

God, I don't want to simply read these proverbs, I want to live them so that my life is full of light and joy. I want to bring your Word into the darkness that surrounds me. Please teach me these truths so that I apply them and reflect your light wherever I go.

MAY 31

Proverbs 14–16

We can gather our thoughts, but the Lord gives the right answer.
—Proverbs 16:1

Solomon teaches that the Lord's wisdom is pure, good, and right; while the wisdom of the world is foolishness. Mockers never find wisdom. Wisdom is not found among fools. Fools cannot give good advice. Fools plunge ahead with great confidence. The effort of fools yields only folly.

How gracious of God to provide pure, good, and right wisdom when we seek his wisdom.

I have heard it said that in a room full of people, if you can't spot the fool, it is probably you. No one wants to be the fool, I surely don't, I'm sure you don't. How can we be confident that we are not the fool? How can we be confident that the person advising us is not the fool? Any wisdom that we give or receive that does not align with the words of God is foolishness. In order to not be the fool, we must seek God's wisdom in his Word. We must pray and ask for wisdom. God promises that when we do, he will give generously (James 1:5).

When you receive advice, if it causes you to behave or think in a way that is contrary to God's Word, you can know with certainty that a fool has advised you.

How carefully do you run your advice (whether giving or receiving) through the grid of Scripture? How confident are you that you have not given or received the advice of a fool?

> God, please give me wisdom, I don't want to be the fool in the room. Until I know that I am dispensing your truth with your wisdom, please help me to remain silent. When I hear foolishness, please give me boldness to speak wisely.

grace JUNE

JUNE 1

Proverbs 17–19

A person's words can be life-giving water; words of true
wisdom are as refreshing as a bubbling brook.
—Proverbs 18:4

Solomon asks for wisdom and God gives Solomon true and
refreshing words of wisdom. Solomon records wisdom regarding
true friendship. He writes of the refuge and safety found in the name
of the Lord who is a strong fortress. His words convey the assurance
of security and protection that accompanies the fear the Lord. And
his words promise the Lord's purposes will prevail.

How gracious of God to provide words of encouragement,
refreshment, and life.

God chose to use words to reveal himself to us. Jesus is the final
Word. Jesus is the complete revelation of God; he is the true Word
(John 1:1, Hebrews 1:1–2).

As we read God's Word, we experience a myriad of emotions and
thoughts. God's words convict, challenge, rebuke, encourage, and
comfort us (2 Timothy 3:16). They show us the way to abundant
life. They draw us to the Father. They lead us to salvation. God's
words reveal God!

Words are important to us and to the people who listen to us.
How would you describe your words? Do your words encourage or
discourage your listener? Are your words as refreshing as a bubbling
brook or do your words cause anxiety like a raging rapid? Do you use
life-giving words, or life-draining words? Do you speak with God's
wisdom, or worldly wisdom?

> God, my heart's desire is to be a truthful witness and to
> represent you well with my words. Please keep me from being
> so zealous to speak the truth that I forget to season my words
> with grace, compassion, gentleness, and love. Help me to always
> use refreshing, life-giving words that draw my listeners to you.

JUNE 2

The godly walk with integrity; blessed
are their children after them.
—Proverbs 20:7

Solomon experiences God's integrity as God keeps every promise he makes. Solomon knows the importance of keeping one's word and he knows the Lord despises double standards. Solomon knows the Lord examines the heart and that the Lord's searchlight penetrates the human spirit, exposing every hidden motive.

How gracious of God to establish and maintain a high bar of integrity for his people.

We know that as Christians what we do and say matters; we represent the God whose name we bear. When we fail to act with godly integrity, we slander God.

God does not have a double standard—one set of rules for one group of people, and another set for others—so neither must we. God searches the heart (Psalm 139:23–24); he knows when it is divided, he knows when there is compromise, he knows when we fail to meet the bar of integrity.

Has there been a time when you compromised God's reputation because you failed to act with integrity? Is it important to you to keep your word in all things? If you say you'll be there, do something, pray for someone, keep a secret, or make a promise, do you follow through? Do you hold yourself to the same bar to which you hold others? How well do you keep the rules you expect others to follow?

God, please search my heart and expose my hidden motives.
Please examine me and show me where I am not in alignment
with you. Help me to live as a person of integrity in every
area of my life.

JUNE 3

I am teaching you today—yes, you—
so that you will trust in the Lord.
—Proverbs 22:19

Solomon calls his readers to listen to the words of the wise. Solomon writes thirty wise sayings filled with advice and knowledge—wisdom for the way in which people should live. Solomon teaches truths about God and people so that people will learn to trust the Lord, the defender of the poor and the redeemer and protector of the weak. Solomon writes that God gives discipline, discernment, and wisdom to his children. God knows all hearts and he sees and watches over souls. He always judges rightly.

How gracious of God to teach his people that he is faithful and worthy of trust.

It is impossible to trust someone who acts inconsistently, is arbitrary, has favorites, changes like shifting sand, and is unfaithful (James 1:17–18). God is none of those things. God is true, trustworthy, and unchanging. He will never let us down and he will never be anything less than perfect (Hebrews 13:6–8). He is on our side.

Fear, though, can be devastating, even paralyzing. Fear promotes disobedience. The antidote to fear is developing a deeper understanding of God's character. As we meditate on God's nature we begin to understand what it means to be more than conquerors. We learn to trust God when he tells us that nothing can separate us from his love (Romans 8:37–39).

Do you live in fear? Will you study God's Word and discover who he is in regard to the things you fear most?

God, I confess that when I am afraid it is because I do not trust you. Please forgive my shortsighted vision of your majesty, glory, and power. Help me to grasp the reality that you are exactly who you claim to be: The Almighty.

JUNE 4

Song of Songs 1–8

This is Solomon's song of songs, more wonderful than any other.
—Song of Songs 1:1

Solomon writes his most wonderful song and it is about the beauty and glory of sexual love and intimacy within a marriage relationship. Repeatedly the Young Woman and the Young Man profess their adoration of each other and their commitment to one another. Solomon describes the joy and delight they experience in each other's arms.

How gracious of God to ordain the gift of marriage and sexual intimacy.

Marital love is a treasure that God has entrusted to us. His glorious plan is that we experience an intimate and loving sexual relationship based on mutual trust, and shared within the boundaries of marriage. When we choose marriage, we choose to be open, transparent, and vulnerable with our spouse. There is great joy as husband and wife delight equally in one another, respecting and upholding their marriage vows.

This is the ideal but sometimes it isn't the reality. Marriages often include mistrust, brokenness, and fatigue. Young families struggle to balance careers and/or children that consume their energy and attention. Spouses and their needs often find their way to the bottom of the priority list. Worse yet, there may be abuse, adultery, pornography, or a host of other trust and intimacy destroying evils wreaking havoc within marriage.

What might you do today to assure your spouse that he or she is the most important person to you? If your marriage is broken, will you work with God and your spouse to repair it?

If you are single, what is your plan to protect your possible future marriage purity?

God, please purify my heart and help me to enjoy my spouse and protect the gift which you've given us.

JUNE 5

1 Kings 11; 2 Chronicles 9:29–31; Ecclesiastes 1:1–11

The God of Israel, says: "I am about to tear the kingdom from the hand of Solomon … But I will leave him one tribe for the sake of my servant David … For Solomon has abandoned me."
—1 Kings 11:31b, 32a, 33a

Solomon marries many wives and they turn his heart to worship other gods. The Lord warns Solomon against this, but Solomon doesn't listen. Then the Lord tells Solomon he will tear the kingdom away from him, but he will not do it while Solomon is alive. The Lord raises enemies against Solomon. After Solomon dies, the Lord removes the kingdom from Solomon's son, but for David's sake, God allows Solomon's son, Rehoboam to be king over Judah. God raises Jeroboam, the son of one of Solomon's officials, as king over the remaining tribes of Israel.

How gracious of God to judge sin in his children. God's judgment proves God's love. Judgment also establishes value because it shows that who we are and what we do matters to God.

Today, God judges our sin and convicts our hearts so that we might repent and return to him (1 John 1:9). Any circumstance that God allows or brings to pass, no matter how devastating it might be, is an act of grace administered to draw us back to God while there is still time to repent (2 Peter 3:9).

Have you aligned with people who are leading you away from God and toward sin? How is God judging that sin? Are you responding to him in repentance or rebellion?

> God, please forgive me for allowing idols into my life. Thank you for the conviction and heartache as you judge my sin, because it prompts me to run to you.

JUNE 6

Ecclesiastes 1:12–6:12

God has made everything beautiful for its own time.
He has planted eternity in the human heart …
—Ecclesiastes 3:11 a, b

King Solomon, by now an old man, writes Ecclesiastes. Throughout the course of his life, he learns that everything under the sun is temporary and meaningless. The search for increased knowledge brings increased sorrow and chasing pleasure is as futile as chasing after the wind. Because God has planted eternity in the heart, all people long for more than time. Under the sun, there is never enough of anything. Enjoying one's work and accepting one's lot in life is a gift from God; there is great futility and discontent in the quest to attain more.

How gracious of God to give his people a desire for eternal things.

Too often we think that if only we had more of this or more of that we would be satisfied; but as Solomon learned, this or that never satisfies because this or that is not eternal. Searching for our purpose or meaning in life through things that are temporary is futile. Everything under the sun is temporary; everything temporary will inevitably end.

Upon what are you basing your purpose and enjoyment in life? Is your life a continual search for more and more and more, the next thing or the thing after that? Only the Eternal God will satisfy your soul's desire.

> Almighty God, I don't want to stand before you with nothing to show for my life but exhaustion from chasing after the wind. I don't want the sum total of my days to add up to nothing. I don't want futility to be my destiny. Help me to learn Solomon's lesson and fill my desire with you.

JUNE 7

Ecclesiastes 7:1–11:6

Those who fear God will succeed…
—Ecclesiastes 7:18b

Solomon knows by experience that human wisdom is limited. Though Solomon determines to be wise, wisdom is distant and difficult to find. He concludes that no one can discover everything God has created, for even the wisest people cannot know everything. Solomon is in awe of God, and knows that the key to success is given to those who fear God.

How gracious of God to give success to his people who fear him.

From an historical perspective, if there was anyone who was successful, it was Solomon. He had it all: wealth, women, land, respect—and if he didn't have it, he knew where to get it and had the means to acquire it.

We use the same standards today: wealth, status, position, reputation, education, the size of a house, the number of cars in the garage, the labels on clothing, or even the church we attend.

Rarely do we hear anyone describe success as fearing God and walking in his path (Joshua 1:7). When we stand in awe of God, and seek to please him through fearful obedience, motivated by love (I Samuel 15:22), only then we will be successful.

Which matters most to you: success from the world's perspective or from God's?

God, I want the success that you want me to experience. Please imprint your definition of success upon my heart. I choose to live in reverent fear of you, and I stand in holy awe of you because I love you. Please help me to stop striving to accomplish success as the world defines it, so that I can walk where you are leading, seeking the success that matters: humble submission and loving obedience.

JUNE 8

1 Kings 12; 2 Chronicles 10:1–11:17; Ecclesiastes 11:7–12:14

The older counselors replied, "If you are good to the
people ... they will always be your loyal subjects."
—2 Chronicles 10:7a, c

Solomon's final advice in Ecclesiastes is to not let the excitement
of youth cause you to forget your Creator, rather to fear God and
obey his commands. Rehoboam, Solomon's son, becomes king. He
doesn't heed Solomon's words, or the advice of the older counselors.
He listens to his young friends, alienates his people, and divides the
nation. The ten northern tribes of Israel separate and follow their
new king, Jeroboam. Jeroboam establishes calf idols, shrines, pagan
altars, and a new priesthood in Israel; leading God's people into the
sin of idolatry.

How gracious of God to give wise counsel through experienced
godly people. God's wisdom is timeless and ageless (1 John 3:20);
it will never contradict the principles of his written Word (Hebrews
6:17–18), or his character (1 Samuel 15:29). If we surround ourselves
with fools, we become the fool. If we surround ourselves with yes-
men, we become arrogant. If we surround ourselves with godly
counsel, we act wisely.

Sometimes we choose to whom we listen based on the outcome
we desire or fear. Perhaps that is the time we must be most careful
not to discard the wisdom of godly older believers.

What criteria do you use for giving or receiving advice? Have
you compromised godly biblical counsel in order to follow your own
desired path?

God, please guard my heart and my mind and help me to
seek and dispense your wisdom. Keep me from pursuing my
agenda at the cost of godly counsel.

JUNE 9

1 Kings 13:1–15:15 2 Chronicles 11:18–15:19

> Because Rehoboam humbled himself, the LORD's anger was
> turned aside, and he did not destroy him completely.
> —2 Chronicles 12:12a

In Israel, God judges Jeroboam's sin: the religion he established. God judges the people of Israel for sinning alongside Jeroboam. In Judah, Rehoboam establishes himself as king; he doesn't seek the Lord with all his heart as his grandfather David did; he abandons the Lord. When the King of Egypt invades, Rehoboam recognizes God's hand and justice in allowing the destruction. Rehoboam humbly calls out to God and God responds with compassion.

How gracious of God to allow difficult circumstances.

God allows or ordains hard things in order to show his people that he is their only hope (Daniel 4). Hard times should draw us back to God in humble submission. When we are living in comfort and ease it is easy to forget God (Deuteronomy 6:11–12). When our enemies increase and surround us on every side, defeating us at every turn, that's when we are most likely to remember from where our help comes (Psalm 121:1–2). The moment we cry out to God he acts with compassion.

Do you feel surrounded by a destructive invading enemy? Are you seeking to defend yourself alone? Will you humble yourself before God and yield to his justice?

> God, I confess that I am defeated without you. Please show
> me where pride has a stronghold on my heart, keeping me
> from humbly submitting to you. I don't want to wait until I
> am surrounded by enemies before I call out to you; I submit
> to you and humbly beg you to rescue me today.

JUNE 10

1 Kings 15:16–24; 16:1–17:7; 2 Chronicles 16:1–17:19

As surely as the LORD, the God of Israel lives—the God
whom I worship and serve—there will be no dew or rain
during the next few years … unless I give the word.
—1 Kings 17:1

Judah's king, Asa, remains faithful to the Lord throughout his
life, and leads Judah to worship and serve the Lord. Asa dies and
Jehoshaphat becomes king. The Lord is with Jehoshaphat as he
follows the example of his father and seeks God.

Ahab is king in Israel and is more evil than any previous king.
During this time the Lord uses the prophet Elijah to speak to Ahab
telling him there will be no rain. There is no rain.

How gracious of God to speak through his prophets proving that
he is the one true God. Only God's true prophets accurately
foretold future events because God told them what to say. God
spoke through his prophets and then, because God is sovereign over
all things, he intervened in history to bring the spoken things to pass
(Isaiah 45:18–25).

Anyone can profess to tell the future, however, only God can
foretell the future and then bring it to pass. This gives us great
confidence that the biblical God is God alone. When we look to the
fulfillment of every past prophecy, then we can rest in confidence in
the fulfillment of every future prophecy and every future promise.
The Lord's words are true and therefore his words are trustworthy.

Have you committed your future to the God who already
knows—and holds—the future?

Almighty Sovereign God, thank you for the unquestionable
assurance that you are the one true God above all gods.

JUNE 11

1 Kings 17:8–20:22

But the LORD said to him, "What are you doing here, Elijah?"
—1 Kings 19:9b

There is drought and the people prepare to die. God sends Elijah to the widow in Zarephath where God miraculously feeds Elijah, the widow, and the widow's son for many days. Then the boy dies. God answers Elijah's prayer, restoring the boys' life.

At the showdown between Elijah and the prophets of Baal, God sends fire and defeats the prophets of Baal. Then God brings rain. Elijah flees for his life; when he stops to sleep, God sends an angel with food and water. Elijah travels forty days and nights until he arrives at a cave on Mt. Sinai. Elijah fears he is the last remaining believer and God encourages him with the promise that he will preserve thousands who have never bowed to Baal.

How gracious of God to meet every physical, emotional, and spiritual need of his people.

We may never experience the same miracles that Elijah experienced, but we do experience the same salvation and the same God. God will validate our faith, protect us in danger, comfort us, allow time for rest, reassure us that we are never alone, and provide for every need when we ask him to and believe that he will (Matthew 7:7–11).

Are you at the place where God has led you? Do you feel alone? forsaken? or tired? Have you given your all for God and yet you feel abandoned? Will you ask and trust that God will give to you that which is best for you?

> Lord, you are God, and I know that I am never alone no matter how much my heart tries to deceive me. Thank you for the assurance that you are always with me and will never forsake me.

JUNE 12

1 Kings 20:23–22:9; 2 Chronicles 18:1–8

So I will help you defeat this vast army. Then
you will know that I am the LORD.
—1 Kings 20:28b

When Ahab, the king of Israel, defeats the Arameans in the hills
the Arameans believe that God is merely a god of the hills. The
Arameans decide to fight Israel in the plains. Israel musters their
army. The man of God goes to Ahab and tells him that God will
help him defeat the Arameans so that Ahab will know he is the Lord.
God defeats the Arameans. God reveals himself to Ahab as the one
true God. Ahab disobediently signs a treaty with the king whom
God told him to destroy. God pronounces judgment: Ahab will die
in place of the Aramean king.

How gracious of God to give abundant evidence that he is God
over all.

O, how easy it is for us to pass judgment on Ahab. How could
he not submit to God and obey his every command? God spoke to
him and led him in a military victory. God is God over every nation
and every person. He is not a tribal deity (Jeremiah 44:26–29).

However, are you and I any different? If we want to see God in
our circumstances, all we have to do is open our eyes. He's there! In
everything that we are going through, in every battle, in every calm,
in every storm, in every pain, in every suffering he's there, and he's
at work for our good and for his glory (Romans 8:28–29).

Will you look for God today?

Almighty God, please open my eyes to see you every day.
Open my mind to accept you as truth. Open my ears to
hear your voice. Open my heart to embrace you as the one
true God.

JUNE 13

1 Kings 22:10–40, 51–53; 2 Chronicles 18:9–20:30

Tomorrow, march out against them. But you will not
even need to fight. Do not be afraid or discouraged.
Go out there tomorrow, for the LORD is with you!
—2 Chronicles 20:16a, 17a,d

Jehoshaphat travels throughout Judah encouraging the people to return to the Lord, the God of their ancestors. Jehoshaphat hears that a vast army is marching against him. He stands before the people and prays; acknowledging the Lord alone is God, the ruler of all kingdoms, powerful, and mighty. Jehoshaphat admits that he and the people are powerless against the army that comes against them. He looks to God for help. The Lord speaks to Jehoshaphat through Jahaziel and encourages him to not be afraid for the Lord is with him

How gracious of God to defeat the enemies of his people and give them peace.

How powerless we feel when we come up against an enemy that seems too big, too powerful, or too confusing to fight. We often feel defeated before we can formulate a battle plan. However, there is no enemy more powerful than God is, no problem that is too tangled for him to solve, and no battle that is too difficult for him to win (Genesis 18:14a Romans 8:38–39).

Do you feel powerless in your battle? Have you asked God to fight the battle with you, or for you? Will you trust him to untangle the snarled knot of circumstances that threaten to overpower you? Will you trust him to bring you peace?

> God, I cry out to you, "I am powerless!" I can't fight this
> enemy alone. I know you are more powerful than my enemy,
> and yet I am restless and afraid. Help me to rest in your
> omnipotence and sovereignty.

JUNE 14

1 Kings 22:41–50; 2 Kings 1; 3; 8:16–22; 2 Chronicles 20:31–21:7

> But the LORD was not willing to destroy David's dynasty,
> for he had made a covenant with David and promised
> that his descendants would continue to rule forever.
> —2 Chronicles 21:7

Jehoshaphat dies and Jehoram is king in Judah. Jehoram marries the daughter of King Ahab of Israel and follows in the wickedness of the Israelite kings. Jehoram does what is evil in the Lord's sight. He murders his brothers, abandons the Lord, and leads Judah to worship pagan idols. One evil king after another assumes the throne, and yet the Davidic dynasty continues.

How gracious of God to keep his word despite the failures of his people.

God kept his word to King David as David's dynasty continues through the ultimate and final king: Jesus (2 Samuel 7).

Jesus is the fulfillment of God's promise to David, to you and to me (2 Corinthians 1:20). Though you and I have failed and will continue to, just as David failed, and as just as the successive kings did, God will never fail (1 Peter 4:19). He always keeps his word (Deuteronomy 23:19).

What promise has God kept to you despite your failure? What protection have you experienced in your life because of God's grace to an ancestor of yours?

> God, I recognize that I am a beneficiary of grace. I don't deserve your protection, love, mercy or salvation. Thank you for the blessings that are mine simply because you loved those who came before me and you love me. Help me to live upon the truth that faith doesn't begin with me and it also must not end with me. Cause me to be a conduit of blessings for those who come after me.

JUNE 15

2 Kings 2; 4

Then the river divided, and Elisha went across.
—2 Kings 2:14b

Before Elijah is taken up to heaven, Elisha asks to become his rightful successor. Elijah tells Elisha that if he see him when he is taken, then Elisha will get his request. Elisha sees Elijah go. God lets Elisha know that he is Elijah's rightful successor. God uses Elisha to perform several miracles: the water is made wholesome, forty-two men are overcome by two bears, the olive oil flows, a child is raised to life, the poison is removed from the stew, and hungry people eat until they are full. Elisha always gives the glory to God.

How gracious of God to authenticate his prophets.

Wouldn't it be wonderful to see such magnificent miracles today, to experience the supernatural as Elisha did? That would definitely reassure us of a person's authentic calling as a spokesperson for God.

Nevertheless, God does not leave us without proof when he is at work in a person's life. The benchmark that we do have is the Holy Spirit. In authentic Christian work, where the Holy Spirit is at work, Jesus will be glorified, Jesus will get the credit, and Jesus will be made famous rather than the person doing the work (John 15:26; 16:14).

What about in your work—does your work for the Lord bring glory to Jesus?

> God, I don't want to mislead anyone or misrepresent you. I want to work for your kingdom with authenticity, manifesting the fruit of your Holy Spirit. I want you to receive all the glory for you alone are worthy. Please help me to lift up the Name of Jesus in my life, my work, and my relationships so that I am authenticated as your workmanship.

JUNE 16

2 Kings 5:1–8:15

The LORD opened his servant's eyes, and when he
looked up, he saw that the hillside around Elisha
was filled with horses and chariots of fire.
—2 Kings 6:17

God works through Elisha as he heals the commander of the
Aramean army of leprosy, deals with Gehazi's greed, causes the ax-
head to float, and then gives Elisha insight into where the Arameans
are planning to mobilize their troops against Israel. God never
abandons Israel, or Elisha, his prophet in Israel. When the Aramean
king sends troops to seize Elisha, Elisha's servant is gripped by fear
and Elisha prays. God opens the servant's eyes to see the hillside
filled with horses and chariots of fire.

How gracious of God to protect his people even when his help
goes unseen.

Can you imagine seeing what Elisha's servant saw? We have no
idea how often and in how many ways God is protecting us. When
we see only the danger, the enemy, the obstacles, and all of the things
that make us feel outnumbered, fear often takes over. We may forget
that God is here. But he is and he is working to take care of us,
protect us, and provide for us (Genesis 50:20; Psalm 121).

What makes you feel vulnerable? Do you feel outnumbered in
your own home? at work? or at church? As you look around can you
imagine God's horses and chariots surrounding you?

God, I want to trust you, but sometimes the things I am able
to see cause me to fall into fear. Please open my eyes to focus
on you. Please train my heart to trust you so that I will rest
knowing you are here. Thank you for protecting me from
unknown and unseen dangers. Thank you for continually
watching over me.

JUNE 17

2 Kings 8:23–10:31; 2 Chronicles 21:8–22:9

Then Elijah the prophet wrote Jehoram this letter ...
—2 Chronicles 21:12a

Jehoram is a wicked king. He builds pagan shrines in Judah and leads the people to give themselves to pagan gods. God uses the prophet Elijah to speak to Jehoram. Elijah writes a letter outlining God's charges against Jehoram and the punishment for those actions. God says he will strike Jehoram with a severe disease; and he does. Jehoram dies. No one mourns his passing.

How gracious of God to speak truth to all people.

God spoke through Elijah and told Jehoram what he was going to do. God speaks to us still today through his Word, through the Holy Spirit, through our circumstances, and through godly men and women. He speaks in such a way that our consciences and our hearts will hear him (John 10:3).

No one will be able to stand before God on the Day of Judgment and say, "I didn't hear you," because God speaks so that all can hear (Psalm 19:1–4; Romans 1:20). Those who hear and believe God's words will live (John 1:12). Those who reject will stand condemned (John 3:18).

God has spoken to you. Have you received his words or have you rejected them?

God, your words are life to me. My heart rejoices in your salvation. I cherish the knowledge of knowing that when I open the Bible you are speaking to me. Teach me to listen. Humble me to receive every warning and encourage me with your promises. Teach me to speak your truth in love so that many people will hear your words and turn to you in saving faith.

JUNE 18

2 Kings 10:32–12:16; 2 Chronicles 22:10–24:22

Joash was seven years old when he became king …
Joash did what was pleasing in the LORD's sight
throughout the lifetime of Jehoiada the priest.
—2 Chronicles 24: 1b, 2a

Athaliah, the mother of deceased king Ahaziah, and grandmother of Joash, sets out to destroy the royal family. Joash is secreted away and hidden in the temple of the Lord. He remains there protected by the priest Jehoiada, for seven years. When Jehoiada decides it is time to reveal Joash as the rightful king, the descendant of David, he makes a pact with the army commanders and the Levites to protect the boy-king. Upon Joash's coronation, he is presented with a copy of God's laws.

How gracious of God to use ordinary people to keep his extraordinary promises.

You and I may not be called to extraordinary measures such as secretly hiding and protecting a royal baby, but we are commanded to protect God's word and to make sure the next generation knows God, his Word, and his promises (Deuteronomy 11:18–21). To obey this command we must read, study, and meditate on God's Word.

How are you protecting the next generation by passing God's Word on to them? Are you willing to be used in any extraordinary way or place in which God might call you?

> God, I am an ordinary person; there is nothing spectacular about me except that I am yours. I am a child of the King I am royalty. I surrender to you, my Lord, for you to use me however you desire to further your kingdom and reach the next generation for your glory.

JUNE 19

2 Kings 12:17–13:11, 14–25; 2 Chronicles 24:23–27

So the LORD was very angry with Israel. Then Jehoahaz
prayed for the LORD's help, and the LORD heard his prayer.
—2 Kings 13:3a, 4a

The Israelites continue in the idol worship that Jeroboam established
in Israel. The Lord allows the Arameans, under King Hazael, to
conquer more of Israel's land. The Israelite king, Jehoahaz, cries out
to the Lord for help. The Lord delivers Israel and brings safety to
the land. The people continue in their idolatry and sin. The cycle
continues.

How gracious of God to rescue his people when they call out
to him.

God is longsuffering and patient, holy, and just (Exodus 34:5–
7). In his justice, he must exercise his perfect judgment upon sin. In
his mercy and great love, he rescues his people when they call out
to him. Sometimes our circumstances, like the Israelites', have to
become unbearable before we turn to God and call out for rescue.
And, like the Israelites, we can fall into a cycle of sin, crying out,
and forgiveness.

Are you continually fighting the same sin in a recurring cycle
of sin and forgiveness? Is there an idol entrenched in your land that
God is calling you to uproot? Will you repent: turning fully away
from sin and turning fully toward God?

Has God allowed you to experience defeat? How much more
must you lose before you call out to God for deliverance?

God, I don't want to lose anything more to the sin in my
life. I don't want to swing like a yo-yo between sin and
forgiveness. Please hear my prayer and rescue me. Help me
to live in the victory that you have won.

JUNE 20

2 Kings 13:12–13; 14:1–27; 15:1–5;
2 Chronicles 25:1–26:21; Jonah 1–4

Then the sailors picked Jonah up and threw him into
the raging sea, and the storm stopped at once!
—Jonah 1:15

God sends Jonah to Nineveh, however, Jonah boards a ship bound for the opposite direction. A storm arises and Jonah, confronted by the sailors, confesses that he is running away from the Lord: The God of heaven who made the sea and the land. The terrified sailors try to row ashore but can't. They cry out to the Lord begging for mercy. Jonah commands them to throw him overboard. The storm calms. Awestruck, the sailors vow to serve the true God.

How gracious of God to reveal himself as the God who is sovereign over land and sea and everything in them (Luke 8:24).

It is amazing how God intertwines lives and circumstances in ways we could never imagine. Our lives, like Jonah's, affect everyone with whom we have contact. Who would have thought that pagan sailors would come to faith in God through the consequences of the disobedience of God's prophet? Yet, that is exactly how God works. God uses every circumstance for the good of those who love him, including the consequences of our sin (2 Corinthians 1:8–11; Romans 8:28).

How is God using the storms that are the consequences of your sin, for your good, the good of others, and his own glory?

God, you could let the consequences of my sin just be ugliness—a storm I must endure— but you don't. I trust you to redeem these storms and use them for your good purpose.

JUNE 21

Now this is what the LORD says to the family
of Israel: "Come back to me and live!"
—Amos 5:4

Uzziah is king in Judah; he seeks the Lord and God gives him success. Jeroboam II is king in Israel, and though he refuses to turn from idolatry, the Lord sees the bitter suffering of Israel and uses Jeroboam II to save them. Both the southern tribes of Judah and Israel in the north are in a time of prosperity and relative peace. They enjoy practicing their religion, but their hearts are far from God. God uses Amos to call them back to himself. They reject the Lord and refuse to obey him. God gives a warning: return to him and live, or face judgment and exile.

How gracious of God to warn his people when they begin to wander away from him.

The ancient hymn says it well, *prone to wander, Lord, I feel it, prone to leave the God I love.* God continually calls us to return to him and live (John 1:12). He calls out to us for the same reasons that he called out to Judah and Israel: we pervert justice, steal, trample the helpless, indulge in sexual sin, oppress the poor, crush the needy, and then turn and brag about our offerings. God has withheld rain, brought floods, blight, and mildew, sent our young men and women off to war, and devastated the economy yet many people still refuse to return to him.

What devastating circumstance has God allowed in your life to get your attention? Is he warning you that it's time to stop playing at religion and time to return to God and live?

Gracious God, *Here's my heart, O take and seal it, seal it for thy courts above.*

JUNE 22

2 Kings 14:28–29; 15:6–29;
2 Chronicles 26:22–23; Isaiah 6; Amos 7–9

In the year King Uzziah died, I saw the Lord. He was sitting
on a lofty throne, and the train of his robe filled the Temple.
—Isaiah 6:1

A series of kings come and go in Israel; but in Judah, King Uzziah
reigns fifty-two years. In the year Uzziah died, the Lord calls Isaiah
as the prophet in Judah. Isaiah sees a magnificent vision of God upon
his throne. Isaiah recognizes his own sinfulness and the sinfulness of
the entire human race. God cleanses Isaiah's lips, removes his guilt,
and calls him to be God's mouthpiece to the people. Isaiah asks how
long his ministry will last. The Lord tells him until their cities are
destroyed and no one is left in them.

How gracious of God to reveal himself in majesty. Isaiah needed
a vision of God that would sustain him throughout a lifelong
ministry that will not bring about change in the hearts of the people.

God reveals himself to you and me through the Bible, the
universe, and our own personal experiences. Whatever task he has
for us, the vision he has given us of himself should encourage and
sustain us whether we experience success or failure (Revelation 4).

What is your vision of God? Is he the majestic Holy One, the
Lord Almighty who fills the earth with his glory? Is he holy, holy,
holy? Has he cleansed you from your filthy sin? Does the train of
his robe of righteousness cover you? Do you believe he is sufficient
to sustain you for the work he has called you to do?

Lord, I will go! Send me! My Mighty, All-sufficient Holy
God, I submit to wherever, whenever and for however long.

JUNE 23

2 Kings 15:32–16:9; 2 Chronicles 27:1–28:15; Isaiah 7; Micah 1

> Then the LORD said to Isaiah, "Go out to meet
> King Ahaz. Tell him to stop worrying."
> —Isaiah 7:3a, 4a

Ahaz is king in Judah. He doesn't do what is pleasing in the sight of the Lord. His enemy Aram allies with Israel against him. Ahaz sends the temple treasures as gifts to Assyria in an attempt to secure their help. God sends Isaiah to tell Ahaz that Jerusalem will not fall. God reassures Ahaz of Israel's and Aram's coming destruction. God tells Ahaz that if he wants God to protect him, he must learn to believe what God says. God gives Ahaz a sign to prove that the kings Ahaz fears soon will be dead.

How gracious of God to send his word of assurance to those in battle.

God is always aware of the battles his children fight. He knows our enemies. He knows what we need for victory (Psalm 35:1–3). He knows how long the battle must rage (Psalm 62:1–2). He knows what ground will fall. He knows who will be defeated.

We will fight many battles. Sometimes our enemy will appear to be strong and well armed, but our God is waiting to help us. We don't have to give away our treasures. We don't need to secure allies. Our victory is in God and his word assures it (Psalm 118).

What battle are you fighting? Are you trusting God to be your strength and your defense during this time of war?

> God, in the heat of battle, please help me to remember that
> you have already defeated my greatest enemy. Please keep me
> from fighting apart from you—my strength and my defense.

JUNE 24

Isaiah 8–11

In that day the LORD will end the bondage of his people. He will break the yoke of slavery and lift it from their shoulders.
—Isaiah 10:27

Isaiah prophesies that Judah rejects God's gentle help so God allows Assyria to sweep into Judah. God also allows Assyria to devour Israel. Assyria blackens the land and takes the Israelites into exile. Destruction is certain for Assyria because of the arrogance of her kings. The remnant that remains in Judah and Israel will return to the Mighty God. God promises that out of the stump of David's family a shoot—a new Branch—will grow.

How gracious of God to explain his wrath so that we might understand his grace.

God's wrath is his settled hatred of sin. His wrath is poured out upon the evil that comes from within his people and from without. However, God is gentle, he will not destroy his child; he will not crush the bruised reed nor will he snuff out the smoldering wick of the flame of faith (Isaiah 42:3). God allows slavery and he alone frees the enslaved when his people respond to his word and run to him (John 8:31–32; Romans 6:15–18).

Isaiah's words were for Judah, but they also hold promises for us today. Jesus Christ is the Branch. There was no king on David's throne for four hundred years until the coming of the Lord Jesus Christ: our King.

What devastation has God allowed in your life so that you might turn to him? Are you experiencing slavery? Will you repent and enjoy the freedom of its removal?

> God, your wrath is just, and your grace is amazing. Thank you for the reality of your wrath that calls me to my knees so that I can experience your grace.

JUNE 25

2 Kings 15:30–31; 16:10–18; 17:1–4; 18:1–8;
2 Chronicles 28:16–25; 29:1–2; Isaiah 12; 17; Hosea 1:1–2:13

Go and marry a prostitute. This will illustrate the
way my people have been untrue to me.
—Hosea 1:2b, c

God's people turn from the God who saves them, the Rock who hides them, to idols. They worship what their own hands make. King Ahaz builds an altar and offers sacrifices on it to the gods of Damascus. He shuts the doors of the Lord's temple. He sets up altars to pagan gods in every corner of Jerusalem.

God tells Hosea, the prophet in Israel, to marry a prostitute and have children with her to illustrate Israel's unfaithfulness.

How gracious of God to use his prophets as object lessons to reveal truth as they live out their sermons.

As Hosea chose his wife, God chose the Israelites as his treasured possession and he chose you and me. And, as in a marriage relationship, when we seek our purpose and our pleasure apart from God, we commit spiritual adultery. When we put anyone or anything above God in our hearts we become the unfaithful spouse.

Do you know the humiliation caused by an unfaithful spouse? God does. Do you know the hurt of disrespect? God does. Have you experienced the stabbing pain of being forgotten and cast aside by a loved one who desires to be with their new love? God has. Is it time to commit to faithfulness in your relationship with God?

Dear God, I am so sorry. Precious Lord, please forgive my wretched and callous unfaithfulness. Please accept my repentance and restore me to the intimacy that you desire.

JUNE 26

Hosea 2:14–8:14

> I want you to be merciful; I don't want your
> sacrifices, I want you to know God.
> —Hosea 6:6

Cursing, lies, theft, murder, and violence fill Israel. The priests and leaders lead the people into idolatry. Israel, arrogant and guilty of sin, has no knowledge of God in the land. She plants the wind and harvests the whirlwind of God's wrath. The people love their religious rituals that bring a false sense of security. To God, their sacrifices are meaningless. Hosea speaks God's promises to Israel. God woos Israel; he will make her his wife. God tells Hosea to bring his adulterous wife home illustrating that God still loves Israel.

How gracious of God to tell his people clearly what he expects of them.

Violence, theft, and murder mark our times much like they did Hosea's, and many people have abandoned the knowledge of God (Romans 1:21–33). Religion, for some of us, has becomes more ritual and rote than relationship, and yet God continues to woo us. He continues to tell us exactly what he wants: a relationship.

How difficult it must be for our faithful God to persevere in wooing unfaithful sinners into his saving grace. How difficult it must be to watch as his beloved moves away from the warmth and intimacy of a relationship into the coldness of ritual (Isaiah 1).

Which is more precious, more cherished to you, your relationship with God or the ritual of your religion?

> Precious God, I thank you for making it clear to me that what you desire from me is an intimate relationship. Please help me understand that the relationship you desire is intimacy with me and not rote ritualistic religious adherence from me.

JUNE 27

Hosea 9–14

Return, O Israel, to the LORD your God, for your sins have
brought you down. The Lord says, "Then I will heal you of your
idolatry and faithlessness, and my love will know no bounds."
—Hosea 14:1, 4a

Hosea pronounces coming punishment for Israel's unfaithfulness:
they will be carried off to Egypt and Assyria where they will not
be able to worship God as God requires. They will be wanderers,
homeless among the nations. God sends prophets to warn them,
but they reject the prophets and spurn God. However, the Lord still
promises he will restore them when they repent.

How gracious of God to promise healing and love after repentance.

While nothing can separate us from God's love (Romans 8:38–
39) there have been, and probably will be times when you and I
must suffer in exile until we recognize and repent of the sin that
separates us from intimacy with God. God warns us about sin and
calls us to repentance. For true repentance we must identify and
confess specific sin. We cannot heal ourselves of sin, only God can
heal us. When sin is confessed, God pours the healing salve of his
love and forgiveness into our hearts which cleanses us and makes
us whole (Hebrews 9:13–15). God's love has no bounds: while we
were sinners, Christ died for us breaking the bonds with which sin
enslaves us (Romans 5:8).

What sin is God calling you to confess? Will you sincerely repent
so that God can cleanse your heart with the healing blood of Christ?

> God, the thought of exile frightens me. Please reveal the
> sin that prohibits my intimacy with you. Please accept my
> sincere sorrow and repentance and restore me to you with
> your healing love.

JUNE 28

2 Kings 17:5; 18:9–12; 17:6–41; Isaiah 1:1–20; 28

So the Lord will spell out his message for them again, repeating
it over and over, a line at a time, in very simple words.
—Isaiah 28:13

God continues giving the same message to Israel and Judah: foreign
armies cannot save you, if you want to live, you must abandon your
idols and choose God. Return to God and live. Israel refuses to
return to God. In the ninth year of King Hoshea's reign in Israel,
Samaria (the capital city of Israel) falls. The Israelites are deported
to Assyria. Only Judah remains in the land. Isaiah preaches: If you
continue turning away and refuse to listen, Judah will be destroyed.

How gracious of God to repeat continually, in simple words,
what we must do to live.

How many times have we said, "How many times do I have to
say …?" Typically it is a simple message that we are trying to get
across: Clean your room, brush your teeth, pick up your towel, fill
the paper tray. I wonder if God thinks, "How many times do I have
to say, it is a matter of life and death!" Either we choose Jesus and
live, or we don't and we die. (John 3:18).

Salvation is simple: you can't earn God's favor, you can only
accept his grace (Ephesians 2:8). Have you? Or is this plan of
salvation too simple? It sounds simple, but the cost to God—the
life of Jesus Christ—makes it invaluable.

> Oh God, I trust you, your plan, and my Savior Jesus Christ
> for my salvation. I choose you. I choose life. Thank you
> for lavishing your love and grace upon me. Thank you for
> choosing me and for offering me this gift of salvation.

JUNE 29

Isaiah 1:21–5:30

I will turn against you. I will melt you down and skim
off your slag. I will remove all your impurities.
—Isaiah 1:25

Because of her many sins, Judah is worthless. The people partner
with pagans and fill their land with idols. The Lord cannot ignore
the sins and forewarns them that they will be humbled and brought
low; their leaders and their women judged and held accountable.
Because the Lord is just and righteous, he redeems the repentant
and destroys the sinner who refuses to come to him.

How gracious of God to purify repentant people.

It is not difficult to see similarities between ancient Jerusalem
and the world we live in today. Without a second thought, Christians
make alliances with pagans. We purchase pagan entertainment. We
strive for more things in order to find satisfaction and happiness.
Our leaders are more interested in self-promotion and camera time
than in actually leading. Moreover, pornography is fast becoming
the standard by which we define our sexuality, if we can define it
at all. Even though we've been washed with the blood of Jesus and
belong to him (Psalm 51:7), we are not immune to the filth of the
world (John 13:10).

What filth are you carrying into your home, workplace, school,
or church? Will you repent today and be cleansed?

> O God, I ask you to burn away the slag that keeps me from
> reflecting your glorious person. Purify my mind so that I
> desire holy things. Purify my heart so that I love you above
> all. Purify my hands so that my work for you is worthwhile.
> Thank you for washing away the world's filth from my soul
> and my life.

JUNE 30

2 Kings 16:19–20; 2 Chronicles 28:26–27; Isaiah 13–16

> The LORD Almighty has sworn this oath: "It will all happen
> as I have planned. I have a plan for the whole earth, for
> my mighty power reaches throughout the world"
> —Isaiah 14: 24a, 26

Isaiah prophesies destruction for Babylon. Destruction for Assyria. Philistia is doomed. Moab ends in destruction. God assigns the armies of the world to punish the world for its evil, and the wicked for their sin.

How gracious of God to include every nation and individual in his plan for the world. To accomplish his perfect plan, God will use any tool he desires, including war.

As we read this passage, it is as if we are sitting at a train crossing and we see one train car of destruction after another. We cannot understand what God is doing or why. However, God sits on his throne high above the earth and not only sees the train, but its origination and destination. God is bringing about his perfect plan for all humanity (Revelation 4, 5).

You and I have a part in God's perfect plan. God created us in Christ Jesus us for a specific purpose—to do good works—and he will use us for that purpose (Ephesians 2:10). Just as God will assign tasks to the armies of the world, he will assign tasks to you and me.

Have you thought of yourself as a tool in God's hand (Isaiah 10:15)? Could it be that you are one soldier in an army with which God will change the world?

> God, help me to understand that I am part of something
> bigger than I can imagine. Please open my mind to see more
> of what you see, and to understand more of your purpose
> for the world.

grace JULY

JULY 1

2 Chronicles 29:3–31:21

For the LORD your God is gracious and merciful. If you return
to him, he will not continue to turn his face from you.
—2 Chronicles 30:9

Hezekiah is king in Judah and sets about to reopen the neglected
temple. He calls the Levites to purify both themselves and the
temple. He offers sacrifices for the atonement of the sins of all
Israel. He bows in worship with the people. He sends messengers
throughout Israel and Judah asking them to return to the Lord, the
God of Abraham. God gives the people in Judah a strong desire to
unite in obedience to the king and officials who are following God's
word. Most of the people in Israel laugh at the messengers.

How gracious of God to respond with mercy when his people
turn to him in repentance.

Neglecting the temple was the result of neglecting God. When
we neglect our walk with God it is as though we have closed the door
of our heart to him, the result of which is accumulated filth. God
will get our attention and, like Judah, he may make us an object of
dread, horror, or ridicule so that we can see how far from him we've
drifted (Deuteronomy 28; Psalm 41:4–13).

When you experience pain, hardship, or suffering do you run
to God or from God? Is God using difficult circumstances as tools
to call you to repentance? Is there filth that needs removed? Are you
aware that God is waiting to cleanse you as soon as you repent and
return to him.

> God, show me the filth from which I must repent so that
> my heart can be purified and I can enjoy the sweet intimacy
> with you that you have planned for us.

JULY 2

Proverbs 25–29

People who cover over their sins will not prosper. But if
they confess and forsake them, they will receive mercy.
—Proverbs 28:13

Hezekiah's advisors collect the proverbs of Solomon. Solomon's
wisdom is for the king and for the people. Solomon's proverbs give
advice on issues ranging from dealing with fools to how to handle
lazy, quarrelsome, wicked, hateful, hypocritical, and bragging people.
He advises truth, humility, steadfast friendships, and wisdom. He
warns against immorality, partiality, and dishonesty. Solomon's
proverbs remind the king and his officials of God's mercy.

How gracious of God to provide guidelines to enhance
interpersonal relationships, strengthen communities, and protect
one's relationship with God.

You and I are in situations every day that require the Wisdom
of Solomon! If we are to live in harmony with others and with God
we must heed God's guidelines. Since we don't live in a vacuum
our actions always affect others, and other people's actions affect
us. Fortunately, God's wisdom is available as a light to guide us
along the paths of righteousness (Psalm 119:105). God's wisdom is
available, but we must seek it to take advantage of it.

Do you seek wisdom? Do you collect it—memorizing it so that
it is readily available to guide you? Will you utilize God's Word to
lead you in all your business and personal decisions?

> Almighty God I love your wisdom and I know that my life
> will bring honor to you as I live by your Word. Please show
> me the sin that I am trying to hide. Please show me where
> I persist in walking in darkness and humble me to turn to
> you and boldly live in the light of your righteousness.

JULY 3

Proverbs 30–31

Charm is deceptive, and beauty does not last; but a
woman who fears the LORD will be greatly praised.
—Proverbs 31:30

Solomon describes the value of a virtuous and capable wife. She is
a trustworthy spouse who greatly enriches her husband. She doesn't
hinder him; she helps him. She works hard. She gets up early. She
plans the affairs of her home meticulously. She is energetic and
strong, a hard worker. She is a bargain hunter. She is busy. She helps
the oppressed and needy. She is clothed with strength and dignity.
She is wise and kind, virtuous and capable. She is greatly praised
because she fears the Lord.

How gracious of God to assure every woman that despite what the
cultures of the world value—her size, body shape, looks, education,
race, job, number of children, size of house, or any other measurable
thing—her true value is praiseworthy as she fears the Lord.

We all desire praise—men and women—and while this passage
is aimed at women, it applies to men as well. Personality and good
looks will only get us so far. Godly character will enable us to
persevere to the end (Romans 5:3–5; James 1:3–4).

Are you building your character in the Lord so that it rises even
as gravity and time take their toll and everything else falls? Do you
apply the Word of God as diligently as you apply moisturizer? Do
you exercise your faith as much as you do your physical body?

Heavenly Father, you know the things that make my heart
and my spirit ugly. Please help me to apply your Word so
that the light in my spirit is a reflection of your beauty for
the entire world to see.

JULY 4

Psalms 42–46

There I will go to the altar of God, to
God—the source of all my joy.
—Psalm 43:4

Hezekiah reestablishes the temple and the use of the Psalms in worship. The Psalms incorporate some of the names of God: God, the Living God, Savior, the Lord, King, Most High, the Lord Almighty, the God of Israel. The people sing and praise God for his character and attributes: hope, kindness, unfailing love, rock, defender, rescuer, safe haven, light, truth, guide, holy, source of joy, worthy of praise, victor, powerful, glorious, warrior, helper, handsome, gracious, majestic, awe-inspiring, conqueror, royal, just, husband, refuge, and indestructible.

How gracious of God to provide songs that remind his people who he is: the all-encompassing God who is with them and dwells among them.

What a privilege it is to sing songs during our times of worship alongside other believers. God tells us to come into his presence with singing (Psalm 100:2). Some of us may sing on key and hit every note and some of us can't carry a tune in a bucket, but I'm sure God joyously receives every song of worship.

Why do you sing? What do you sing? For whom do you sing? To whom do you sing? Do your songs exalt God, who is our joy? Do they praise God for who he is? Does your singing carry your spirit before the Throne of Grace and lift your eyes to God?

God, you are my hope and the source of all my joy. I will praise you with songs. I will celebrate you with my voice. I will teach my children and my grandchildren hymns that speak of who you are. Thank you for the gift of music, for hymn writers, pastors, musicians, and choir directors.

JULY 5

Psalms 47–49; 84–85; 87

For the LORD God is our light and protector. He gives
us grace and glory. No good thing will the LORD
withhold from those who do what is right.
—Psalm 84:11

The Psalms celebrate God's righteousness: His never-failing right character and actions. They exalt the Lord Most High as the great King of all the earth. They speak of his unfailing love. They declare the happiness of those who trust in the Lord Almighty. The Psalms remind the hearers of the blessings of God's forgiveness.

How gracious of God to remind all people of all time that he is always good.

As for Israel, so it is for God's child today: God does not withhold that which is good from his people who do what is right. God knows what is good and he promises to guide us into that good; there is no need to fear (Psalm 25:9). We enjoy happiness when we trust in him. He pours out blessing upon blessing. He forgives guilt and covers sin.

We cannot imagine the heights of God's goodness until we appreciate the depth of our sin. God's goodness reached down into the pit of humanity to lift those of us who trust him out of the slime and filth of our sin-stained pasts.

Are you carrying a load of sin? Does guilt haunt you? Jesus died to remove your guilt and shame, and God is waiting to forgive you (Hebrews 10:19–21). When you confess and repent God will not withhold that which is good from you. Are you ready to experience the joy of trusting in God?

O Lord, your unfailing love and salvation are my foundation;
I glory in your righteousness. O Father, thank you for the
blessings of goodness that you have poured out on me in
mercy and grace.

JULY 6

Psalms 1–2; 10; 33; 71; 91

Those who live in the shelter of the Most High
will find rest in the shadow of the Almighty.
—Psalm 91:1

The Psalms speak of God's people who trust him for their care. The Psalms proclaim God's watchfulness. They speak of God's sovereignty over the kings of the earth. They call upon God to remember the helpless. They praise God as the eternal King. They exalt his true Word and trustworthiness. They declare that God alone is the refuge, rescuer, rock, and fortress; he is the safety of his people.

How gracious of God to provide safety, rescue, and rest for his people.

God is the same today as he was yesterday, and as he will be tomorrow (Hebrews 13:8). He never changes. He still promises rest to the weary who come to him (Matthew 11:28). He promises to be with his children in trouble, to rescue them, and to love them (Isaiah 43:2).

God does not promise us trouble-free lives. Quite the opposite, God tells us not to be surprised by suffering (1 Peter 4:12–19). In the midst of difficulty, when we trust in God, we find rest in the shadow of the Almighty; no evil will conquer us, because Jesus defeated evil. We rest from fear and from dread because God is our refuge, rescue, and rock.

Are you living in the shadow of the Most High? Are you resting in the promise of his rescue? Do you carry with you the sweet refreshment of his promise wherever you go?

> Thank you, Father, for drawing me into your nest, for shielding me under your wings, and for sheltering me with your feathers. Thank you that no matter my circumstances, I am at rest in you.

JULY 7

But the godly will flourish like palm trees and grow strong like the cedars of Lebanon. For they are transplanted into the Lord's own house. They flourish in the courts of our God. Even in old age they will still produce fruit; they will remain vital and green.
—Psalm 92:12–14

It is good to give thanks and sing praises to the Most High. It is good to proclaim God's unfailing love and faithfulness. The Psalmist proclaims that God is a God of miracles and that knowing his thoughts are so deep no one can understand why he does all that he does thrills the Psalmist and causes him to sing for joy.

How gracious of God to plant his children in his own house where they flourish and produce fruit throughout the length of their lives.

God is higher and more magnificent than we can imagine, yet he reaches down to take hold of us and lift us up to live in him. God chose us and appointed us to bear fruit (John 15:16), and he provides everything we need to successfully bear that fruit (Hebrews 13:21). How wonderful to know that neither our fruitfulness nor our usefulness ends as we grow physically older.

Are you abiding in God so that you continually bear fruit (John 15:2–8)? Is God pruning you—cutting away worthless, diseased or dead things in your life—so that you might be even more fruitful?

O God, how blessed I am! How delightful to know that I have been transplanted from the realm of death into the realm of life. I know that you are the Master Gardener, and I trust you as you prune away everything that prevents my fruitfulness.

JULY 8

Psalms 98–100; 102; 104

For the LORD is good. His unfailing love continues forever,
and his faithfulness continues to each generation.
—Psalm 100:5

Psalm 100 praises God for his wonderful deeds, his victories, and his faithfulness. The Psalm calls everyone to break out in praise and sing for joy.

In Psalm 102, the Psalmist cries out to God in his distress, begging God to hear his plea. His heart is sick; he is sleepless, taunted and tearful.

How gracious of God to listen and hear both our praises and our pleas.

When our hearts fill with rejoicing we readily sing praises to God. When our hearts are overwhelmed with the burden of loneliness, despair, grief, anguish, anxiety, depression, fear, or worry we plead with God for help. God is always available and always hears us (Psalm 34).

God hears our prayers for mercy and he receives our praise. There is nothing that can separate us from his love (Romans 8:35–39) and he is always waiting to give us what we need (Hebrews 4:16).

Do your prayers consist of both praise and supplication? Are you teaching the next generation of believers how to boldly approach God's throne of grace with confidence?

> O Lord, my God, how great you are! You are robed with honor and with majesty; you are dressed in a robe of light. You stretch out the starry curtain of the heavens; you lay out the rafters of your home in the rainclouds. You make the clouds your chariots; you ride upon the wings of the wind. The winds are your messengers; flames of fire are your servants. Let all that I am praise the Lord!
> —Psalm 104:1–4

JULY 9

Psalms 105–106

Give thanks to the LORD and proclaim his greatness.
Let the whole world know what he has done.
—Psalm 105: 1

The Psalmist recounts God's miracles to Israel through the years: that God stands by the covenant he made with Abraham. God sends Joseph into Egypt before Israel. God multiplies Israel in Egypt and then sends Moses to deliver them. God spreads out a cloud above them and gives fire to light the darkness. God provides food and water. Though God gives land to Israel they fail to take it; they mingle with the people living in the land and adopt their evil customs. God rescues them repeatedly, but they continue to rebel.

How gracious of God to provide, protect, and guide his people despite persistent rebellion.

The circumstances of our lives are not random, nor are they a by-product of fate or coincidence. God is sovereign over all things including the circumstances of our lives (Acts 4:23–30). In his sovereignty, God promises us that he will bring to completion the work he began in us (Philippians 1:6). Our destiny is holiness (Romans 8:28–30), and God is using our circumstances to accomplish our destiny.

Have you ever pondered all that God has done to get you where you are? How has God led you? Provided for you? Protected you? Gone before you? How has God delivered you despite your rebellion? How will you show your gratitude today?

O Lord, my God, sometimes I look at my circumstances and fail to see you in them. Please forgive my myopic vision. From this day forward I will choose to praise you in my circumstances rather than complain because of my circumstances.

JULY 10

Psalms 107; 111–114

Far below him are the heavens and the earth. He
stoops to look, and he lifts the poor from the dirt
and the needy from the garbage dump.
—Psalm 113:6–7

The Psalmist records the ways in which God responds to rescue his people: God leads them straight to safety, he leads them from the darkness and deepest gloom, he snaps their chains, he speaks and heals them, he calms the storm, and he changes rivers into deserts, and deserts into pools of water.

How gracious of God to stoop down and rescue his people.

The Lord rescued you and me when, with the life-blood of Christ Jesus, he purchased us out of the marketplace of sin (1 Peter 1:18–19). He removed us from the garbage dump of pride, envy, laziness, complacency, guilt, shame, depravity, bitterness, self-righteousness, worry, fear, hatred, jealousy, and selfishness. He stooped down and lifted us from the filth and dirt of this world and set us with Jesus, high above, in the heavenly realms (Ephesians 2:6).

Do you need rescuing? Have you called out to Jesus to calm your storm, or lead you out of the darkness of your gloom and despair? Will you follow him to a place of safety? Will you surrender the chains that hold you down so that he can snap them? Jesus is the refreshing Living Water for which your soul yearns, will you drink from him (John 4:10–14; 7:37–38)?

God, I am overwhelmed by the love, mercy, and grace that you lavished on me when you reached down into the pit of sin and despair in which I existed and lifted me up to you. Your love is deeper than my mind can fathom. How can I thank you enough?

JULY 11

Psalms 115–118

Give thanks to the LORD, for he is good!
His faithful love endures forever.
—Psalm 118:1

The Psalmist sings of the faithful love of the Lord. He calls on the congregation of Israel, Aaron's descendants, and all who fear the Lord to praise his faithfulness. The Psalmist sings of God: he answers prayer, he rescues the distressed, he is trustworthy, he is strength, he is glorious, he is triumphant, he is accessible, he saves, and he is the cornerstone. He is God.

How gracious of God to love with a never ending, always faithful love.

Fortunately, God's love doesn't depend upon our ability to be lovable, but upon God, who is love (1 John 4:4–11). It doesn't depend on our faithfulness or obedience, but upon God who is faithful. God's love isn't arbitrary or fickle, it does not change because God doesn't change (1 Samuel 15:29).

It is God's choice to love us (Ephesians 1:4–9). He loved us when we were sinners (Romans 5:8) and he will love us eternally.

Is it difficult for you to believe and accept that God loves you unconditionally? God loves you because he is God and it pleases him to love you. God is good. His love does not grow dim. He loved you before you were born and he will love you through all eternity.

> Father, I know how unlovely I can be and yet you love me.
> Oh, God, thank you for loving me despite my ugly rebellion,
> independence and sin. Thank you for never ceasing to love
> me. Thank you for loving me into obedience. Thank you
> for loving me eternally.

JULY 12

Psalm 119

Open my eyes to see the wonderful truths in your law.
—Psalm 119:18

The Psalmist reminds his listeners of the beauty and necessity of God's law. God's law enables purity. God's law gives understanding. God's law renews one's life with goodness. God's law is hope. It is the path to happiness. It teaches good judgment and knowledge. It disciplines. God's law stands firm in heaven. It is entirely trustworthy. God's law is perfectly true and always fair. It is eternal and unchanging. It is the delight of God's people.

How gracious of God to give his people his righteous law as a guide for righteous life.

It has been said that we cannot break the law—rather, we break ourselves against the law. God's law always has and always will stand firm. While we treasure God's law and memorize it to keep us from sin, we cannot meet the righteous demands of God's law (Romans 8), therefore, our only hope is to run to the Savior, Jesus Christ, who fulfilled the law (Romans 3:19–22). It is Jesus's own righteousness, imputed to us, that enables you and me to meet the standard for righteousness that God requires (2 Corinthians 5:21).

As you read God's law, study it, memorize it, and try to live by it—and as you find that you cannot keep it—will you run to Jesus (Romans 3:10, Isaiah 64:6)?

> God, your law is my delight. Open my eyes that I may see more and more of the wonderful truths in your law. Your law disciplines, rebukes, convicts, comforts, and assures me. It shows me how much you love me. Thank you for Jesus's righteousness that covers me and brings me into alignment with your perfect law.

JULY 13

Psalms 120; 121; 123; 125; 126

My help comes from the LORD, who made
the heavens and the earth!
—Psalm 121:2

During festival times, God's children sing these songs as they approach
Jerusalem and the temple. They sing of God's character and attributes—
of the God who answers prayer and rescues them. They sing of God
who made the heavens and the earth, and who does not sleep, never
tires, and watches over his people. God, who is their protective shade,
who stands beside them, keeps them from all evil, and preserves their
lives. They sing to the Living God who is enthroned in heaven, is
merciful, is their security, and who does amazing things.

How gracious of God to inspire songwriters and musicians to
write worship songs.

Songs are threads that weave throughout the fabric of our lives.
We sing lullabies, wedding songs, and funeral songs. We worship God
with songs; and this portion of Scripture is a God-breathed hymnal
that can enhance our relationship with God (2 Timothy 3:16).

Singing worship hymns that recount the glory of God fills our
minds and hearts with a deeper desire to worship God, which makes
us sing even more. It is a sweet cycle of worship and remembrance.

What prompts you to sing? What silences you? In joy or in
sorrow, what will you sing to Jesus today?

> God, in every event of my life, whether a joyful celebration,
> or a time of deep sorrow and grief, I will choose to sing
> praises to you. O God, may my songs be a sweet aroma of
> worship before your throne, for you are my strength and my
> song. You are the one from whom my help comes. You alone
> are worthy of my song.

JULY 14

Psalms 128–130; 132; 134; 135

LORD, if you kept a record of our sins, who,
O LORD, could ever survive?
—Psalm 130:3

The Psalmist sings of salvation, the reward for those who fear God. He sings of the Lord's goodness and of his blessings. He sings to the Lord who hears his prayer. He sings of the Lord's forgiveness, and unfailing love. He sings praises to the Lord for his greatness, his miracles and his name. The Psalmist calls upon all who fear God to praise the Lord!

How gracious of God to give his children an abundance of reasons to sing.

That we are God's children, adopted into his family when we accepted Jesus Christ as our Savior and followed him as our Lord, is reason enough to sing (Romans 9:4). Confessing our faith in Jesus Christ, and receiving eternal life in him, is yet another reason to sing (1 John 2:24–25). Knowing that God assures our salvation and removes our sin from us as far as the east is from the west—how can we keep silent (Psalm 103:12)? And as if that isn't enough, God's word tells us that God does not keep a record of our sin; let us sing out!

It costs us nothing to become a child of God. It cost God his one and only Son to make our adoption possible.

What song of gratitude will you sing to God today?

God, you have removed my sin from me, you have cast it into the depths of the sea at great cost to you. Oh how I love you. O how I love my Savior, the Lord Jesus Christ who died for me. God forbid that I should mope or remain silent. My song of rejoicing will be heard throughout this day.

JULY 15

Psalms 136; 146–150

> Rather, the LORD's delight is in those who honor him,
> those who put their hope in his unfailing love.
> —Psalm 147:11

The Psalmist calls all people to give thanks to the Lord for his faithful love endures forever. His song honors the God of gods, and the Lord of lords; God who does mighty miracles. God is the one who made heaven and earth. He is the one who keeps every promise. He is the one who will reign forever. He heals the brokenhearted. He calls the stars by name. His power is absolute. He supports the humble. He sends peace across the nations. He delights in his people. He crowns the humble with salvation. Let everything that lives sing praises to the Lord!

How gracious of Almighty God, the Maker of Heaven and Earth, the Sovereign Lord, the All-powerful One to delight in those who honor him.

When we are confident that God will do what he says he will do, and completely trust him to do it, we honor God. Perhaps one of the things that brings honor to God most is when we place our hope in him (Romans 15:13). Christian hope is not mere wishful thinking, it is a settled expectation of the fulfillment of God's word.

Are you wishfully thinking that God's Word is true? Or are you confidently settled in your expectation that God will fulfill his Word? Does your hope honor God?

> Precious Lord, my hope is in you! I know that you will bring to pass all that you have spoken. I know that your plan for me and for the world is perfect. Because my hope is in you, my soul sings. Because my hope is in you, I know that I will praise you for all eternity. Praise the Lord!

JULY 16

Isaiah 18–23

When the people cry to the LORD for help against those who
oppress them, he will send them a savior who will rescue them.
—Isaiah 19:20

Isaiah prophesies God's warning to the nations. He speaks of
destruction for Ethiopia, yet promises a day when they will worship
God. Isaiah sees Egypt handed over to her enemies yet eventually
Egypt will follow God. Isaiah sees Babylon plundered and destroyed
and Edom and Arabia coming to their ends. Even Jerusalem doesn't
escape crushing trouble because she refuses to ask God for help.
Isaiah foresees both destruction and redemption.

How gracious of God to send a Savior to rescue repentant people.

If we, like Isaiah, could see into the future what would we
would hope to see: wealth and fame, health and happiness? But,
what if we see the destruction that comes because of rebellion and
disobedience? Or if we see enemies advancing and every plan failing
because we refuse to ask God for help? If we knew that disaster was
coming in the future, would that cause us to act differently today?

We do know the future: There will be salvation for those who
receive Jesus (John 3:36), and disaster is certain for those who reject
the Lord and refuse to repent (Revelation 9:20–22).

Are you fortifying your walls, storing up supplies, and fixing
your gates against the enemy? In your preparation for defense, have
you sought the only Savior who can rescue you?

> Almighty God, only you can save me from physical,
> emotional and spiritual destruction. Oh God, I cry out to
> you. Please rescue me from the external enemies that seek
> to destroy me as well as the enemies that dwell within my
> own heart and personality.

JULY 17

Isaiah 24–27, 29

You will keep in perfect peace all who trust in
you, whose thoughts are fixed on you.
—Isaiah 26:3

Isaiah praises God for his faithfulness and salvation. He praises God for who he is: A just judge, a refuge for the poor, and a shelter for those in distress. He praises God—the victor over death, the Sovereign Lord who wipes away all tears, the Lord who punishes the people of the earth for their sins, and the God who purges sin. Even as Isaiah sees the destruction of all things while sin is being purged, he also sees the remnant praise God, and the Lord's rule over Jerusalem.

How gracious of God to keep his people at peace when they fix their thoughts on him.

Fixing our thoughts on the truth that God is always good and right, even when everything around us seems bad and wrong, is what keeps God's people in peace (2 Corinthians 4:16–18). Focusing on the Lord keeps our feet on solid ground when all around things are slipping away. Focusing on the Lord anchors us in the storm so that we are not blown away. Focusing on the Lord as the ultimate Victor and Ruler over all gives us a proper perspective; and that is the way to peace.

On what do you tend to focus in difficulty? Do you dwell on your circumstances or on the God who allows and controls your circumstances as he brings about his perfect plan for your life?

Almighty Sovereign Lord, I know that I cannot understand your thoughts and your ways, but I thank you that when I focus on who you are—a Holy, Good and Just God whose actions are always right—then peace and trust surround me.

JULY 18

Isaiah 30–33

But the LORD still waits for you to come to him so
he can show you his love and compassion.
—Isaiah 30:18

God gives Isaiah a vision of Jerusalem's destruction by the Assyrians who have already conquered the northern tribes of Israel. God calls upon Judah to trust him; instead, they go to Egypt for help. God warns them that calamity is coming because they refuse his word and choose to trust in lies. God waits for them to come to him. Destruction is certain if they continue to look to Egypt for help. Isaiah foresees the time when God's people ask for help and God responds instantly. Isaiah sees the day when God forgives the sins of his people.

How gracious of God to exercise patience, showing love and compassion.

God is longsuffering; he waits for his people but he doesn't wait idly. God is continually at work bringing about what is best for us. As he waits, God may allow calamity, war, destruction, grief, famine, poverty, oppression, lies, affliction, and adversity to fall upon us to lead us to repentance (Romans 2:4). God waits for us to turn to him for help. When we turn to him, he will show us his love and compassion (Psalm 32:5).

Have you turned to God in your distress? If not, is it because you are afraid to trust him? Will you consider that there is no one else to turn to, no one else who is as mighty as God? Will you return to God and experience his deliverance?

> God, I thank you for the calamities in my life that have been clarion calls to repentance. And, thank you for never withholding your grace, compassion and mercy from my repentant heart.

JULY 19

Isaiah 34–35; Micah 2–5

But as for me, I am filled with power and the Spirit of the Lord.
—Micah 3:8a

Micah, God's prophet, charges the people of Israel and Judah with wickedness. He rebukes them for listening to false prophets who speak only what Israel wants to hear. He convicts the leaders for their injustice and corruption. Micah, filled with the Spirit of the Lord, fearlessly points out Israel's sin and rebellion. He also promises a day when a remnant will be gathered and the Lord rules from Jerusalem as their king forever.

How gracious of God to give Spirit-filled leaders who are not afraid to speak the truth.

Whose truth is true? When we hear one person saying one thing and another saying something different, how can we know what is true?

God's leaders will not contradict God's inspired Word in the Bible (James 1:17). God's Spirit-filled teachers will exalt the Lord Jesus Christ (John 15:26; 16:14). God's leaders will not tolerate injustice or condone sin, and they will always adhere to the sound instructions of Jesus (1 Timothy 6:2b-5).

To whom do you listen? Do you listen for God's truth, even if it may not be what you want to hear? Do you apply what you hear to your life so that God's Word changes you?

God, I thank you for giving us your written Word as the standard against which we can measure all spoken words. Please give me wisdom and discernment to know and understand your truths. Thank you for giving Spirit-filled leaders who are bold enough to speak your truth; truth that causes me to examine and root out the things that draw me into sin.

JULY 20

2 Kings 18:13–37; 2 Chronicles 32:1–8; Isaiah 36; Micah 6–7

> ..this is what he requires: to do what is right, to love
> mercy, and to walk humbly with your God.
> —Micah 6:8

After all that King Hezekiah did to restore a right relationship with God, including the repair and opening of the temple, the leaders and the people continue to turn away from God. God sends Micah to condemn their empty worship, warn them of God's judgment, and remind them of God's faithfulness. Micah tells them that God wants them to do what is right: To love mercy and walk humbly with their God. Micah exhorts them to fear the Lord for the armies of destruction are coming. They come: Assyria invades Judah, laying siege to the fortified cities with Judah's capital, Jerusalem, in her sights.

How gracious of God to clearly state how to avoid his judgment and just wrath.

God does not ask much of his people. He wants us to do what is right—and he tells us what that is; even our consciences tell us (Romans 2:15). The Bible tells us that God wants us to love mercy, to be kind and forgiving toward others. He wants us to walk humbly with him, to submit to him as the Lord over our lives. And he tells us that he disciplines those he loves, you and me, to draw us back to a right relationship with him (Hebrews 12:5–7).

Is God allowing an enemy to advance against you? Is the hardship in your life the Lord's discipline? Is God calling you to repentance? Will you do what is right, love mercy, and walk humbly with God?

Oh God, please help me to do what is right, to love mercy and to walk humbly with you.

JULY 21

2 Kings 19; 2 Chronicles 32:9–23; Isaiah 37

This is what the LORD, the God of Israel,
says: I have heard your prayer ...
—2 Kings 19:20b

Jerusalem is in the cross-hairs of Sennacherib's Assyrian army. King Hezekiah sends a contingent to the prophet Isaiah asking him to pray. Sennacherib sends Hezekiah a letter touting Sennacherib's victories over all other kings and their gods. Hezekiah prays to the Lord God and begs for rescue. Isaiah prays. God hears their prayers and sends Isaiah a message for Hezekiah: Sennacherib has insulted the Holy One of Israel and because of Sennacherib's arrogance, he will be defeated. God destroys the army of the Assyrians.

How gracious of God to hear and respond to the prayers of his children.

God's Word reminds us that it is not against flesh and blood that we fight, but against the spiritual forces of evil (Ephesians 6:12). This is true, no matter what form that evil takes. We may be surrounded and under siege by illness, foreclosure, long work hours, brutal commutes, crying babies, fighting siblings, addiction, death, mourning, broken relationships, debt, red tape, paperwork, legal action, failing grades, loneliness, fatigue, or any other conceivable enemy. Yet, there is no enemy bigger than God is. God is sufficient to defeat every enemy.

Will you ask God to rescue you today?

O Lord, God of Israel, you who sit enthroned between the mighty cherubim! You alone are God over all the earth. You are the Creator of heaven and earth. Please listen to me, O Lord, and hear! Open your eyes, O Lord, and see! Rescue me from my enemy, then all will know that you alone, O Lord, are God; you alone are my God.
—Isaiah 37:16–17a

JULY 22

2 Kings 20:1–19; 2 Chronicles 32:24–31; Isaiah 38–39

I will heal you … I will add fifteen years to your life … I will do
this to defend my honor and for the sake of my servant David.
—2 Kings 20:5c, 6a,c

Hezekiah becomes deathly ill. The Lord says he will die. Hezekiah
turns his face to the wall and prays to the Lord. The Lord hears his
prayer. God heals Hezekiah to defend his own honor and for the
sake of his servant David.

How gracious of God to intervene in history to bring about his
plan for all humanity.

This passage invites many questions. We know that God's ways
and thoughts are infinitely higher than our ways and thoughts and
we struggle to reconcile God's sovereignty with his call to us to
pray (Isaiah 55:8–9). We don't know what would have happened
if Hezekiah had not prayed. We know that he did. And we know
God's response.

We know that God calls us to pray—that he has ordained
prayer as a means to his ends (Romans 12:12). While we may not
understand how prayer changes things, we do know that prayer
changes us. Prayer assures us that fate does not own us; rather, our
sovereign God loves us and watches over us.

Does it comfort you to know that God has a plan for you, and
nothing can thwart it (Jeremiah 29:11).

> Lord, I try to be faithful to do what is pleasing, and yet
> I often fail. You, though, are always faithful and in your
> sovereignty you act on my behalf to accomplish your perfect
> plan for me. Thank you for the assurance that you will bring
> to completion the work which you began in me.

JULY 23

I am the LORD; that is my name! I will not give my glory
to anyone else. Everything I have prophesied has come
true. I will tell you the future before it happens.
—Isaiah 42:8a, 9a, c

God gives Isaiah a glimpse into the future when Israel's sins are
pardoned, her punishment is complete, and her God comes. Isaiah
sees the Sovereign Lord, the one who rules in awesome strength, the
one who holds the oceans in his hands, the one who spoke before the
world began, the only living God, the one without equal, the one
who is beyond compare, the Lord, the everlasting God, the Creator
of all the earth come in his glorious power! God calls Israel to witness
that he alone is God—he alone declares what he will do, and then
he does it. He is God, from eternity to eternity.

How gracious of God to reveal his glorious majesty in pardoning
sin when punishment is complete.

We base our faith on the fact that God punished our sin at the
cross—that Jesus, our substitute endured God's just wrath for our
sin—and that because of the atonement of Jesus, our punishment is
complete and we are pardoned. God has declared us to be in right
standing before him based on the finished work of the Servant, the
Lord Jesus Christ. From eternity to eternity, God is God and he
holds our salvation secure (Jude 1:24).

When we examine the evidence there is only one conclusion
that makes sense: the God of the Bible is the one true God and he
is trustworthy for all eternity (Micah 7:18–19). Will you stake your
eternal life on this truth?

Holy One of Israel, you are the incomparable God.

JULY 24

"I am the Lord'" he says, "and there is no other."
—Isaiah 45:18b

Isaiah tells the Israelites to put away their lifeless idols, idols that neither see nor hear. Isaiah declares that only a fool makes his own god; never stopping to see that it is just a block of wood. God tells his people that he is the living God who delivers them. No idol can save them. He is not an idol who needs carried; he is the one true God who carries his people.

How gracious of God to clearly reveal the worthlessness and captivity of idols.

We would never think to allow a lifeless idol to carry us into captivity, would we? Yes, that is what we do when we place our trust and hope in anything other than God. When our confidence is in our religion, church, pastor, job, education, intelligence, worldliness, health, bank account, or anything other than God we make that thing our idol.

We must not be afraid to ask ourselves, "Is this thing I am holding onto a lie?" Why would we choose to carry our idols into captivity instead of allowing God to carry us into freedom (Romans 6:16–18)?

Do you rely upon anything other than God? What do you trust in that has become more powerful, important, loving, freeing, trustworthy, faithful, or more alive than God? What is bigger, stronger or wiser than God is? Has this thing—this lie—taken the place of God in your life?

> God, please free me from this captivity. Show me the deeper idols of my heart that are weak and lifeless substitutes for you and that bind me in captivity. Help me to break free as I seek the freedom that comes with serving only you.

JULY 25

Isaiah 48:12–52:12

Can a mother forget her nursing child? Even if that were possible, I would not forget you! See, I have written your name on my hand.
—Isaiah 49:15a, c, 16a

Isaiah speaks of the Sovereign Lord—the one who creates light and makes darkness, who promises a day of salvation and restoration for Israel. It is the Sovereign Lord who sends Israel to captivity. The same Lord refines them and rescues them. Then God raises Cyrus up, a Gentile king who does not know God, and prepares Cyrus to fulfill God's righteous purpose: to restore his city and free his captive people.

How gracious of God to use whatever and whomever he chooses to rescue his children.

God went to great lengths to rescue the Israelites and he went to great lengths to rescue us. As you think back on the day you came to faith, who did God use to get your attention? Who did he use to share the gospel with you (Romans 10:17)? Ultimately, God gave his one and only Son to free us from our sin (John 3:16–18) and he continues to refine us through the sanctifying work of his Holy Spirit.

Do you feel forgotten in sin's captivity? God knows where you are and what it is that enslaves you. He will rescue you when you cry out to him. He will lead you out with the same mighty and majestic hand upon which your name is written.

> Lord God, thank you for the Sunday School teachers, the family members, and the friends who prayed for my salvation. Thank you for the Bible study class where I heard the truth of your salvation. Thank you for going to great lengths to rescue your wayward child.

JULY 26

> All of us have strayed away like sheep. We have
> left God's paths to follow our own. Yet the LORD
> laid on him the guilt and sins of us all.
> —Isaiah 53:6

Isaiah speaks of the Lord's Servant who is highly exalted. The Servant is beaten, bloodied and disfigured. Kings stand speechless in his presence. He carries our weaknesses and our sorrows weigh him down. He is wounded and crushed for our sins. He is oppressed and treated harshly, but never says a word. He is led as a lamb to the slaughter. He suffers our punishment. He is buried in a rich man's grave. He makes it possible for many to be counted righteous.

How gracious of God to provide a Servant to bear our sin and carry our guilt.

Isaiah foretold God's plan for handling our unrighteousness, and the path to righteousness leads through the Lord Jesus Christ (John 14:6). The people in Isaiah's day looked forward to the promise of the Servant; we look back to the same promise. Our vision intersects at the cross. Jesus died for all. One man, Jesus, who was, is, and always will be the infinite God (John 1:1), died for an infinite number of sins, so that you and I might be saved.

The exchange Isaiah spoke of takes place at the cross—our unrighteousness is exchanged for Jesus's perfect righteousness. God made the exchange possible (2 Corinthians 5:21). Either we carry our own unrighteousness, or Jesus does. Have you conducted this very personal transaction with Jesus at the cross?

> Jesus, I know that you are the only way to truth and life. Thank you for bearing my personal sin, and all my guilt, on the cross. Thank you for imputing to me your glorious righteousness.

JULY 27

Isaiah 58:1–63:14

I will not stop praying for her until her righteousness shines like the dawn, and her salvation blazes like a burning torch.
—Isaiah 62:1b

Judah's pastor and prophet, Isaiah, loves Israel. He prays for her. He posts watchmen to pray for her day and night. He commits to pray until Jerusalem becomes the object of praise. His prayers remind Israel of God's promises. Isaiah tells of the Lord's unfailing love. He praises God for all he has done and he announces Israel's future salvation.

How gracious of God to provide prayer warriors to intercede for his people.

Oswald Chambers says, "The real business of your life as a saved soul is intercessory prayer." We know that it is our responsibility to pray for others, and like Isaiah, we must not stop praying. We pray for others as Jesus prays for us (Hebrews 7:25).We pray to God the Father as Jesus taught the disciples (Matthew 6:9). We pray to God based on the completed work of the Lord Jesus Christ (Hebrews 4:14–16). We pray in the Holy Spirit (Ephesians 6:18).

We may never know who has prayed for us. We may not know for what they have prayed. God knows, and that is enough.

For whom do you pray? Are you tempted to give up? Will you persevere until you see God's purpose accomplished in them? Will you pray as if you are the only one praying for that specific person?

Forbid it Lord that I should stop praying for the salvation of the lost, whether they are led astray by false prophets, or simply deceived and practicing a form of religion that has no power. Father, should I grow weary or complacent and start to slack off, please remind me that eternity is at stake.

JULY 28

2 Kings 20:20–21; 2 Chronicles 32:32–33; Isaiah 63:15–66:24

> We are constant sinners, so your anger is heavy
> on us. How can people like us be saved?
> —Isaiah 64:5c

Isaiah prays for God to burst from the heavens as he did at Sinai when Israel was a fledgling nation. He acknowledges that they are far from God, infected and impure with sin. Any righteousness they try to display is in reality filth. Their sin sweeps them away. The Lord responds to Isaiah and promises a remnant, a new heaven and a new earth where there is rejoicing and happiness and where weeping and crying are heard no more.

How gracious of God to save undeserving sinners and promise them a glorious future.

Our potential for sin is amazingly vast and deep. We are born with the same bondage to sin as every murderer, tyrant, pedophile, thief, liar, adulterer, and abuser who ever lived (Romans 6, 8). We have no righteousness of our own (Romans 3:9–18). If what we think is good, or righteous, is filthy to the Lord, can you imagine how despicable our sin must be to him? Like Isaiah, we ask, "How can people like us be saved?"

God's response: By grace, through faith, so that none can boast (Ephesians 2:8–9).

Have you acknowledged before God that you are a sinner in need of grace? Will you confess your sin before it sweeps you away? Will you receive his gift of salvation by grace through faith today?

> God, please forgive my filthy self-righteousness. I recognize that apart from you, I am a constant sinner, unable to save myself. Thank you for your grace, which is sufficient to save even me, and provides me with the very real hope of a glorious eternal future with you.

JULY 29

2 Kings 21:1–22:2; 2 Chronicles 33:1–34:7;
Jeremiah 1:1–2:22

For I am with you, and I will take care of
you. I, the LORD, have spoken.
—Jeremiah 1:19b

The Lord tells Jeremiah that before he was born the Lord set him apart to be his spokesman. Now that it is time to speak, Jeremiah hesitates. The Lord touches Jeremiah's mouth and appoints him to stand against kingdoms and nations. God gives Jeremiah visions and then assures Jeremiah that he is with him and will take care of him.

How gracious of God to prepare work in advance for his people, and prepare his people for the work.

God doesn't explain his foreknowledge; if he did, we wouldn't understand it. However, we know that he knows the end from the beginning (Isaiah 46:10). And somehow, before we existed, before we were born, before we could do anything good or bad, he knew us and he chose us (Romans 9). In his foreknowledge and planning God knew who we would be and determined what work to prepare for us (Ephesians 2:10).

What work has God prepared for you? Is it bigger, or harder, than you imagined it would be? Are you afraid? Will you step out in faith, trusting that as you rely on God, you will be enabled to do the work (Philippians 4:13)?

> Lord, I will do this job one step at a time. I won't borrow tomorrow's trouble instead I will trust you to be with me, to equip me, and to accomplish your plan in me and through me.

JULY 30

Jeremiah 2:23–5:19

"My wayward children," says the LORD, "come back
to me, and I will heal your wayward hearts."
—Jeremiah 3:22

Israel, like an adulterous wife, prostitutes herself with many lovers
and Assyria takes her captive. Judah follows Israel's example: seeking
other lovers and giving herself to idols. The Lord calls Judah to
confess, repent, and return to him. Judah's preacher, Jeremiah,
sounds the alarm: destruction is coming! The people set their faces
like stone and refuse to repent. Jeremiah sees the coming destruction.

How gracious of God to continue calling to his people despite
their rejection of him.

When we disrespect God by refusing to abandon all other gods,
we are adulterers. When we embrace things other than God for our
comfort or security, we are adulterers. When we chase after things,
other than God, to which we have assigned our happiness, we are
adulterers. When we reject God as the sole source of our salvation,
we are adulterers. When we pin our hopes and dreams on anything
other than God, we are adulterers (Hosea 1:2).

Are you an adulterer? Is God calling you to come back to him so
that he might heal your wayward heart? Must massive destruction
occur before you return to your first love?

Heavenly Father, I acknowledge that I am a spiritual prostitute.
Every time I receive the things of the world in exchange for
my loyalty to you, I sell myself to sin. Oh God, please forgive
me. Sear the pain of adultery and infidelity upon my heart.
Show me the ugliness of my choices from your perspective.
Help me to see that my love for you must outshine any other
love. Help me to be faithful in my relationship with you.

JULY 31

2 Kings 22:3–20; 2 Chronicles 34:8–28; Jeremiah 5:20–6:30

> This is your last warning, Jerusalem! If you
> do not listen, I will empty the land.
> —Jeremiah 6:8

The people are stubborn. The prophets give false prophecies and the priests rule with an iron hand. Disaster is coming. The Lord calls them to stop, to look for the old, godly way and walk in it. The people don't listen.

Meanwhile, King Josiah supervises the temple's restoration uncovering the Book of the Law. Josiah realizes the Lord's anger burns because they haven't obeyed the Lord's words. Josiah understands that the Lord's holiness and justice demand that the people be punished. The Lord promises Josiah that the punishment won't happen in Josiah's lifetime.

How gracious of God to act mercifully even as he metes out divine justice.

The Lord is patient with rebellious people, but he is not eternally patient with them. Ultimately, there will be a final day of reckoning. He will return and judge the earth. He has given us fair warning in his word, the Bible. His warnings are clear and his promises are sure: there will be devastation for the unrepentant, and salvation for the repentant (2 Peter 3).

Are you heeding the warnings God has given you as he calls you to repent? How will you know when it is the final warning?

> God, please help me to embrace the truth that your appointed day of judgment will come soon. Please ignite a desire within me to share your words of warning and promise with lost people before it is too late for them to confess, repent and turn to you for salvation. God, please help me to understand that your delay must never become an excuse for complacency. Please give me the same sense of urgency that Jeremiah had.

grace AUGUST

AUGUST 1

2 Kings 23:1–28; 2 Chronicles 34:29–35:19; Nahum 1–3

O my people, I have already punished you once, and I will not
do it again ... Celebrate your festivals, O people of Judah ... for
your enemies from Nineveh will never invade your land again.
—Nahum 1:12b, 15c, e

Josiah restores both the temple and worship in Judah. He leads the
people of Judah, the priests, Levites, and some of the survivors from
Israel in a celebration of the Passover.

However, Judah lives in fear of the Assyrians, of Nineveh's
military might and ferocious wickedness. They have seen and heard
what Assyria did to their brothers in Israel. Through the prophet
Nahum, God promises that in his justice he will punish the Assyrians
for their wicked atrocities upon Israel.

How gracious of God to justly punish the wicked even as he
protects the innocent.

How God works on the international stage is a mystery to us.
While it often seems that nations and kings fight and act outside of
the realm of God's sovereign will, we know that God's rule is all-
encompassing (Psalm 103:19). He knows the side of righteousness,
even when it looks to us like there is no right side. He knows who
to punish and who to encourage (Psalm 9:4–6).

In a day of terrorism, bombings, economic strife, moral
degeneration, and mass apostasy will you choose to rest in God's
sovereignty? Despite the confusion and fear that tries to pull you
away from God, will you celebrate his steadfast faithfulness with
other Christians?

God, in the midst of worldwide unrest and terror I will place
my hope in you—in your wisdom, justice, and mercy. I will
rest in your character. I will find peace in your unfolding plan.

AUGUST 2

Habakkuk 1–3; Zephaniah 1:1–2:7

Yet I will rejoice in the LORD! I will be joyful in the God
of my salvation. The Sovereign LORD is my strength!
—Habakkuk 3:18, 19a

Habakkuk, a prophet in Judah has his eye on the world scene.
God gives him a vision of the next super-power that God is raising
up to replace the Assyrians: Babylon. God tells Habakkuk that
Babylon is his instrument of judgment upon Judah for her many
sins. Habakkuk doesn't understand why wicked Babylon will be
allowed to destroy righteous Judah. God assures Habakkuk that
Babylon will be judged for her arrogance and sin.

How gracious of God to bring clarity into the confusion of life's
circumstances.

We may not understand any more than Habakkuk did how
God uses the wicked to punish the righteous. However, we know
that God can, and will, use any tool he desires to accomplish his
plan for his people. We also struggle to reconcile the sovereignty of
God with the fact that each person and nation stands responsible
for their own actions.

There will always be things that we do not understand about
God's ways (Deuteronomy 29:29). However, we must strive to
understand the character of God. As we focus on God's character, we
will find clarity in the knowledge that he is wisdom, his judgments
are perfect, and his love is unfathomable (Romans 11:33–36).

When you are confused, will you take your confusion to the
Lord? Will you choose to focus on God and trust his wisdom, as
you trust him to accomplish his plan for you?

God, when world events confuse and overwhelm me, when
doubt starts to settle in, I will trust in you, the Sovereign Lord.

AUGUST 3

2 Kings 23:29–30; 2 Chronicles 35:20–27;
Jeremiah 47–48; Zephaniah 2:8–3:20

And the Lord himself, the King of Israel, will live among you!
—Zephaniah 3:15b

The Lord tells the prophet, Zephaniah, that he will destroy Judah because of her idolatry, theft, and murder. Zephaniah calls the people to pray while there is still time, but the city of violence and crime refuses correction. The leaders, judges, and prophets know no shame and seek self-promotion and gain. The Lord, in his justice, punishes his people while he also punishes the people who destroy her. Through Zephaniah, God promises a day of restoration when he gathers the exiles, deals justly with oppressors, and brings his people home with glory.

How gracious of God to give a vision of hope on the eve of imminent disaster.

God kindles hope in every believer. We know there is a day of great tribulation that is still future to us (Revelation 8:6–9:21). As we await that day, we know that the King of Israel, Jesus Christ, is with us. He lives within every believer (John 14:20). He rejoices over you and me. His love calms our fears. He is our hope. He is our solid ground in every storm. He goes before us and he has our backs (Psalm 139:5).

Are you living in fear of the next disaster? What vision of hope has God given to sustain you? How does knowing that Jesus is with you calm your fear?

Lord, you are my great Savior! You live within me! I will not fear; for knowledge of you casts out fear. I trust that whatever disaster comes upon me I am not alone. Whatever path you have laid before me, you are waiting at the end, even as you walk beside me.

AUGUST 4

2 Kings 23:31–24:4; 2 Chronicles 36:1–5;
Jeremiah 22:1–23; 25:1–14; 26

Each time the message was this: "Turn from the evil road
you are travelling and from the evil things you are doing."
—Jeremiah 25:5

Through Jeremiah the Lord calls the king and the people to do what is right: Quit their evil deeds, stop mistreating others, and stop murdering the innocent. If they do not listen to him or his prophets God will destroy the palace and the temple. God warns that he will make Jerusalem an object of cursing in every nation on earth. Jeremiah finishes speaking and the religious leaders want to kill him. After a brief trial, the officials declare he does not deserve the death sentence for he has spoken in the name of the Lord. Some of the wise old men agree: Jeremiah's prophecy is consistent with God's previous words.

How gracious of God to speak the truth even when the truth is not popular.

Neither God's words nor his opinions will change. God's holiness doesn't change, nor does his justice (1 Samuel 15:29). God always speaks the truth and therefore God's prophets will speak truth. It behooves us to search the Scriptures and know the truth so that we can stand with Christians who teach the truth; especially when truth is not popular or opposes the current of the culture.

Are you willing to receive and live by truth that aligns with God's word, even if it means standing alone or in a shrinking minority?

Almighty God I pray that you would humble my heart to accept and apply your Word of truth. Help me to stand firm for truth. And help me to apply your truth so that my mind is renewed and my thinking is transformed to align with yours.

AUGUST 5

Jeremiah 25:15–38; 36; 45–46

But do not be afraid, Jacob, my servant; do not be dismayed,
Israel. For I am with you. I will not destroy you. But I
must discipline you; I cannot let you go unpunished.
—Jeremiah 46:27a, 28b,d

The Lord tasks Jeremiah with telling all the nations that God will
judge them for their sins; none less than Judah. Yet, the Lord gives
the people opportunity to repent. Jeremiah records God's messages
to the people and the scroll is read. The king burns the scroll piece
by piece. Jeremiah re-writes the scroll at God's command. God will
punish the king and Judah will experience disaster, but God will
bring Judah home again for he is always with them.

How gracious of God to stay with his people even as he
disciplines them.

When life gets hard; especially when the difficulties are the
consequences of our sin, it is easy to forget that God is right there
with us. However, just as a good parent will not leave the house when
a little child is sitting in time out, God will not leave his children
alone. In difficulty, in despair, in discipline, in defeat, and in the
consequences of sin, God is there (Psalm 27).

What is the most difficult thing you are enduring today? Does
it comfort you to know that God is with you and that he will never
abandon you, even as he disciplines you?

> God, when the consequences of my sin seem disastrous and
> overwhelming to me, when darkness threatens to engulf me,
> when I am rejected and scorned, help me to remember that
> I am not alone; that you are with me, holding, disciplining
> and loving me.

AUGUST 6

Jeremiah 19–20; Daniel 1

> But the LORD stands beside me like a great warrior.
> —Jeremiah 20:11a

Jeremiah delivers God's words of judgment against Jerusalem and is promptly arrested, whipped, and put in stocks. Upon his release, Jeremiah prophesies that God will hand the people of Judah over to the king of Babylon and many people will become captives, including the priest's family.

King Nebuchadnezzar of Babylon besieges Jerusalem and the Lord gives Nebuchadnezzar victory. He takes captive some of the young men from Judah's royal family, including Daniel, who is renamed Belteshazzar.

How gracious of God to strengthen his obedient servants in their weakness.

Simply because we are Christians we will face scorn and mistreatment—probably not to the degree Jeremiah did—but it will happen. Our enemies watch us closely and root for us to slip in our faith; anticipating the day when we trap ourselves with our words.

Like Daniel, we have opportunities to stand firm for the Lord when our faith is challenged. We need not fearfully shrink back in our weakness, we can stand firm because we know that the Lord stands beside us. Our Great Warrior is our strength (2 Corinthians 12:9–10).

What hard thing has God asked you to say or do? What message of truth are you willing to speak regardless of the consequences? Will you choose to stand firm for the Lord, letting the pieces fall where they may, because you trust him to be your strength?

> God, I never want to compromise your truth. Please give me grace to stand firm in you. Remind me that you are the warrior who stands beside me; and that before you, all my enemies will stumble and fall.

AUGUST 7

Jeremiah 7:1–8:3; Daniel 2–3

Daniel handled the situation with wisdom and discretion.
—Daniel 2:14b

Daniel, a Judean captive in Babylon, becomes one of the king's advisors. The king has a dream. No one can interpret the dream so the king orders the execution of all the wise men, including Daniel. Daniel doesn't panic; he handles the situation with wisdom and discretion. He urges his friends to ask the God of heaven to show them his mercy and tell them the secret. God reveals the dream to Daniel in a vision. Daniel praises God and goes to the king and tells him that God has given the king a vision of coming events. Daniel is made ruler over the whole providence of Babylon, as well as chief over all the wise men.

How gracious of God to place his servants in spheres of influence for his glory.

Hopefully, you and I will never experience exile to a foreign country with an unfamiliar culture and an unknown language. However, if we were, would we choose to spend our days wallowing in varying degrees of self-pity and commiserating with other captives or would we integrate and thrive, without compromising our faith, as Daniel did? Nevertheless, in whatever circumstances God chooses to place us, we must commit to be a godly influence to the people around us.

In what sphere of influence has God placed you? Have you asked him for wisdom so that you might adapt, thrive and represent him well (1 Corinthians 12:7–11)?

God of heaven, as I ask for your wisdom, please humble me to receive it. Please give me the stature that is required to serve you well wherever I am.

AUGUST 8

Jeremiah 8:4–11:23

Then why do these people keep going along their self-destructive
path, refusing to turn back, even though I have warned them?
—Jeremiah 8:5

The Israelites follow prophets who lie and teachers who reject the
Word of the Lord. The Lord promises judgment and Jeremiah weeps
for the destruction that is to come. The Lord tells Jeremiah to
remind the people of their covenant with him and that he wants to
keep it; but they refuse. The people choose their idols instead of God
and rejoice in doing evil. They plot to kill Jeremiah.

How gracious of God to demand holiness in his people.

We live in a world of ever-changing fads. Many of us jump
on and off bandwagons so frequently it could be considered our
main source of exercise. We are fickle and we change our minds
on a whim. However, God does not change (1 Samuel 15:29). He
does not tolerate sin because he is eternally holy (Leviticus 19:2).
His people, who are called by his name, have a responsibility to
represent him and his holiness. Holiness is never too much to ask
of us because holiness aligns us with God. Holiness is a not only a
protective boundary, it is our destiny (Philippians 1:6).

From what self-destructive, sinful path is God calling you to
repent? How long will you wait? How much destruction are you
willing to endure before you repent?

> God, I trust that your Word is the lamp that lights my path,
> illuminating the truth and revealing the dark shadows of
> false teaching. Please hold my feet to the path that leads to
> holiness.

AUGUST 9

Jeremiah 12–15

Give glory to the LORD your God before it is too late.
Acknowledge him before he brings darkness upon you.
—Jeremiah 13:16a

God speaks to and through Judah's pastor, Jeremiah, as the people of Judah turn away. Through Jeremiah, the Lord calls the people to repentance to avoid the coming disaster. Jeremiah speaks clearly and preaches that the coming disaster will be horrific; it will bring complete destruction. Finally, God forbids Jeremiah to pray for the people of Judah any longer. Jerusalem will be an object of horror for all to see. God promises to protect Jeremiah.

How gracious of God to warn his people that rebellion brings disaster.

The stopping point of God's patience is the starting point of his judgment (2 Peter 3:9–10). The moment when God says that enough is enough, is the moment when evil has reached its full measure. The day when one hardens one's heart completely is the day when God stops speaking to him or her (Hebrews 3:7–13). The minute that a sinner genuinely repents is the minute when God pours out grace and mercy upon him (1 John 1:9). However, there will come a time when, as in the days of Noah, the door closes (Matthew 24:37–41).

Are you living in rebellion? Are you choosing to disregard God's call to repentance? What if you were to die before this day is through? What do you risk by waiting until later?

> God, thank you for showing me the rebellion that was destroying me and for saving me, a sinner lost in darkness. Thank you for purchasing me out of the sin that enslaved me. God, I pray for the people who do not yet know you— might today be the day of their salvation!

AUGUST 10

Jeremiah 16–18; 35

LORD, you are my strength and my fortress,
my refuge in the day of trouble!
—Jeremiah 16:19a

The coming disaster will touch every life in Jerusalem bringing death, disease, war, and famine. Dead bodies will litter the ground; there will be funerals without mourners, no comforters, no singing, no celebrations, there will be only deceit and wickedness. The destruction comes because the people defile the land with lifeless gods and evil deeds. Yet God continues to send Jeremiah to preach to the people and call them to repent. Again, they refuse and continue to live as they want.

How gracious of God to allow pain and suffering.

We have no idea how much pain God has spared us, however, we do know the heartache, suffering, and destruction he allows. We often pray and ask God to remove our suffering or help us endure. Perhaps we should ask God what rebellion he is revealing, what childishness he is maturing, what perseverance he is strengthening, or what disobedience he is disciplining (Romans 5:3–4; Hebrews 12:7). Pain and suffering are not always bad things, often it is our pain and suffering that compels us to repentance and to cling tightly to God.

Will you ask God to show you a glimpse of his mighty, loving hand at work in your suffering? Will you ask him to show you how he is working in you for his good purpose?

> God, thank you for knowing exactly what is best for me, both today and in the future. Thank you for all the wonderful things you have allowed in my life and thank you for the pain you have allowed, for it is in the pain that I seek you more sincerely and rely on you more deeply.

AUGUST 11

2 Kings 24:5–9; 2 Chronicles 36:6–9;
Jeremiah 22:24–23:32; 49:1–33

If they had listened to me, they would have spoken my
words and turned my people from their evil ways.
—Jeremiah 23:22

Jerusalem is besieged by Nebuchadnezzar; it is the beginning of the end for the people of Judah. The prophets commit adultery and love dishonesty; they encourage the people toward evil instead of turning them away from sin. Not one of them knows the Lord enough to hear what he is saying. The priests are like the prophets. Destruction is certain for all. However, God promises to put a righteous Branch on King David's throne, and gather the exiles back to their fold.

How gracious of God to guide his people with his Word.

We know that God's Word is powerful, alive and penetrating (Hebrews 4:12) and when we hear God's Word it burns in our hearts, refines impurities, and convicts us of sin. God's Word reassures us that we are God's own children and draws us into holiness. God's Word reveals where we are out of alignment with God. His Word corrects, rebukes, and teaches (2 Timothy 3:16–17). God's Word turns people away from evil, and toward God. Any other message is just idle words and lifeless chatter.

Will you thank God for your pastor who is not afraid to preach the whole counsel of God? If you are a leader over God's people, will you commit to study God's Word so that you hear what he is saying before you speak?

Lord, I pray that each day your Word will penetrate the
core of my being, and burn away the pride and idolatry that
reside there. Please purify my ears to hear before my mouth
begins to speak.

AUGUST 12

Jeremiah 23:33–24:10; 29:1–31:14

I have sent them into captivity for their own good. I will see that
they are well treated, and I will bring them back here again.
—Jeremiah 24:6

God's tool, Nebuchadnezzar, exiles the king, the princes, and the
skilled craftsmen to Babylon. Jeremiah writes to the exiles and tells
them to settle in Babylon, build homes, marry, have children, and work
for peace. Jeremiah tells them they will be in Babylon for seventy years
and then the Lord will bring them back. There will be joy, celebration,
singing, and praise in Jerusalem—but not until God's punishment is
complete. Until then, Jerusalem faces unimaginable horror.

How gracious of God to send his people away from certain
destruction.

How many times has God removed us from something or
someone—a job, community, group of acquaintances, school,
church, family member, mentor, or even a very close friend? We
may not have realized at the time that God was moving us; perhaps
the circumstances were harsh or unfriendly, or maybe we did not
want to go. God uses whatever tool he desires to place us where he
would have us be (Acts 8:1; 16:6–7).

From what has God removed you? Perhaps you've lived in the
same town, or even the same house all your life. Maybe God has
moved things or people away from you. Have you asked God how
he is protecting you? Have you kept true to him? Are you drawing
closer to God, or moving away from him?

> God, sometimes I feel like I am far removed from things that
> are comfortable and familiar. Help me to see your guiding
> hand wherever I am and to understand that your sovereign
> plan protects me even when I don't see a need for protection.

AUGUST 13

Jeremiah 31:15–40; 49:34–51:14

I have heard Israel saying, "You disciplined me severely, but I deserved it. I turned away from God, but then I was sorry."
—Jeremiah 31:18a, 19a

God reassures Jeremiah that he still loves Israel. The people weep for the sons of Jerusalem who are led into captivity but there is also hope for the future. In that future, Israel recognizes her sin, repents, and God has mercy upon her. God doesn't abandon Israel to Babylon forever. God gives Jeremiah a glimpse of the day when Israel's restoration is complete, and Babylon is punished for defying the Lord.

How gracious of God to promise restoration and eternal love.

Like little children, when we are caught in our sins we often get defensive—blaming others, sugar-coating the seriousness of the offense, attempting to justify it, or believing we can hide or bury it under acts of self-righteousness, or even deny it with a lie.

Christians, unfortunately, commit sins. Our sins do not separate us from God eternally (Romans 8:1), but they do inhibit our spiritual growth and become a barrier between us and an intimate relationship with God and God will discipline us (Hebrews 12:4–7). God's discipline prompts us to own our sin, confess it, repent of it, and turn to him for cleansing and restoration (Psalm 32; 1 John 1:9).

Does God's discipline lead you to repentance? Have you repented: a definitive turning away from your sin and turning toward God? Have you experienced the joy of his eternal love?

God, I am a sinner, and I deserve punishment, even death. Thank you for saving me from eternal death through my precious Lord Jesus Christ, who bore the punishment of my sin when he died in my place, on my behalf, on the cross.

AUGUST 14

2 Kings 24:10–20; 1 Chronicles 3:10–16;
2 Chronicles 36:10–14; Jeremiah 37:1–10; 51:15–58; 52:1–3a

The LORD says to Jerusalem, "I will be your lawyer
to plead your case, and I will avenge you."
—Jeremiah 51:36a

Jeremiah's hymn praises God as the maker of heaven and earth—
sovereign over nature. Jeremiah praises God, the Creator of
everything that exists, including his people.

God will not let Babylon go unpunished for her disastrous
treatment of Jerusalem. God will destroy Babylon for her wickedness
and idolatry. The exiles' time in Babylon will be brief, and then
Babylon will fall. But for now Jerusalem must fall, though the end
has not yet come.

How gracious of God to avenge his people.

God knows when we are harmed, mocked, disrespected,
persecuted, or oppressed. God sees everything, and understands it
completely (Genesis 16:11–13). God allows persecution for our own
good, yet he also punishes our persecutors for having sinned against
him and us. God is just: he punishes all sin and he humbles the proud
(Daniel 4:37). His holy character assures his just treatment of all
people; God never acts wrongly and he never overlooks wickedness
(Colossians 3:25). Therefore, we have no need to plot vengeance or
revenge; God will avenge his people (Deuteronomy 32:35).

In your mistreatment, will you trust God to avenge you in his
time and in his way?

God, you know the persecutions and the persecutors in my
life. I release this to you. I know you alone are wise enough
to punish the wicked and avenge me in a way that will
honor you.

AUGUST 15

Jeremiah 37:11–38:28; Ezekiel 1:1–3:15

And whether they listen or not—for remember, they are rebels—
at least they will know they have a prophet among them.
—Ezekiel 2:5

In Jerusalem, Jeremiah is flogged, imprisoned, nearly killed, and yet
he continues to give God's word to King Zedekiah, telling him to
surrender to the Babylonians or die.

In Babylon, the Lord calls Ezekiel as his prophet. Ezekiel has
visions that reveal the glory of the Lord. The Spirit comes into
Ezekiel and speaks to him, commissioning him to give the Israelites
God's messages whether they listen or not. God makes Ezekiel as
stubborn and strong as the Israelites so that he is not afraid. God
holds Ezekiel in his grip.

How gracious of God to strengthen his people to speak truth
without fear.

God has given us his Word in the Bible, his Spirit within us,
and he holds us firmly in his grip therefore we shouldn't be afraid
to speak God's truth (Ephesians 1:11–14, Jude 1:24). Yet, are there
moments when you or I search for excuses because we are afraid?
Why is that? What do we fear most: That we won't have anything
to say, or that people won't listen to us?

Does fear prevent you from speaking boldly for God? Will you
ask God to give you a holy fear of him that is greater than any fear
that keeps you silent?

> God, I trust that your grip is strong enough to hold me. Help
> me to understand that should I fall, I am falling into your hand.
> Humble me to deal with rejection in a godly way, and encourage
> me to speak with boldness. Protect me from fearing anything
> more than I fear you, and strengthen me in my weakness.

AUGUST 16

Jeremiah 27–28; 51:59–64; Ezekiel 3:16–4:17

At the end of the seven days, the LORD gave me a message.
I have appointed you as a watchman for Israel.
—Ezekiel 3:16a, 17b

Ezekiel must live his sermons in Babylon just as Jeremiah lives his sermons in Jerusalem. God uses their lives as object lessons for his people. God gives Ezekiel a vision of the coming siege in Jerusalem. Ezekiel illustrates the siege for 430 days, tied up, lying on his side, and eating only bread and water.

In Jerusalem, Jeremiah wears a yoke showing the people that they must submit to Babylon's king and serve him or they will die.

How gracious of God to illustrate his messages to spiritually deaf people.

We enjoy messages from the Lord when they are good and sweet. We enjoy singing songs that promise God's presence and salvation. We enjoy talking to others about the great things the Lord has done for us.

However, do we stop listening when the words of the sermon hit a little too close to home—when they call for change, discomfort, or repentance? Do we refuse to hear good words about bad things (Psalm 95)? How far must God go to get our attention?

Are you willing to change the way you live in order to bring God's message to a lost or hurting soul? Will you let God put your faith on display?

> God, it is often easier for me to sing *I Surrender All* than it is to surrender all. I want to be an instrument for you, but I dread the cost or inconvenience. Please open my ears, renew my heart and make me as willing as Ezekiel and Jeremiah to be used for your purposes on earth.

AUGUST 17

Ezekiel 5–9

Son of man, have you seen what the leaders of Israel are
doing with their idols in dark rooms? They are saying,
"The LORD doesn't see us; he has deserted our land!"
—Ezekiel 8:12

God gives Ezekiel the message that the end has come for Jerusalem.
Transported by the Spirit of God, Ezekiel sees in a vision the
unspeakable wickedness that God sees. He knows that no one can
hide their sin. He knows the destruction will be horrific. Ezekiel
realizes that the people in Jerusalem deserve the wrath of God
for their sinful rebellion, idolatry, and extreme violence. Ezekiel
understands God's justice is always right.

How gracious of God to reveal truth.

God's spokespersons never treat sin lightly because God doesn't
treat sin lightly; therefore, we must also hate sin (Psalm 97:10). Sin must
become as loathsome to us as it is to God, including the hidden secret
sins that we enjoy so much. We must stop protecting, nurturing, or
trying to hide our preferential sins from God's view. Instead, we must
look at that sin from God's perspective, recognizing that every sin, no
matter how large or small, is heinous and brings death (Romans 6:23).

Is God bringing to mind a specific sin that you enjoy, protect,
and try to keep secret? Will you choose to see it as God does: as
horrific and unspeakable wickedness? As you experience sorrow over
your sin, will you follow that sorrow as it leads you to repentance (2
Corinthians 7:9–11)?

God, I thank you for opening my eyes to see how destructive
my sin is. Thank you for calling me out of my sin, rather
than abandoning me to it, when I tried so desperately to
hide in it.

AUGUST 18

Therefore, give them this message from the Sovereign
LORD: No more delay! I will do now everything I have
threatened! I, the Sovereign LORD, have spoken!
—Ezekiel 12:28

The Spirit of God transports Ezekiel in a vision to Jerusalem. Ezekiel
sees the glory of the Lord leave both the temple and the city of
Jerusalem. God gives Ezekiel a message for the exiles in Babylon:
God will be their sanctuary, he will gather them, restore them, and
remove the idol worship from their homeland. God gives Ezekiel a
message for the false prophets in Israel: their destruction is sure. God
will stand against them and everyone will know that God is Lord!

How gracious of God to fulfill his word in his sovereign time.

We do not know God's timetable; but seeing the fulfillment
of ancient biblical prophecies gives us assurance that all prophecies
still future to us will be fulfilled. When God intervenes in history,
and does what he says he will do, he proves that he is the only true
and sovereign God over history (2 Peter 1:20–21). God will do what
God says he will do (Mark 14:49b). The greatest prophecy future to
us is the return of Jesus Christ to judge the world and reign as King
forever (2 Peter 3:1–15).

Do you believe God's Word that the Lord Jesus will return and
judge all things? Or, like the people of Israel, do you believe that
time makes a liar of all prophets? Do you scoff at the notion that
Jesus might return in your lifetime? Would you live differently if you
knew Jesus was returning tomorrow? How do you know he isn't?

Sovereign Lord, please help me to live every day as if it were
the last day.

AUGUST 19

Ezekiel 14–16

Yet there will be survivors. You will see with your own
eyes how wicked they are ... you will agree that these
things are not being done to Israel without cause.
—Ezekiel 14: 22a, c, 23b

God teaches Ezekiel that his judgment and punishment of Jerusalem
is just. The nation of Israel is punished because of the sin of all the
people. When Jerusalem falls and survivors come to Babylon, Ezekiel
sees by their behavior that God is right in judging the nation. The
people of Jerusalem are useless to God in their unfaithfulness. They
are adulterous, shameless prostitutes running after their lovers—
their idols. They are loathsome and should be ashamed because of
their terrible sins.

How gracious of God to judge justly.

Judgment establishes value; without judgment then who we are
and what we do would not matter. However, who we are does matter
to God. We are valuable to him; we have been purchased not with
silver or gold, but with the precious blood of Jesus (1 Peter 1:18–19).
Not only do we matter, what we do matters. We represent God to
the world. When God judges our sin, and then, in grace forgives it,
we see both the horror of our sin and the unsurpassable glory of his
grace (Colossians 2:13–14)

How brilliantly does God's grace shine in your life as you behold
it against the darkness and repugnance of your sin?

> God, I know my wicked heart. I see with my own eyes how
> wicked I am, and even more, how wicked I would be apart
> from your saving grace. O God, help me to live worthy of
> the life you have purchased for me at such great cost.

AUGUST 20

"Do you think," asks the Sovereign LORD, "that I like
to see wicked people die? Of course not! I only want
them to turn from their wicked ways and live."
—Ezekiel 18:23

God teaches Ezekiel his rule: The person who sins will be the one
who dies. Children do not die for their parents' sins. Righteous
people are rewarded and wicked people are punished. Wicked people
can turn away from their sin and all their past sins will be forgotten.
The Lord is just, yet the people of Israel say the Lord is unjust.
Therefore God judges each Israelite according to their actions. God
calls Israel to turn back and live! God gives Ezekiel a funeral song;
it is now time for the funeral.

How gracious of God, even in the face of death, to give an
option of life.

Probably more than any other single event, death causes us to
ponder life. Because God has planted eternity in our hearts we long
for it (Ecclesiastes 3:11). However, death reigns because the wages
of sin is death (Romans 6:23). In the sphere of death, God tells us
how we can obtain eternal life: we must believe on his one and only
son, Jesus Christ. Whoever believes in him shall not die, but have
eternal life (John 3:16). The choice is life or death, and each one of
us must choose.

Have you turned to Jesus Christ, the one and only Son of God,
for salvation? Have you asked him to save you completely? Will you
do that now? Will you thank him for saving you?

Almighty God, I choose life! I choose to believe on Jesus.
Thank you, Jesus, for saving me. Thank you for changing
my eternal destiny from death to life.

AUGUST 21

Ezekiel 20:1–22:16

When I bring you home from exile, you will be as pleasing
to me as an offering of perfumed incense. And I will
display my holiness in you as all the nations watch.
—Ezekiel 20:41

With unbelieving and rebellious hearts, Israel's leaders come to
Ezekiel requesting a message from the Lord. God has no message
for them. Rather, God lists Israel's offenses from the days of their
enslavement in Egypt to the present. God speaks of every generation's
rebellion. However, God tells Ezekiel that one day Israel will look
back at their sins and hate the evil they have done, then God will
treat them mercifully in spite of their wickedness.

How gracious of God to show his people their sin.

Sometimes God must remove us from all that is familiar in order
to hone our vision. When we live in the midst of sinful people it's easy
to adapt to their wicked behavior, and to approve it (Romans 1:32).
Only as we ask God to show us our sin, do we see the destruction,
suffering, and confusion that our sin has caused. Sin separates us
from God. It is only through the death of Jesus that God mercifully
and graciously reconciles us to himself (Romans 5:9–11).

From what have you been exiled so that God might purify you?
Have you looked deep into your heart and identified the sin that is
there? Will you confess the wickedness that separated you from God
and seek reconciliation through the work of Christ on your behalf?

> Heavenly Father, when past sin rears its ugly head and
> overwhelms me with guilt and shame, your Word reminds
> me that because I have trusted in Jesus for my salvation, I
> am no longer under condemnation; I am yours, reconciled
> to you.

AUGUST 22

2 Kings 24:20b–25:2; Jeremiah 39:1; 52:3b–5; Ezekiel 22:17–24:14

> You will be judged on the basis of all your wicked actions.
> —Ezekiel 24:14b

God condemns Israel's leaders for destroying people's lives for profit. God condemns Israel's prophets for announcing false visions and speaking false messages. God condemns Israel for her idolatry. God brings the king of Babylon to begin the final siege of Jerusalem. Destruction is certain for the city of murderers. Jerusalem is filled with corruption. The people refuse God's cleansing so God doesn't hold back, he doesn't change his mind. Judgment begins.

How gracious of God not to let sin go unnoticed, uncharged, or unpunished.

God is a just judge (Psalm 96), and his judgment is unbiased. God sees everything clearly and he understands everything completely. He knows every heart thoroughly. He understands intentions, motives, and actions. He knows our thoughts. He knows every secret sin. Nothing is hidden from God and every wicked action will be judged. The only way to escape God's judgment is to be made right with him through the work of Christ Jesus (Romans 5:1–2).

Will you stand before God on the Day of Judgment with your wickedness upon your own shoulders? Or have you received the cleansing that only Jesus brings? Has your wickedness been washed away by the blood of the Lamb (John 1:29)?

> Almighty Judge, my only plea is the cleansing blood of Jesus shed for me. Thank you for making it possible to stand faultless before your throne because I am dressed, not in my own good works, but in the spotless righteousness of Jesus—my Sacrificial Lamb. I am justified because he died for me. Thank you for this perfect and holy salvation.

AUGUST 23

Jeremiah 21; 34; Ezekiel 24:15–25:17; 29:1–16; 30:20–31:18

Tell all the people, "This is what the Lord
says: Take your choice of life or death!"
—Jeremiah 21:8

In Babylon, Ezekiel's wife dies. God tells him not to show sorrow or weep, using Ezekiel as an example of how the captives will mourn— or not— when they hear the news of Jerusalem's destruction and the downfall of the temple.

In Jerusalem, the battle continues. Though the people seek God's help through the prophet Jeremiah, they will not repent. God does not stop the destruction. The people have a choice: stay in Jerusalem and die; or surrender to Babylon and live. The city will be destroyed.

How gracious of God to give free will and choice to all people.

Free will and God's sovereignty—we will never understand how these two seemingly contradictory principles operate in God's plan for humankind. We have freedom to choose or reject God, freedom to choose spiritual life or death. God tells us that everyone who calls on the name of the Lord will be saved (Acts 2:21; John 3:16). Yet, we know that God chose those appointed to salvation before the foundation of the world (Acts 2:47b; Ephesians 1:4). We may not be able to reconcile these two doctrines, but we know we must not embrace one at the expense of the other, for God's Word teaches both. Our responsibility is to choose.

What will you choose? Life or death?

God, in so many arenas of my life I have made choices that I regret. However, I know I will never regret my decision to choose you. Therefore, it is with humble gratitude, that I thank you for choosing me and drawing me to yourself for salvation.

AUGUST 24

Jeremiah 32–33; Ezekiel 26:1–14

So, I bought the field at Anathoth. I signed
and sealed the deed of purchase.
—Jeremiah 32:9a, 10a

Jerusalem is under siege. Jeremiah is a prisoner. God sends Jeremiah a message to buy a field, so Jeremiah buys the land. Afterward, God assures Jeremiah that real estate will one day be bought and sold in Jerusalem again, and there will be rejoicing; nothing is too hard for God. God promises that he will never abandon the descendants of David. God tells Jeremiah, that though his people will be scattered, he will bring them back again and do the good things he has promised.

How gracious of God to confirm that his ways are never foolish.

Sometimes, like Jeremiah, the Lord asks us to do things that don't make sense to the people around us. He might ask us to share our home with a missionary family for months at a time. He might ask us to forgive someone who has hurt us deeply. He might ask us to reconcile with an unfaithful spouse. He might ask us to give someone a second, third, or even fourth chance. He might ask us to give away an item that we could sell.

Has God asked you to do something that appears foolish to you or to other people? Do you trust the perspective of the world or the wisdom of the Lord (1 Corinthians 1:25–31)? Are you willing to take a risk in order to obey what God has asked you to do?

> All wise God, I want to be a person who chooses to obey you no matter what the world might think, and no matter what it might do to my reputation. Please remove the pride that prevents me from doing what you would have me do.

AUGUST 25

2 Kings 25:3–7; Jeremiah 52:6–11; 39:2–10;
Ezekiel 26:15–28:26

Son of man, give the prince of Tyre this
message from the Sovereign LORD ...
—Ezekiel 28:2a

The nation of Tyre rejoices over the fall of Jerusalem. God gives Ezekiel a message for Tyre: You will fall and the whole coastline will tremble at the sound of your fall. God tells Ezekiel to sing a funeral song for Tyre. God gives a message for the prince of Tyre: You think you are a god, but you are not; you will come to a terrible end.

How gracious of God to speak truth to unbelievers in advance of judgment.

As we sit in our living rooms and watch the news unfold we see dictators, tyrants, and other wicked people who think they are gods. We hear of terrorists who kill their own people and who desire our destruction. We see regimes fall only to have the leadership vacuum filled with men even more wicked than the last. We see people and cultures celebrate our own nation's defeats and failures. We may wonder if God is in control. Does he see the wickedness? Will he act? Will he judge? The answer is yes! There will be a day of reckoning and everyone has received the warning (1 Thessalonians 5:1–10; 2 Peter 3:9–11).

Does it comfort you to know that God knows what is going on, has a plan, and is in control? Does knowing that there is a final Day of Judgment set on God's calendar give you hope?

Sovereign Lord, I pray that the leaders of all nations would
listen to you and choose to follow you. Lord, I especially
pray for the leaders of my country: That they would humbly
seek your will for every decision they make.

AUGUST 26

2 Kings 25:8–21; 2 Chronicles 36:15–21;
Jeremiah 39:11–40:6; 52:12–27; Lamentations 1

But I will rescue you from those you fear so much.
Because you trusted me, I will preserve your life
and keep you safe. I, the LORD, have spoken!
—Jeremiah 39:17–18

The chained captives walk out of Jerusalem. Jeremiah is released from prison and allowed to stay in Jerusalem. The temple of the Lord is destroyed. The walls of Jerusalem are torn down. Everything of value is removed to Babylon. The poorest of the poor are permitted to stay in Jerusalem. Priests and leaders are put to death as well as the young and old, men and women, and the healthy and sick. The most horrific destruction in Jerusalem's history is taking place. Jeremiah weeps for Jerusalem.

How gracious of God, to keep safe in the midst of disaster, all who trust in him.

By God's grace, we may never experience the devastation of the fall of our nation, but God does allow destruction: marriages fail, businesses collapse, natural disasters rip apart towns, homes, and lives, car accidents destroy normalcy, age robs us of physical and mental agility, mental illness steals hope, and addictions bind our hearts and souls. Destruction is inevitable, but God rescues us (Psalm 27). God is big enough to preserve our lives and keep us safe (Psalm 25:20–21).

Are you living in destruction now? Will you call out to God to rescue you?

> God, I trust you. I know that when disaster tries to pull me
> into a sea of fear and doubt that you anchor my soul in your
> peace. I know there is no destructive force on earth that is
> greater than you and from which you cannot save me.

AUGUST 27

Lamentations 2–4

I will never forget this awful time, as I grieve over my loss. Yet I still dare to hope when I remember this: The unfailing love of the LORD never ends! Great is his faithfulness; his mercies begin afresh each day.
—Lamentations 3:20–22a, 23

Jerusalem is totally destroyed. No house stands. There is no food, no walls, no protection, no temple, and no presence of God. The people sit in sorrow and despair. The children starve. The women eat their own offspring. The dead lay in the streets—young and old, boys and girls. Jeremiah, Jerusalem's pastor, grieves the loss of Jerusalem; his only comfort is found in the character of his God.

How gracious of God that he is always good, always faithful, always trustworthy.

How awful it would be to experience heartache if we were not able to trust that God is at work in the devastation. He is always at work (John 5:17). He is always good (Psalm 25:7–8; 52:9). He is always at work for the good of those who love him (Romans 8:28). It's not always easy to see God's goodness in the midst of destruction and that is when, like Jeremiah, we must hold unswervingly to his character (Hebrews 10:23).

Have you lost sight of God's goodness in the devastation that surrounds you? What is the most horrific thing in your life right now? Will you believe that God is big enough, good enough, trustworthy enough, and faithful enough to be working for good in that situation?

O Lord God, in the midst of my devastation, I cry out to you. When the darkness overwhelms me, I choose to look for your light. When life seems hopeless, I put my hope in you.

AUGUST 28

2 Kings 25:22–26; Jeremiah 40:7–41:18;
Lamentations 5; Obadiah 1

Restore us, O Lord, and bring us back to you
again! Give us back the joys we once had.
—Lamentations 5:21

Jerusalem is a land of orphans and widows. The women and girls are raped. The young men are forced into labor or killed. There is no joy. Jerusalem's enemies celebrate her demise. God gives Obadiah a message for Jerusalem: It will become a refuge and a holy place. God promises Jerusalem will be the royal throne of the Lord Himself.

How gracious of God to give a message of hope for the future in a hopeless day.

When darkness surrounds us we know that evil is at work; and where Satan is active there is no joy. His followers celebrate the demise of God's people (1 Peter 5:8). However, we also know that his time and his power are limited; he is a defeated foe (John 16:11). One day, when Satan is bound and cast into the lake of fire and brimstone forever (Revelation 20:10), evil will end. On that day, there will be no more darkness and no more pain. This is part of our eternal hope (Revelation 22).

Do you feel as though evil has won the day in your life? Will you choose to trust God's word and live in hope—the assurance that after a night of weeping, joy does indeed come in the morning (Psalm 30:5)

Almighty, victorious God, I know that Satan's time is limited, he is a defeated foe. Please help me to resist him so that he will flee from me. Please restore me to your side. Please fill my heart with the joy that comes from trusting and resting in your victory over evil.

AUGUST 29

Jeremiah 42–44; Ezekiel 33:21–33

Stay here in this land. If you do, I will build you up and
not tear you down; I will plant you and not uproot you.
—Jeremiah 42:10a

The people who remain in Jerusalem ask Jeremiah to pray for them
and seek God's guidance. God tells them to stay in Jerusalem and
he will be with them, save them and rescue them from the king of
Babylon. They refuse to obey and instead follow their own plan to
flee to Egypt. God tells Jeremiah that the king of Babylon will also
destroy Egypt and bring death and captivity. The people will not
listen to the Lord's message, they do as they want and continue to
worship their idols.

How gracious of God to lead us even when his guidance is
insincerely sought.

Are we any different from the Israelites? Even though they've
seen destruction around them, they cling to their worthless idols and
dismiss God's wise leadership because it is not what they want to do.

We may think that we can fool some of the people some of the
time, but we can never fool God (Luke 16:14–15). He knows when
we insincerely seek his wisdom and guidance pretending that we want
his direction, when we have already determined what we will do.

What destruction have you brought upon yourself, or those you
love, because you set your mind to do what you wanted to do despite
God telling you something different?

Lord God Almighty, for all the times I've been insincere,
asking others to pray for me, even praying myself when I had
no intention of following your perfect way, please forgive
me. Teach me to listen to you and to set aside my will and
embrace yours.

AUGUST 30

> I am bringing you back again but not because you deserve it. I
> am doing it to protect my holy name. I will show how holy my
> great name is—the name you dishonored among the nations.
> —Ezekiel 36:22b, 23a

God gives Ezekiel a message for Israel: when they lived in Israel,
they defiled and polluted the land with their evil deeds, but he is
bringing them back. He will gather them and bring them back. He
will cleanse them. He will give them a new heart and put a new spirit
in them. They will be his people and he will be their God. When all
this is accomplished, all the nations will know that God is the Lord.

How gracious of God to protect his great name.

Like Israel, we are to represent God to an unbelieving world; like
Israel, we often fail. We fail because we cease to behold the glory of
God, to dwell on him, or gaze on his beauty. When we focus on God
we reflect him (2 Corinthians 3:18). Like Israel, when we focus on
our rights, and ourselves, we fight for what we want, we use hateful
words, we cheat, steal, or swear, we belittle others, we are selfish, and
we act irresponsibly. When we dishonor God in this way, we can
trust that he will act to protect his name.

Do your words or actions honor or dishonor God? Does your
life draw people toward or away from God? What must change in
your life so that you are a protector of God's name?

Almighty God, please forgive me for dishonoring your
name. Please cause me to behold you throughout every day
so that I continually reflect your good name to others.

AUGUST 31

Ezekiel 32:1–16; 37–39

Can these [dry] bones become living people again?
—Ezekiel 37:3

The Lord takes hold of Ezekiel and he is carried away by the Spirit to a valley of dry bones. Ezekiel sees the Lord breathe life into the bones. A great army of bones comes to life. The bones represent the people of Israel. God promises that Israel will rise again. God tells Ezekiel that Judah and Israel will reunite as one nation. There will be one king to rule them. God's visions and messages to Ezekiel reach far into the future and cover many nations and events.

How gracious of God to reveal himself as sovereign over people, nations and times.

Only the one true God accurately foretells the future (Deuteronomy 18:21–22). Only the sovereign God intervenes in history to bring his prophecies to fulfillment (2 Peter 1:20–21). The God of the Bible is the one true, living, and sovereign God, who created all things, is sovereign over all things, and will accomplish his eternal plan in all things. Only the living God can breathe life into spiritually dry bones.

Have you received the life-giving breath of the Holy Spirit into your being? Have you committed your life to serve the one true King? Do Ezekiel's visions comfort you and give you hope for the future? When you have questions, doubts or fears about future events, do you find comfort in the knowledge that God is in control? Are you resting in God's sovereignty over your life no matter how dry the circumstances may seem today?

> God, I trust you for life now and throughout all eternity. I trust that you have perfectly planned the future and will bring it to pass. I trust that the life you breathed into me will live for all eternity.

grace
SEPTEMBER

SEPTEMBER 1

1 Chronicles 4:24–5:17; Psalm 137;
Jeremiah 52:28–30; Ezekiel 32:17–33:20

But if the watchman sees the enemy coming and doesn't sound
the alarm to warn the people, he is responsible for their deaths.
—Ezekiel 33:6a

God appoints Ezekiel as the watchman over Israel to warn the people of their impending doom: if they do not change their ways, they will die in their sins. God holds the watchman accountable to tell the people that he takes no pleasure in the death of the wicked; God wants them to turn from their wicked ways and live. The good works of righteous people will not save them if they do not turn from their sin. God will judge each person according to their deeds.

How gracious of God to set watchmen to sound the alarm to warn us of sin.

We hear the alarms of the watchmen in many ways: The Holy Spirit convicts our hearts of sin, our pastors preach sermons about sin, we watch the news reports and see the effects of sin in the world, and our Bible study groups discuss the dangers and deceptions of sin. But, oh how easy it is to overlook the sin in our own lives as we point out the sin in others. We must repent—turn away from sin and turn to God—if we want to live (Acts 26:20).

Do you hear the alarm? From what is God calling you to wake up? There is no time to hit the snooze. Today is the day of salvation.

> Gracious God, I thank you for the watchmen in my life.
> I pray that I might also prove to be a vigilant watchman.
> Please give me love, gentleness, compassion, and empathy as
> I sound the alarm that you have commissioned me to sound.

SEPTEMBER 2

1 Chronicles 5:18–26; 6:3b–15, 49; 7:1–8:28

Seraiah was the father of Jehozadak, who went into
exile when the LORD sent the people of Judah and
Jerusalem into captivity under Nebuchadnezzar.
—1 Chronicles 6:14b–15

The northern kingdom of Israel is exiled to Halah, Habor, Hara, and
the Gozan River. The southern kingdom of Judah is exiled to Babylon.
The genealogies of both kingdoms are carefully recorded and protected.
There are priests, descendants of Aaron, going with the exiles into
Babylon to lead in worship and assist them in drawing close to the Lord.

How gracious of God to provide worship leaders and intercessors
for his people.

God provides for us as well: we have a Great High Priest, the
Lord Jesus Christ, who lives to intercede for us (Hebrews 7:23–28).
Because of the work of Christ Jesus on the cross, we are a holy
people, a royal priesthood, and therefore we can come into the
presence of God and draw close to him (1 Peter 2:9). We have
the privilege of worshipping anytime, anywhere, and anyway. God
desires our worship, not because he needs it, but because we need
to worship him. Apart from worship our joys are incomplete, our
sorrow is inconsolable, and our lives are meaningless.

In your circumstances today, will you worship God? Will you
come into his presence with praise and thanksgiving? Will you spend
time with God giving him the worship that he is due?

> Father, I thank you that I can come into your presence at
> any time because of the blood of Jesus. I also thank you for
> the gift of corporate worship. Thank you for the men and
> women who lead me away from the busyness of life toward
> the precious sanctuary of heaven where I can worship you.

SEPTEMBER 3

1 Chronicles 8:29–9:1a; Ezekiel 40:1–37; Daniel 4

Now I, Nebuchadnezzar, praise and glorify and honor
the King of heaven. All his acts are just and true,
and he is able to humble those who are proud.
—Daniel 4:37

Nebuchadnezzar, the king of Babylon, has a dream that none of his
wise men can interpret. He calls for Daniel, and God gives Daniel
the interpretation: Nebuchadnezzar will be driven from human
society to live with wild animals until he learns that the Most High
rules over the kingdoms of the world and gives them to anyone
he chooses. When Nebuchadnezzar declares that it is by his own
might he built up his empire, the prophecy is fulfilled at that very
hour. Nebuchadnezzar lives as a wild animal for seven years until he
praises and worships the Most High. At that time, his sanity returns.

How gracious of God to humble the proud.

We don't really enjoy being humbled. It's not fun to fall, or be
pushed, off any pedestal. We don't like the idea of being less than
we think we are. The problem is: we think we are more than we are
(Romans 12:3b–8). When we think we are more than we are, it is
harder to accept that God is more than we think he is.

What do you have that God did not give you? (1 Corinthians
4:7). If God gave it, why do you take the credit? To what lengths
must God go to remind you that he alone is worthy of worship? How
far must you fall before you begin to look up?

> Almighty God, I confess: I am prideful. Please help me to
> overcome the ugliness of my pride and help me to become
> the humble person you created me to be.

SEPTEMBER 4

Ezekiel 40:38–43:27

Son of man, describe to the people of Israel the Temple
I have shown you. Tell them its appearance and its
plan so they will be ashamed of all their sins.
—Ezekiel 43:10

In a vision God takes Ezekiel to see many things and tells him to
pay close attention so that he can tell the Israelites all that he sees.
God shows Ezekiel a temple, and in it: the Holy Place and Most
Holy Place. God's glory comes into the temple and God speaks from
within the temple declaring it to be the place of his throne, where he
will rest his feet. He promises to remain there forever, living among
the people of Israel and calls them to put away their idols. The Lord
tells Ezekiel that the basic law of the temple is absolute holiness!

How gracious of God to give a vision of his holiness and
forgiveness.

Lord willing, we will never live through the horror that the
Israelites experienced. Nevertheless, we will probably have periods of
devastation, despair, and failure. We may wonder if we are beyond
God's restoration. We are not. God restores repentant people
(Jeremiah 15:19). God is accessible (Ephesians 3:12) and he forgives
repentant people (2 Chronicles 7:14).

What vision is God using to bring your sin and idolatry into
focus? Do you feel like you are beyond restoration? Will you trust
his word that you are not?

> God, my body is your temple and I want the place where
> you dwell to be a clean and holy place. Help me to recognize
> where I have let purity fall by the wayside as sin creeps into
> the dark corners. Please cleanse me, restore me, and fill me
> with your glory.

SEPTEMBER 5

Ezekiel 44–46

I looked and saw that the glory of the LORD filled the Temple
of the LORD, and I fell to the ground with my face in the dust.
—Ezekiel 44:4

In Ezekiel's vision, the Lord's glory fills the temple. The Lord gives
Ezekiel regulations regarding the temple. He reminds Ezekiel of
Israel's rebellion and how they profaned the temple. In the new
temple, only God's people may enter. There will be teachers to
teach the difference between what is holy and what is common, and
judges will resolve disagreements. There will be an end to violence
and oppression, and there will be festivals and rest.

How gracious of God to explain the difference between what is
holy and what is not.

There is much conversation today regarding this temple and
there is much we won't understand until God reveals all of history,
however, there are some applications for us.

We are a nation of priests and yet we often fail to act like it (1
Peter 2:9–10). We are not above rebellion, profaning the name of the
Lord, abandoning the Lord, or drifting into idolatry; we do it every
time we put our desires ahead of the Living God

Our culture has forgotten what is holy and what is common.
Have we profaned God's temple—our bodies—by surrendering to
the common thinking of our culture? Have we exchanged holiness
for happiness as the primary motivator of our lives?

Is it time to embrace a fresh call to holiness (Romans 12:1–2; 1
Corinthians 6:19–20)?

God, please forgive my casual attitude toward holiness. Please
teach me the difference between what must be holy and what
is common in my life, and humble me to embrace holiness.

SEPTEMBER 6

2 Kings 25:27–30; Jeremiah 52:31–34; Ezekiel 29:17–30:19; 47–48

Here is the list of the tribes of Israel and
the territory each is to receive.
—Ezekiel 48:1a

Ezekiel sees a healing river flowing out of Jerusalem. He sees the city restored with citizens in the land. He sees the land divided among the tribes: Dan, Asher, Naphtali, Manasseh and Ephraim (Joseph's sons), Reuben, Judah, Levi, Benjamin, Simeon, Issachar, Zebulun, and Gad. He sees Israel's future redemption and restoration.

How gracious of God to give a vision of redemption and restoration to the captives.

How easily and without thinking do you and I defy God daily? We defy God in our rebellion: when we insist on doing things our way, in our time, and for our own purposes. We establish idols as we seek comfort and satisfaction in things other than God. We deserve exile and captivity—which is in fact the description of our lives apart from Jesus (John 8:34).

Nevertheless, God promises restoration and redemption. Jesus has paid the price for our redemption (Hebrews 9:11–22). It is our choice whether to receive the freedom he purchased for us. If we choose redemption then rivers of living water will flow through us and we will receive an eternal inheritance (John 7:38–39; Ephesians 1:14; 1 Peter 1:4).

Have you received the gift of redemption that enables your restoration and assures you of an inheritance? Are you working to spread the name of Jesus throughout the territory in which you live?

Glorious One, what a blessing it is to know that you have redeemed me and restored me. Thank you for the Holy Spirit that empowers me to establish your great name in the territory in which you have assigned me.

SEPTEMBER 7

Daniel 5; 7–8

Earlier, during the first year of King Belshazzar's reign in Babylon, Daniel had a dream and saw visions as he lay in his bed ...
—Daniel 7:1

God is with the captives in Babylon. God shows them through visions and dreams that he has a plan for the future and for them. Daniel sees visions that are simultaneously frightening and comforting. He sees the Ancient One sit down to judge. He sees the Eternal King given authority, honor, and royal power over all the nations of the world. He sees the wrath of God. He sees the end of time. And years later, he sees the writing on the wall declaring God's judgment upon Belshazzar.

How gracious of God to give wisdom, understanding, and insight to his people.

God's ways are higher than our ways and God's thoughts are higher than our thoughts (Isaiah 55:8–9), therefore, we can't know all that will happen regarding the end of time. However, we can know the things that God has clearly revealed (Deuteronomy 29:29). We know Jesus will return, and when he does he will judge all people: the living and the dead (2 Timothy 4:1). We know that we will live with Jesus eternally if we belong to him (1 John 5:11–12). We know that God's people are not destined for wrath but for eternal life (1 Thessalonians 5:9).

Do you live confidently in the knowledge of truth, or fearfully in the unknown? What must you do to increase wisdom and understanding of God's Word to eliminate fear in your life?

O Ancient of Days, I rest in the knowledge that you are sovereign over all things, the known and the unknown. Your divine and eternal omniscience provides rest for my soul.

SEPTEMBER 8

1 Chronicles 3:17–19a; 2 Chronicles 36:22–23; Ezra 1; Daniel 6; 9

> But the Lord our God is merciful and forgiving,
> even though we have rebelled against him.
> —Daniel 9:9

Daniel is God's man in Babylon. As Daniel studies the writings of Jeremiah, he learns that the Israelite captivity will last seventy years. He prays that God will forgive the captives' sins and restore Jerusalem. He confesses his sin and the sin of the people. God sends a messenger, Gabriel, to Daniel to give him insight and understanding. God fulfills Jeremiah's prophecy by stirring the heart of King Cyrus to allow the captives to return and rebuild the temple of the Lord.

How gracious of God to intervene in history to accomplish his plan for his people.

When we look at the series of events that led to the captives' return it is amazing how specifically and thoroughly God directed history. Jeremiah recorded that the captivity would be seventy years. Exactly seventy years later Daniel reads Jeremiah's prophecy. Daniel prays for the people and at the same time, God moves the heart of the king to free the captives (Proverbs 21:1).

What coincidences have you seen in your life recently? Could it be that God is directing them? What has God put on your heart to pray? Could it be that God wants to answer that prayer for his glory? How might God be directing your history to bring honor to his name?

God, of course you are intensely involved in the lives of men and women to bring honor to your name, so why should I doubt or question whether or not you are specifically involved in the events of my life. Please open my eyes to see your mighty hand at work in the circumstances of my life.

SEPTEMBER 9

1 Chronicles 3:19b–24; Ezra 2:1–4:5

With praise and thanks, they sang this song to the LORD:
"He is so good! His faithful love for Israel endures forever."
—Ezra 3:11

Ezra, the scribe, records the families of the exiles who return to Jerusalem with Zerubbabel. Despite their fear of the local residents, the returned exiles rebuild the altar of the God of Israel and immediately sacrifice burnt offerings. They assemble building materials and begin construction of the temple. They pause to celebrate when the foundation is completed. There is joyful shouting and weeping mingled together. Even though the local residents try to deceive, discourage, and frighten them, they press on.

How gracious of God to fortify his people to accomplish their work.

Seventy years—that's a long time. It's enough years for generations to grow old and die, and new generations to be born. It's enough time to forget the past and establish a new life, home, friends, and career. Yet, some of the Israelite captives chose to uproot and return to Jerusalem. They return to a land of strangers, enemies, fears, and destruction.

Following their example is not easy. It means believing the truth that if God is in the plans there will be success. When God initiates the work, God will fortify his people and assure them that the work will be accomplished (Isaiah 44:24–28, 55:11; Philippians 1:6; 2 Timothy 3:17).

Are you willing to leave your comfortable, settled, and established life; or let your children leave you to follow God's call? Will you trust him to equip you for success?

God, I know in my heart that if you initiate the work, the work will be successful. Please help me to live in faith, trusting you to fortify me to stand firm and accomplish your work.

SEPTEMBER 10

Ezra 4:24–5:1; Daniel 10–12; Haggai 1

But at that time every one of your people whose
name is written in the book will be rescued.
—Daniel 12:1c

In Babylon, Daniel has a frightening vision of future events and God sends a visitor to comfort him. The horrific trials Daniel sees are necessary to refine the people. Daniel also sees a resurrection of the dead: some to everlasting life and some to everlasting contempt. Daniel is assured that the people who know their God will be strong.

How gracious of God to promise his people they will overcome.

Daniel saw frightening things that neither he, nor we, fully understand. As we read and study the visions of future judgment and tribulation in God's Word, we may wonder if we will be strong enough to endure if we are alive in that day. However, as in Daniel's vision, God assures us that we will overcome (Revelation 7:3, 12:11). The Evil One may be able to destroy our bodies but he cannot touch our souls. We should not fear the judgment that God has in store for the wicked (1 Thessalonians 5:9; Matthew 10:28).

Are you living in fear of God's wrath or in the assurance that your eternal destiny is secured? Salvation is sure for those who trust in the Lord Jesus Christ and believe that he defeated death by death and lives that we might live (1 Corinthians 15:12–24).

Father, I thank you for the promise that you will sustain me no matter what. Whether your plan for me is to endure the final days of tribulation or current persecution, I know that I will stand firm because of you, because of your promise: that you have not appointed me to suffer wrath but to experience salvation.

SEPTEMBER 11

Ezra 5:2; Haggai 2; Zechariah 1–5

Take courage and work for I am with
you, says the LORD Almighty.
—Haggai 2:4d

God, through his prophet Haggai, sends the message: does anyone
remember the temple as it was before? In comparison the new temple
must seem like nothing at all! God encourages the people by telling
them he is with them and he promises to fill this temple with his
glory; it will be greater than before.

How gracious of God to assure his people that he is with them
when they work for him.

Unless the Lord builds the house, the builders labor in vain
(Psalm 127:1). And when the Lord builds the house through laborers
who rely on him, who work for his glory, who trust his plan then
no matter how small or insignificant the structure may seem—it is
glorious. Whatever God is in, is glorious (Psalm 19:1). Whatever
God has commissioned us to build we must remember that nothing
is small when God is involved. When we focus on things around
us, rather than the God who works within us, we begin to make
comparisons with a faulty perspective. The Lord is with us and he
brings his glory with him, and nothing compares to that.

Are you distracted from the task God has set before you because
you are comparing your life, your ministry, or your mission to someone
else's. Will you commit to work with God and set your eyes only on him?

God, please forgive me for thinking that anything you
are involved in could be small, insignificant, or less than
glorious. Please cause me to focus only on you and work for
you above all other things, no matter the size of the task that
you have assigned to me.

SEPTEMBER 12

Ezra 5:3–6:14a; Zechariah 6–8

This is what the LORD Almighty says: All this may
seem impossible to you now. But do you think this
is impossible for me, the LORD Almighty?
—Zechariah 8:6a,c

God's words spoken through his prophets, along with the gifts sent
from the exiles in Babylon, encourage the remnant in Jerusalem.
Opposition leaders try unsuccessfully to bring the building project
to a halt. King Cyrus has the royal records searched and discovers
the decree to rebuild the temple of God at Jerusalem. Cyrus orders
the opposition to stay away! Moreover, Cyrus decrees the opposition
is to pay the full construction costs.

How gracious of God to remind the remnant that nothing is
impossible for him.

We know that the Sovereign God directs the hearts of kings
(Proverbs 21:1). We also know that if God is doing a work, it will be
finished. No one could prevent the rebuilding of the temple because
God promised it would be rebuilt. God promises the same thing to
us. The work he began in our hearts and lives when he saved us will
be brought to completion (Philippians 1:6). Your destiny, and mine, is
holiness (Romans 8:28–30). God will accomplish his building projects
in us and no matter how strong the opposition is it cannot stop him.

Do you believe that nothing is impossible with God? Will
you bring your impossible things to him: Your excuses, your busy
schedule, the opposition, failures of the past, struggles of the present,
and fears of the future?

> God, I'm sorry I limit you. Help me to remember your
> promise, that when your power is at work within me, when
> I trust you completely, that you are able to do immeasurably
> more than I can possible imagine (Ephesians 3:20).

SEPTEMBER 13

Zechariah 9–14

Rejoice greatly, O people of Zion! Shout in triumph,
O people of Jerusalem! Look, your king is coming to
you. He is righteous and victorious, yet he is humble,
riding on a donkey—even on a donkey's colt.
—Zechariah 9:9

Zechariah preaches to the remnant who are rebuilding God's temple. He speaks of their coming King, the Messiah. He speaks of the glorious future when their King removes all weapons of war and brings peace to the nations. He foretells the arrival of the Lord Almighty to look after his people. He speaks of the King who pours out a spirit of grace and prayer; cleansing them from all their sins and defilement. In that day, everything is fulfilled and prophecies end; the Lord is king over all the earth and his name alone is worshiped.

How gracious of God to foretell his glorious plan for the future of the world.

We know the Messiah of whom Zechariah spoke is the Lord Jesus Christ (Acts 2). We know that he was born, lived a perfect life, died on the cross, was resurrected on the third day, and lives exalted in heaven (Philippians 2:6–11). We know this same Jesus will return (Acts 1:11). We know he will reign over a new heaven and a new earth where evil and sin have been defeated, and where there will be no tears, death, mourning, crying, or pain (Revelation 21).

You know the facts, but do you let them penetrate into your heart, into your daily decisions, and into the way you live? Will you commit to live today just as you will when Jesus returns?

God, cause me to be that person who lives fearlessly for you.
When doubt creeps in, I choose to boldly claim you as the
Eternal, Victorious King!

SEPTEMBER 14

Ezra 4:6; 6:14b–22; Esther 1–4

What's more, who can say but that you have been
elevated to the palace for such a time as this?
—Esther 4:14b

While the returned exiles dedicate the temple in Jerusalem, many
other exiles remain scattered throughout the provinces of Persia.
King Xerxes' Prime Minister plots to destroy all of the Jews and
Xerxes agrees. Xerxes' new queen, Esther, who is secretly a Jew, is
asked to make an appeal to the king on behalf of all Jews. Esther, at
risk of death, agrees to go to the king.

How gracious of God to place his people exactly where they need
to be to accomplish his purpose.

We know that it is not a coincidence that Esther is Xerxes'
queen, or that she is a Jew. However, her circumstances are still quite
frightening. If she says nothing, she dies. If she goes to the king, she
could die. Yet, she is willing to die in order to obey. Despite her fear,
she exercises her faith; faith that trusts God will do what is right,
even if it means her death (Matthew 10:28).

God knows our circumstances better than we do; he knows
our past, our present, and our future and tells us not to fear (Isaiah
41:10–14). Nevertheless, when fear creeps in we must deal with it
and the antidote to fear is faith. Fear and faith cannot coexist.

Does fear keep you from doing the things God would have you
do, in the position in which he has placed you?

> God, I believe that there are no coincidences regarding the
> circumstances of my life. Please help me overcome fear by
> choosing to place my faith in you, your promises, and your
> Word.

SEPTEMBER 15

Esther 5–10

When he saw Queen Esther standing there
in the inner court, he welcomed her.
—Esther 5:2a

As the plot to kill the Jews unfolds, Esther approaches King Xerxes at risk of her life. He welcomes her. Esther asks the king to spare her life and the life of her people. Xerxes, enraged by what he learns, hangs Haman then issues a decree that the Jews are given permission to defend themselves. Throughout the Persian provinces the Jews defend themselves on the day they were to be killed. The Jews hold Xerxes in high esteem.

How gracious of God to direct the heart of the king and protect his people.

We see throughout biblical history that God's plans cannot be thwarted (Job 42:2). It doesn't matter who sits on the throne, in the statehouse, the Senate, the governor's mansion, or the mayor's office. It doesn't matter who runs the company or the school. It doesn't matter how much one is hated or loved. God is ultimately in control of all things (Psalm 47:7–8) and establishes his people in places of influence to accomplish his plan for the world.

Does it frighten you to watch the events of the world unfold? Do you fear losing your life, job, income, house, family, or spouse if you speak up for God? Do you believe that God has a perfect plan for you, and even if the entire world is against you, that God is on your side and therefore nothing can separate you from his love (Romans 8:31–39)?

> God, I know that you are all powerful and that nothing can thwart your plans, but sometimes my fears overshadow that truth. Please help me to walk boldly where you have me, trusting you to do whatever you must to accomplish your plan.

SEPTEMBER 16

Ezra 4:7–23; 7–8

I felt encouraged because the gracious hand
of the LORD my God was on me.
—Ezra 7:28b

In Jerusalem, opposition to the rebuilding of the city continues. None of the surrounding peoples wants Jerusalem rebuilt. God calls Ezra, a godly descendant from a godly family, a priest and scribe born in exile to go to Jerusalem to encourage and teach the people. God moves the heart of the king to allow Ezra to go. Ezra travels with great wealth and offerings for the Lord. God puts it on the heart of many others to go with Ezra.

How gracious of God to work in and through his people with his mighty hand.

Ezra was successful because God's hand was upon him. Because we belong to God, his hand is upon us, leading and directing us to accomplish his great purposes. Apart from God, we can do nothing (John 15:5). With God's mighty hand strengthening us, we can do every amazing thing he calls us to do (Philippians 4:13). There is no hurdle that we can't overcome, no mountain we can't climb, and no wall we can't scale.

As you look back over your life, how have you seen God's gracious hand upon you to protect, lead, discipline, train, or use you? How have you seen God's mighty hand in your present successes? Does knowing that God guides you with his mighty hand provide you with the courage you need to go wherever he sends you and to do whatever he asks you to do?

Father, I know that you prepared me for work, and you have prepared a work for me to do. Please help me to step out in confidence knowing that you are with me and your mighty hand is upon me.

SEPTEMBER 17

Ezra 9–10; Nehemiah 1–2

O LORD, please hear my prayer! Listen to the prayers
of those of us who delight in honoring you. Please
grant me success now as I go to ask the king for a
great favor. Put it in his heart to be kind to me.

—Nehemiah 1:11

When visitors from Jerusalem inform Nehemiah (in Susa) that Jerusalem is still in trouble and disgrace—the wall is torn down and the gates are burned—Nehemiah prays then asks the king's permission to return to Jerusalem. King Artaxerxes grants permission and arranges for Nehemiah to go. He sends letters to insure Nehemiah's safety and secures building materials. He sends army officers and horsemen as protection. In Jerusalem, Nehemiah secretly inspects the wall before he tells the city officials his plan to rebuild.

How gracious of God to bring his people into the favor of those in authority over them.

Nehemiah respected authority. He respected the authority of the unbelieving king, and he respected the authority of the city officials in Jerusalem.

When God gives us a task, he sends us with his authority to accomplish that task (Matthew 28:18). However, that doesn't allow us to overlook the human authorities that God has also placed over us (Romans 13:1). God expects that we will obey him while simultaneously submitting to the local governing authorities.

Does accomplishing the work that God has assigned to you hinge on someone in authority over you? Will you ask God to allow you to find favor in their eyes?

God, I am sorry for the times I have let my fear of approaching someone in authority over me keep me from obeying you. I am sorry for not trusting you to go before me and open the necessary doors to accommodate my obedience.

SEPTEMBER 18

Nehemiah 3:1–7:3

But we prayed to our God and guarded the
city day and night to protect ourselves.
—Nehemiah 4:9

Nehemiah leads the Jerusalemites as they rebuild the wall. Side by side men, women, old and young, merchants, and priests work together. Their enemies angrily mock them and make plans to fight against Jerusalem. Nehemiah prays to God and the Jerusalemites stand guard as they continue to work through the piles of rubble. Each man carries a weapon with him at all times. Fifty-two days later, the wall is completed and the gates are hung.

How gracious of God to protect his people as they accomplish their work for him.

There will always be opposition when we are working for the Lord, and the greatest weapon against opposition is prayer. Though God promises to protect us, we are not absolved from seeking his help or from acting wisely in the face of danger (Psalm 91). We must remain vigilant to the circumstances around us and we must work faithfully, side by side with other believers, even as we pray continually for protection. We must trust God to protect us in whatever way he chooses. He may lead us to protect ourselves and each other, he may supernaturally intervene, or perhaps he will use a bit of both.

To what project has God called you? Who are you working alongside? Can they trust you to protect them and their reputation, even as you know God protects you?

Almighty God, I know that you will protect me; you are my fortress and my refuge. Your faithfulness is my shield against the Evil One. Help me to complete the work that you have given me even as I stand guard against the forces of darkness and deception around me.

SEPTEMBER 19

Nehemiah 7:4–8:12

They read from the Book of the Law of God and
clearly explained the meaning of what was being read,
helping the people understand each passage.
—Nehemiah 8:8

Under God's direction, Nehemiah registers the residents of Jerusalem. Later, the people assemble and Ezra brings out the Book of the Law. Ezra stands on a special platform. He reads to the people from early morning until noon while the people stand and listen. The people bow and worship the Lord. The Levites explain to the people what they hear. The people weep, but Nehemiah tells them to go and celebrate! They celebrate with great joy because they hear and understand God's Word.

How gracious of God to give teachers to help his people understand his Word.

If there is anything at all that we know with certainty, it is that we are not born knowing everything. We begin learning the moment we take our first breath. We learn by experience, observation, reading, listening, and by sitting under sound teaching. This is especially true of the Bible. When we believe on the Lord Jesus Christ, we are given the Holy Spirit who teaches us (John 14:26), but we also need the pastors and teachers whom God provides (Ephesians 4:11–13). It is our responsibility to listen, study, learn, and apply what they teach. There is no excuse for not learning, knowing, and applying God's Word.

Are you regularly studying God's Word? How is your life changing as you learn more?

Almighty God, thank you for the teachers you've put in my life and for the Bible studies that are readily available to me. Open my mind to understand, and soften my heart to apply what I learn so that your Word continually transforms my life.

SEPTEMBER 20

Nehemiah 8:13–10:39

The family leaders and the priests and Levites met
with Ezra to go over the law in greater detail.
—Nehemiah 8:13

The Israelites study God's Word and discover there is much they're not applying. They renew the Feast of Shelters. They spend hours confessing their sins and worshiping. They praise God as they recall all he did for their ancestors, and the sin and rebellion that brought about the exile. They praise God for showing them his love and sending the prophets to warn them about sin. They praise God for his mercy; that he didn't abandon or destroy them completely. They praise God for his justice in punishment. They promise to obey God.

How gracious of God to reveal his glorious character through his Word.

When we dig deep into God's Word, we find God in all his splendid beauty. We see God as merciful and just, gracious and kind, the loving Father who disciplines his children, the one who mourns over sin, the Sovereign who directs the hearts of kings, and the Savior who lifts us out of sin's grasp. We find the one true God in all his majesty (Psalm 11:4–7; 18:1–3; 27:1; 40:2–3; 136; Job 37:4–5, Isaiah 63:7–9).

As you read the Bible how has God's revelation of himself changed you, your heart, your perspective, and your hope? Will you pause and praise God for each one of his attributes?

> God, please forgive me for settling into a complacency that
> is content to skim your Word and glimpse the vision of
> who I think you are rather than study your Word to pursue
> a deeper understanding of your glorious person. Please
> keep me from settling for a fleeting glance when I could be
> settling my soul by gazing on your beauty.

SEPTEMBER 21

1 Chronicles 9:1b–34; Nehemiah 11:1–12:26

Now the leaders of the people were living in Jerusalem. Here is a list of the names of the provincial officials who came to Jerusalem.
—Nehemiah 11:1, 3

Nehemiah lists the people in Jerusalem. Some Israelites live in Jerusalem and some settle in their ancestral homes throughout Judah. There are temple workers, public administrators, guards, priests, singers, family leaders, and gatekeepers. Nehemiah overlooks no one and everyone has a responsibility.

How gracious of God to establish order and assign responsibility.

From the rising of the sun to its setting, God is a God of order; spring follows winter, and autumn follows summer (Genesis 1:14). In his ordered universe no one gets lost in the crowd; he knows you and me, and we are precious to him (Matthew 10:29–31). In his ordering of the world he has a job for each one of us and it is perfectly fitted to who we are (Ephesians 2:10). When we all do our job with care, keeping our eyes focused on the Lord and working for his glory, there is order in the church (Romans 12:3–8). When one or more of us chooses not to work, there is disorder, disharmony, and a heavier load falls upon everyone else.

Are you a person of order or disorder? Do you bring order or disorder into your areas of responsibility? How does that affect people around you?

> God, understanding that you know who I am, where I am, and what I am to be doing for your kingdom challenges me to get to work. Please help me to organize and carry my load in the place you have assigned to me.

SEPTEMBER 22

Nehemiah 5:14–19; 12:27–13:31; Malachi 1:1–2:9

The purpose of my covenant with the Levites was to bring
life and peace. They passed on to the people all the truth
they received from me … and they turned many from
lives of sin. But not you! You have left God's paths. Your
"guidance" has caused many to stumble into sin.
—Malachi 2:5a, 6a,d, 8a

Ezra and Nehemiah lead the Israelites in joyous worship as the wall of
Jerusalem is dedicated. Nehemiah returns to Babylon to serve King
Artaxerxes. While he is away, the people neglect the temple of God
and profane the Sabbath as their ancestors have done. The Lord gives
a message to the people through Malachi: despite his love for them,
they are despising his name with their defiled sacrifices! Through
Malachi, God calls the priests to account for their corrupt guidance.

How gracious of God to hold his leaders to a high standard of
obedience.

When our leaders are absent we must not fall away; rather, we
must remember that we are never without God's guidance. When
a church is between pastors, it is never without God. When a Bible
study takes a summer break, we must not break from God. When
our small group disbands, God continues to hold us close. When
a mentor moves away, God always listens and teaches. God never
leaves his children (John 14:16; Joshua 1:5, 9).

Who are you leading? Are you leading them in such a manner
that if, or when, you are no longer able to lead, they will continue
to follow God?

God, as I have been led to follow you, so will I lead others.
Thank you for calling me to a high standard of obedience
so that the people I lead will always be led to follow you.

SEPTEMBER 23

Malachi 2:10–4:6; Joel 1–3

"Now return to me, and I will return to
you," says the LORD Almighty.
—Malachi 3:7b

The LORD says, "Turn to me now, while
there is time! Give me your hearts."
—Joel 2:12

Malachi calls upon the Israelites to give up their hypocritical lives:
They are faithless in marriage, they oppress widows and orphans,
and they withhold justice. Malachi speaks of a day of judgment to
come—when the wicked are burned like straw.

God gives the prophet Joel a message of destruction: The day of the
Lord is coming. It will be a day of despair, sorrow, weeping, mourning,
and famine. It is a day of darkness and gloom, of thick clouds and deep
blackness. The earth will quake and the heavens tremble. Who can
endure? The Lord calls out to turn to him while there is time!

How gracious of God to hold out his hand of hope to disobedient
people.

God cannot overlook sin; it must be punished and he has
declared that the wages of sin is death (Romans 6:23). The entire
world is under a curse because of sin (Genesis 3:17–19). Nevertheless,
all day long, God holds out his hand to a sinful people (Isaiah 65:2).

God is holding out his hand to you, have you chosen to run
to him for salvation from the destruction that is sure to come? If
not, why not? If you have, from what must you repent in order to
experience God's complete restoration?

O God, I know that when I do not flee to your open arms
for cleansing, that I forfeit peace, relationships, and power in
my life. I see your open arms. I hear you call to me. Gracious
God, I come! Here is my heart; I come!

SEPTEMBER 24

Matthew 1:1–17; Mark 1:1; Luke 1; 3:23b–38; John 1:1–18

This is a record of the ancestors of Jesus the Messiah,
a descendant of King David and of Abraham.
—Matthew 1:1

The promised Messiah, the Son of God, the Word, God, the one who created all things is born as a human and lives on earth. The world does not recognize him. His genealogy proves he is a descendant of both Abraham and of King David, a priest and a king. He is born of a virgin: the Holy Spirit comes upon her and the power of the Most High overshadows her. He is God.

How gracious of God to send the Savior, just as he promised (Genesis 3:15).

Throughout all of history God promised, protected, and preserved the genealogy of the Messiah. God promised Abraham a descendant who would bless all nations (Genesis 12:1–3). God prophesied through Isaiah that the Messiah would be born of a virgin (Isaiah 7:14). God foretold that the Messiah would be born in Bethlehem (Micah 5:2). God promised David an eternal kingdom (2 Samuel 7:5–17). Jesus fulfills every prophecy regarding the Messiah. No other person in history meets the specific criteria that Jesus met. Jesus is the Messiah: God's Word proves it, eyewitnesses prove it, and history proves that God faithfully sent the Savior.

Do you struggle with the idea that Jesus is the Messiah, born of a virgin, and the only means of salvation? Will you take your struggle directly to God and ask him to help you overcome your doubt (Mark 9:24).

God, I do believe, please help me to accept the things I don't understand. Please help me to trust your fulfilled promises so that my faith will not waver.

SEPTEMBER 25

Matthew 1:18–25; Luke 1:39–2:40

The Savior—yes, the Messiah, the Lord—has been
born tonight in Bethlehem, the city of David!
—Luke 2:11

Mary prays, praises God, and submits to his plan. John the Baptist, Jesus's cousin is born. Zechariah, John's father, prophesies that John will be a prophet of the Most High—preparing the way of the Lord. Joseph, Mary's betrothed, hears that Mary is pregnant and ponders divorce. An angel of the Lord reassures Joseph that the child is conceived by the Holy Spirit. Mary and Joseph travel to Bethlehem where the child is born. Angels herald his birth. Shepherds come to worship him. When Mary and Joseph bring Jesus to the temple to dedicate him to God, Simeon and Anna recognize their Messiah and praise God.

How gracious of God to condescend to come and live on earth among sinful people.

Immanuel: God is with us! It seems almost impossible to grasp the reality that Jesus, the eternal second person of the divine triune God stepped out of heaven and became a man to identify with our sins (Philippians 2:6–11). He left the glory of heaven to live in the realm of the Evil One in order to save us (John 12:31–32).

This is a foundational truth to Christianity: that Jesus, though he lived as a fully human man, never ceased to be fully God, the Creator and Sustainer of all things—do you believe it?

> Father, help me to more fully understand who this unique God-Man Jesus is, and how believing in him reconciles sinful me to holy you. Holy Spirit, please give me the inner peace that comes with understanding. Precious Jesus, please live out your life in me as I surrender all to you.

SEPTEMBER 26

Matthew 2–3; Mark 1:2–11; Luke 2:41–3:18, 21–22

Jesus came up out of the water. And a voice came from heaven
saying, "You are my beloved Son, and I am fully pleased with you."
—Mark 1:10a, 11

After the wise men visit King Herod is greatly disturbed. An angel
of the Lord tells Joseph to flee to Egypt to save Jesus's life. Joseph
leaves immediately. Herod murders all the baby boys. After Herod
dies, Joseph returns and settles in Nazareth. About thirty years later
Jesus's cousin, John, begins preaching and baptizing. Jesus comes to
John; John knows he is baptizing the sinless Lamb of God.

How gracious of God to publicly affirm Jesus's divinity and
righteous life.

If there were any sin in Jesus he would have repented. There was
no sin (1 Peter 2:22). There was no repentance. There was only full
obedience and complete pleasure from the Father.

We know that any offering in the sacrificial system—whether
a bull, ram, sheep, lamb, goat, or bird—must be perfect, without
defects of any kind (Leviticus 1:3, 10, 14). So must be the final
sacrifice, the sacrificial Lamb who takes away the sin of the world
(John 1:29). Jesus is the perfectly righteous sacrifice who died for the
unrighteous (1 Peter 3:18). The sacrifice of Jesus's body on the cross
cancelled our sin and settled God's holy wrath (Romans 3:25–26).

Do you believe this foundational truth: that Jesus is God's only
Son and that he lived a sinless life, and is therefore the only sufficient
sacrifice for your sin?

> Heavenly Father, I thank you for your Word which tells me
> that I have been made holy through the sacrifice of the body
> of Jesus Christ once for all (Hebrews 10:10).

SEPTEMBER 27

Matthew 4:1–11; Mark 1:12–13; Luke 4:1–15; John 1:19–2:25

> Immediately the Holy Spirit compelled
> Jesus to go into the wilderness.
> —Mark 1:12

The Spirit compels Jesus into the wilderness; for forty days he eats nothing. The Devil tempts him and Jesus resists every temptation. The Devil leaves and angels tend to Jesus. Jesus, filled with the Holy Spirit, begins his public ministry teaching in the synagogues. He calls disciples; they believe he is the Messiah and follow him. At a wedding Jesus turns water into wine. He chases the moneychangers out of the temple. Because of the miraculous signs he does in Jerusalem during the Passover many people are convinced that he is the Messiah.

How gracious of God to reveal to us Jesus's authority, divinity, and power.

That Jesus is both fully human and fully God is a difficult concept to grasp. It is even more overwhelming to try to understand how God the Father filled God the Son with God the Holy Spirit. None of us can completely comprehend these great truths, but God has revealed them to us and by faith we accept them as God's true Word (1 Corinthians 2:10–16).

Though there are hidden things that you and I will never fully understand in this life, however, will you apply the truths that you are accountable for—the truths God has revealed—and trust him with the things he has chosen not to reveal (Deuteronomy 29:29)?

> Father, I thank you that I do not have to understand everything about you to know that you are the truth that enlightens me and the authority that leads me. Thank you for your Word that equips me for the life to which you've called me and for your Holy Spirit who leads me in truth.

SEPTEMBER 28

Luke 3:19–20; John 3:1–4:45

After dark one evening, a Jewish religious leader named
Nicodemus, a Pharisee, came to speak with Jesus.
—John 3:1

After dark one evening Nicodemus comes to Jesus and confesses that
everyone knows God has sent Jesus to teach them. Nicodemus says that
Jesus's miracles are sufficient proof that God is with him. Jesus tells
Nicodemus that he must be born again to see the Kingdom of God.

John the Baptist's disciples are concerned that John is losing
followers to Jesus. John replies that he is not the Messiah, he is there
only to prepare the way for him.

The woman at the well recognizes Jesus as the Messiah. He
knows everything about her. She brings others to him and many
believe.

How gracious of God to have time, and answers, for everyone
who seeks truth.

We know that God's Word tells us that we are all under the
power of sin and no one seeks God (Romans 3:10). Yet, we also know
as believers that we were drawn to the truth (John 6:41–45), and
when we sought truth, we found Jesus (John 14:6).

Have you sought and received truth? Have you been born again—
not by a physical act, not by your own will—but by the power of the
Holy Spirit, just as Jesus explained to Nicodemus? Like the woman
at the well, who in your life needs to see Jesus as he really is? Are you
willing to decrease so that Jesus might increase in your life?

> O Lord God, Almighty, I thank you for drawing me to seek
> the truth that saves me—to seek Jesus. Please humble me
> so that it becomes my sincere desire to decrease so that he
> might increase.

SEPTEMBER 29

Matthew 4:12–25; 8:14–17; Mark 1:14–39;
Luke 3:23a; 4:16–44; John 4:46–54

But the truth is, no prophet is accepted in his own hometown.
—Luke 4:24

Jesus goes to Nazareth, his boyhood home. In the synagogue, Jesus stands to read and then proclaims that the Scripture is fulfilled in their hearing. The people reject him and want to kill him but Jesus slips away. On the shores of Galilee, Jesus calls Simon, Andrew, James, and John as disciples and they immediately leave all and follow Jesus.

How gracious of God to teach us how to understand Scripture in context.

As we read the Law, the Prophets, and the cycle of rebellion and repentance that is the Old Testament, we may forget that it is not only Israel's history but also God's story of the redemption of humankind. However, as we read the Bible focusing on Jesus, seeing him as the true north of Scripture, we understand both the Old and the New Testaments more fully. The Gospel writers consistently tell us that Jesus fulfills Scripture and Jesus himself tells us that he is the fulfillment of Scripture (Matthew 5:17). All of Scripture points to Jesus (Luke 24:27; John 5:39). If we reject any portion of Scripture for any reason, like the people of Nazareth, we reject Jesus.

Why do you read the Bible, is it simply to gain knowledge, to know Jesus, or both? How is your increasing understanding of who Jesus is increasing your understanding of Scripture?

> Father, there is much in Scripture that I don't understand, but I don't want to reject or set any part of it aside. I want to discover Jesus on every page, please open my eyes to see him so that I am compelled to leave all and follow him.

SEPTEMBER 30

Matthew 8:1–4; 9:1–17; Mark 1:40–2:22; Luke 5

Oh, Lord, please leave me—I'm too much
of a sinner to be around you.
—Luke 5:8b

Jesus preaches and great crowds press in on him so he gets into a boat and Simon pushes out. After he finishes preaching, Jesus tells Simon to let down the nets. Simon tells Jesus he's fished all night without a catch; but he tries again and the nets are full. Simon falls to his knees and confesses he is too much of a sinner to be around Jesus.

How gracious of God to convict the heart of the sinner, and bring him to repentance.

You and I know the secret sins in our lives. We know how we have tried to cover our unrighteousness with church activities, Bible study, religious work, and community service. We know that at one time we stood rightly condemned. Moreover, we know that when we fell on our knees in humble submission and repentance before our Lord Jesus Christ that we were cleansed and redeemed (Romans 5:6; Hebrews 9:12, 1 Peter 1:18–19).

What is your response to Jesus's holiness? Do you turn away, disgusted at your own sin? Do you ask Jesus to leave; overwhelmed by his righteousness? Do you recognize and confess your sinfulness? Do you follow Jesus?

> God, I know that Jesus didn't come to patch up my old life, but to pour out his life for me and create in me a completely new life. Thank you that I, a sin-sick seeker, have been healed and redeemed. Thank you for the precious blood of Jesus—the only thing that can cleanse me of sin, remove my guilt and shame and secure my eternal life with you.

grace OCTOBER

OCTOBER 1

Matthew 12:1–21; Mark 2:23–3:6; Luke 6:1–11; John 5

You search the Scriptures because you believe they give you
eternal life. But the Scriptures point to me! Yet you refuse
to come to me so that I can give you this eternal life.
—John 5:39–40

When Jesus's disciples break off heads of wheat and eat the grain, the
Pharisees protest because it is the Sabbath. When Jesus heals a lame
man the Jewish leaders object because it is the Sabbath. Jesus declares
he is the master of the Sabbath and the Pharisees discuss plans to
kill Jesus. Jesus knows what they are planning and leaves the area.

How gracious of God to promise and provide eternal life that
we seek.

The religious leaders had every opportunity to accept Jesus as
the Messiah, the Son of God, the Savior of the world, and the one
who could provide the eternal life they sought to attain through
their rules and traditions (Galatians 1:11–16). Because Jesus didn't
fit their ideals they rejected him.

We know that God planted the desire for eternal life within each
one of us (Ecclesiastes 3:11), but what we must learn is that nothing
outside of the eternal God can satisfy that desire. Like the religious
leaders, we may try to fill the void with things outside of God; even
religious activities and rituals.

Are there things about Jesus that don't fit your idea of who he
should be? Are you searching for a sense of completeness outside of
God? Are you searching for eternal life? Will you look to Jesus?

Almighty One, the Scriptures point to you and reveal you
as the source and completion of all my yearnings. Help me
to rest in you today so that I can rest in you for all eternity.

OCTOBER 2

Matthew 5:1–6:4; Mark 3:7–19; Luke 6:12–36

"There were people from all over ... They had
come to hear him and to be healed ... and they
were all cured." (Luke 6:17b, 18a, 19b)

News of Jesus spreads and huge crowds come to see him for themselves. Jesus goes up a mountain and sits down to teach the people about God's blessing. God blesses people who realize their need for him, who mourn, who are gentle and lowly, who have a hunger and thirst for justice, who are merciful, who have a pure heart, who work for peace, and who are persecuted. Jesus teaches that his followers must be salt and light. He teaches that what they think matters as much as what they do. He teaches with authority.

How gracious of God to teach publicly the lifestyle his children should live.

Jesus's message is the same for us today: the gospel is not about rule-keeping, but about living out our faith in every area of our lives (Micah 6:8, Isaiah 1:10–17). We must recognize, as Jesus taught, that we have nothing apart from God; we are spiritual paupers who are wretched, pitiful, poor, blind, and naked (Revelation 3:17–18). Only in Christ do we have what we need to live blessed lives (Ephesians 1:3). Our religious rule-keeping purchases nothing.

Have you gone to see Jesus for yourself? Have you received from him what is needed to live a life that receives God's blessings?

> Father, I confess that sometimes I do things for all the wrong reasons; I want to appear righteous and religious, holy and happy. I forget that apart from you I have nothing and I bring nothing. Jesus, you are my righteousness, my holiness, and my wealth. Only in you am I blessed.

OCTOBER 3

Matthew 6:5–7:29; Luke 6:37–49

Not all people who sound religious are really godly. They may refer to me as "Lord," but they still won't enter the Kingdom of Heaven.
—Matthew 7:21

Jesus warns that it is impossible to serve two masters: Money and God. He tells people not to worry about everyday things because God will meet their needs.

Jesus teaches believers to beware of false prophets who appear as sheep, but who are really wolves out to kill and destroy. Jesus teaches that words and actions reveal false prophets: just as a tree is known by its fruit, so is a person. A wise person listens to and obeys Jesus's teaching.

How gracious of God to open our eyes and meet our need for truth.

We are precious to God and he will meet our needs, as we trust in him (Psalm 23:1). False prophets will try to lead us away from trusting God (Galatians 4:17). They will twist God's words and even use the Bible to teach hatred, or downplay sin. We must listen carefully to what we hear and what we see; not everyone who claims to speak for Jesus actually does. We must never judge or condemn a person's heart—only God knows the heart—but we must weigh the words and the actions of those to whom we listen against the truth of Scripture (1 Thessalonians 5:21); God will never contradict himself.

To whom do you listen? What fruit does their life bear? Do their words point to Jesus, to themselves, to another religious leader, or to a religion?

O God, please give me discernment to be alert to false teaching that tempts me to place my trust in anyone or anything other than my precious Savior and Lord, Jesus Christ of Nazareth.

OCTOBER 4

Matthew 8:5–13; 11; Luke 7

Are you really the Messiah we've been waiting for,
or should we keep looking for someone else?
—Matthew 11:3

Imprisoned, John the Baptist hears about the things Jesus is doing and sends his disciples to ask Jesus if he is the One. Jesus tells John's disciples to tell John what they have heard and seen: the lame walk, the blind see, the deaf hear, and the dead are raised to life.

How gracious of God to give evidence of the truth to the sincere seeker.

In the darkness of prison John needed the light of truth and God provided it. It is not out of the question that you or I, even though we are believers, might also have moments of doubt (Mark 9:24). Is Jesus the One (John 1:1)? Is this the truth (John 14:6)? Is he the only way of salvation (Acts 4:12)? Is the Bible God's true, inerrant word (Matthew 5:18)? Is my eternal destiny secure (Philippians 1:6; Jude 1:24)?

When we are in darkness and need the light of truth, we too, must take our questions to God in prayer. As we seek truth in his Word and learn his character, then we can accept the evidence that he provides.

What evidence has God provided you to verify that Jesus is the One? Have you chosen to believe on him for your salvation? If not, why not today? To whom would God have you share the reassuring truth of the gospel with today?

Father, I thank you for the Light that has overcome the darkness. Thank you for Jesus, the way, the truth, and the light. Thank you for the reassurance that I am in Christ Jesus and no one can snatch me out of his hand.

OCTOBER 5

Matthew 12:22–13:9; Mark 3:20–4:20; Luke 8:1–8, 19–21

> He took his twelve disciples with him ... and
> many others who were contributing from their own
> resources to support Jesus and his disciples
> —Luke 8:1b, 3b

Jesus travels to cities and villages to announce the good news concerning the Kingdom of God. His twelve disciples and some women he healed travel with them. Many others contribute from their own resources to support Jesus and his disciples.

How gracious of God to give ordinary people the privilege of using their resources to support Jesus's ministry.

During the time of his incarnation Jesus accepted the generosity of others and he continues to give us the same privilege and opportunity today; we can contribute to the work that God is doing in the world. Circumstances may prevent us from going to the mission field—either at home or to a foreign country—to take God's Word to lost and hurting people; however, we must support the ones who can go. The world is dying and people need to hear that Jesus is their only hope.

Because God owns everything he does not need our financial help (Psalm 24:1, Exodus 19:5), however, he allows us to give. As God, Jesus has no needs; he was and is self-sufficient and he sustains all things (Job 38; John 1:1; Hebrews 1:3), and yet, he calls us to serve.

How are you supporting Jesus with your finances? your lifestyle? your words? your time? your home? your family? your education? and your knowledge? What are you withholding?

> Father, I thank you for reminding me that all I have, and all
> I am, is yours. Please help me to manage the resources you
> have entrusted to me with an open hand and a generous heart.

OCTOBER 6

Matthew 8:23–27; 13:10–52; Mark 4:21–41; Luke 8:9–18, 22–25

> So be sure to pay attention to what you hear. To those
> who are open to my teaching, more understanding
> will be given. But to those who are not listening, even
> what they think they have will be taken away.
> —Luke 8:18

Jesus tells the disciples why he teaches in parables: People see the things he does, but they don't see or accept truth. They hear the things he says, but they don't hear or receive truth. This fulfills the prophecy of Isaiah: people have hardened their hearts and closed their eyes.

How gracious of God to give to people who are open to Jesus's teaching eyes to see, ears to hear, and a mind that understands.

We've all heard and perhaps even used many excuses for not reading the Bible; and one in particular may be: it's all in parables. Excuses are not reasons. Is there any reason why we would not desire to read and know God's Word—unless we have already hardened our heart (Hebrews 3:7–19)? God promises to give understanding to anyone who seeks it (Psalm 119:125; Luke 24:45). To those who choose to harden their hearts, even what they *think they have* will be taken away.

As you read your Bible, listen to your pastor, or you sit in your Bible study class are your ears, eyes, heart, and mind open only to your agenda—confirming what you think you already know—or are they open to what God wants to teach you?

God, please soften my heart to receive and apply your Word. Open my eyes to see you, open my ears to hear your truths, and open my mind to understand your wisdom as you would have me receive it.

OCTOBER 7

Matthew 8:28–34; 9:18–26; Mark 5; Luke 8:26–56

> For she thought to herself, "If I can just touch his
> clothing, I will be healed." Immediately the bleeding
> stopped and she could feel that she had been healed.
> —Mark 5:28–29

Surrounded by crowds, a sick woman touches Jesus. Feeling the power go out from him, Jesus asks who touched him. The healed woman falls to her knees before Jesus. Jesus tells the woman that her faith has made her well. Jesus continues to Jairus' house where people weep and wail because Jairus' daughter has died. Jesus tells the little girl to get up. Restored to life, the girl immediately stands and walks around.

How gracious of God to put Jesus near people who need to be healed.

All of us have seasons when we need physical, emotional, or spiritual healing. There may be times when we feel as if we are at the end of our rope and holding on by a thread. Perhaps we need restoration and new life (Psalm 34:17–22). Maybe we need to learn how to stand and walk. Whether we are lost in a crowd or isolated and alone, Jesus is our only hope and he is near (James 4:8).

Where are you right now? Are you on the fringe? Are you reaching out to touch Jesus? Are there dying people in your life? Will you intentionally bring Jesus to them?

Almighty God, help me to see the hurting, the sick, the desperate, and the despised who are living on the fringe, and show me what you would have me do to bring them to you. Please keep me from being a barrier that keeps anyone from touching you, but rather help me be a conduit to usher them into your presence.

OCTOBER 8

Matthew 9:27–10:42; 13:53–58; Mark 6:1–13; Luke 9:1–6

The Jesus told them, "A prophet is honored everywhere except
in his own hometown and among his own family." And so
he did only a few miracles there because of their unbelief.
—Matthew 13:57b–58

Jesus's neighbors know Jesus as the carpenter. They are astonished by
his teaching and yet offended that he is teaching them. They question
where he gets his wisdom and his power to perform miracles. They
refuse to believe in him. Because of their unbelief, Jesus could not
do many miracles among them except to place his hands on a few
sick people and heal them.

How gracious of God to give people the opportunity to walk
by faith.

Jesus was the boy these people had grown up alongside, but
he has grown into a man who speaks with divine authority and
performs miracles (Matthew 7:28–29). How big is the leap of faith
that they must take to believe in someone who contradicts what they
think they know?

Ours is the same dilemma: is Jesus a man, or is he God. Was he a
man who became God? Was he God who became a man? We walk by
faith as we believe that Jesus Christ is God who humbled himself and
took on a human form becoming the man we know as Jesus Christ
(John 1:1, 14; Philippians 2:5–11). If we refuse to walk in faith and
believe in Jesus his power among us will be limited. Faith unlocks
the power of Almighty God (1 Peter 1:3–9). Unbelief holds it at bay.

Who is Jesus to you?

God, I know that I experienced the greatest miracle when
you saved me. Please help me to walk humbly by faith so
that your power is displayed in my life.

OCTOBER 9

Matthew 14; Mark 6:14–56; Luke 9:7–17; John 6:1–21

> Send the crowds away so they can go to the
> villages and buy food for themselves.
> —Matthew 14:15c

The apostles return from their mission trip and debrief Jesus. Jesus also hears that John the Baptist has been murdered. Jesus and the apostles slip away to be alone but crowds follow them. Jesus has compassion on the people, and teaches and heals them. It grows late and the multitudes are hungry. The disciples want to send them away but Jesus tells the disciples that isn't necessary; he commands them to feed the crowd.

How gracious of God to use ordinary people to meet the needs of others.

Jesus was tired and grieving but he pressed on despite his pain because he had compassion on the people. The disciples knew their resources were inadequate to meet the need of the crowd. Jesus knew his resources were sufficient. As the disciples kept coming to Jesus, they received and distributed what Jesus gave them and everyone was fed.

The only way we can meet the needs of people who come to us is in Jesus's power (Philippians 4:13).

Have waves of grief overtaken you? Are you exhausted and hungry? Are you in pain? Do needy people surround you? Are your resources limited? Will you take what you have to God and let him multiply it and use it to meet the needs of the people who depend on you?

> God, you know when I'm bone dry, exhausted, and seem to have nothing left to give. In those times, will you please take the little bit of hope that I have, and increase it to meet the needs of those who depend on me so that I never send anyone away hungry.

OCTOBER 10

Matthew 15:1–20; Mark 7:1–23; John 6:22–71

So Jesus said again, "I assure you, unless you eat
the flesh of the Son of Man and drink his blood,
you cannot have eternal life within you."
—John 6:53

After Jesus feeds the five thousand, he teaches that he is the bread
of life: the bread from heaven that gives eternal life to everyone who
eats it. He is the living bread. All who eat his flesh and drink his
blood remain in him, and he in them. Those who partake of Jesus
will live because of him. The people murmur in disagreement. The
disciples are confused. Jesus asks if they are offended. Many turn
away and desert Jesus. Jesus asks the disciples if they, too, will leave.
Peter states that there is no one else that gives eternal life, there is no
one else to follow: Jesus is the Holy One of God.

How gracious of God to give Jesus's disciples the ability to
understand Jesus's teaching.

Sometimes the words of Scripture sound offensive because we
don't understand the actual words, the context, or the application.
When that happens we have a choice: walk away as if God's Word
is irrelevant, or search for further clarity (Acts 17:11–12). Like the
disciples, we must choose to believe God's Words and trust that
with the Holy Spirit's help we will eventually grasp their meaning
(John 14:26).

Is there a difficult concept or truth that you find offensive? Are
you contemplating walking away from God's Word because of it? To
whom would you go? Who else has the words of eternal life?

Almighty God, when I struggle with hard things please
humble me to remember that your ways and thoughts are
far above mine; and that my problem lies within me.

OCTOBER II

Matthew 15:21–16:12; Mark 7:24–8:21

"Yes, Lord," she replied, "but even the dogs are permitted
to eat crumbs that fall beneath their master's table."
—Matthew 15:27

Jesus leaves Galilee and travels into Gentile territory. A woman
approaches Jesus and begs him to heal her daughter. She refers to
Jesus as the Son of David and she knows his ability to heal, yet, Jesus
remains silent. The disciples urge Jesus to send her away; Jesus tells
her he is sent to help the people of Israel. The woman worships Jesus
and pleads for help, using Jesus's own words. Jesus grants her request
and heals her daughter.

How gracious of God to respond to every act of faith without
favoritism (Romans 2:11).

Like this woman, our faith must be in Jesus, not our religion,
denomination, economic status, ethnicity, gender, or any other
discriminating factor. We must also realize that no one is entitled
to Gods' grace and mercy. God is not indebted to us—to save us,
care for us, heal us, protect us, feed us, or love us. Nevertheless, he
graciously does (Isaiah 64:8; Ephesians 2).

When we humbly come to Jesus he will never snuff out the
smoldering wick of faith within our hearts nor crush the bruised reed
of belief (Isaiah 42:3). He always gives hope and he always responds
to acts of faith with abundant grace.

Will you pause today and praise God's glorious grace and mercy
as you acknowledge your unworthiness?

O God, in pride and arrogance I often think I deserve all
that I have and sometimes I even feel entitled to more.
God, help me to realize that a crumb of grace from you is a
treasured gift that is sufficient to sustain me.

OCTOBER 12

Matthew 16:13–17:13; Mark 8:22–9:13; Luke 9:18–36

Then Jesus said to the disciples, "If any of you wants
to be my follower, you must put aside your selfish
ambition, shoulder your cross, and follow me."
—Matthew 16:24

When Jesus asks who the people say he is, Peter replies that Jesus is the Messiah. Jesus predicts his death and Peter takes him aside telling him not to say things like that. Jesus sternly rebukes Peter. Jesus teaches the disciples and the crowds that if anyone wants to be his follower, they must put aside ambition, shoulder their cross, and follow him. Anyone who tries to keep his or her life will lose it. Only by giving up one's life for Jesus's sake can one find true life.

How gracious of God to lay out the full cost of following Jesus. We cannot earn or purchase salvation; it is free (Romans 4:16). However, there is a cost to follow Jesus; a cost we must pay daily. We must lay down our lives and submit to him. We know this as the cross for believers. It is the place where our desires, plans, and will for ourselves intersect with God's desires, plans, and will for us. We must lay down our will and pick up God's plan (Luke 14:25–30). That is the cost of discipleship.

Are you willing to pay the cost?

Heavenly Father, please keep me from thinking of my salvation as a "get-out-of-hell-free" ticket that was punched when I said some words in church. Today, I lay down my life and take up the beautiful true life that you have planned for me. Today, I surrender all to Jesus, so that he might live fully in me.

OCTOBER 13

Matthew 17:14–8:35; Mark 9:14–50; Luke 9:37–50

At the foot of the mountain they found a great crowd
surrounding the other disciples, as some teachers
of religious law were arguing with them.
—Mark 9:14

After Jesus experiences the transfiguration on the mountain, he descends with Peter, James, and John into a crowd of arguing people. One man asks Jesus to heal his son who is possessed by an evil spirit. The disciples can't cast out the evil spirit. Jesus says that anything is possible if a person believes. The man believes and asks for help with his doubts. Jesus casts out the evil spirit.

How gracious of God to demonstrate his power over evil in the real world.

After a spiritual mountaintop experience it can be difficult to return to the real world that awaits us at the foot of the mountain. The real world can be harsh; however, real faith is what enables us to trudge through the ordinary day-to-day where emotions rise and fall. Sometimes it seems wickedness thrives at the foot of the mountain, but we know that evil can only operate where God allows it, and only for as long as God allows (Job 1; Revelation 12:12).

Are you trying to maintain a mountaintop experience with Jesus? Will you trust that Jesus is powerful enough to help you navigate the harsh reality of the real world?

> God, sometimes I don't like living at the foot of the mountain, but I know that this is where you have me. Help me rely on your power to overcome the things the enemy uses to try to discourage and keep me from trusting in you.

OCTOBER 14

Matthew 8:18–22; Luke 9:51–62; John 7:1–8:20

When the crowds heard him say this, some of them
declared, "This man surely is the Prophet." Others said
"He is the Messiah." Still others said, "But he can't be!"
So the crowd was divided in their opinion about him.
—John 7:40–41a, 43

Controversy follows Jesus. There is much discussion about Jesus
among the crowds: some say he is a wonderful man and some say he
is a fraud and a deceiver. The leaders question Jesus's wisdom and the
crowds question if Jesus is the Messiah. The Pharisees accuse Jesus of
making false claims about himself when he refers to his Father. Jesus
tells them that if they knew him, they would know the Father, too.

How gracious of God to bring every individual to a point of
personal decision.

No one can decide for us whether to believe Jesus is who he
claims to be, and no one else's decision can affect our eternal destiny.
We must personally decide: is Jesus the Messiah, the Alpha and the
Omega, the Bread of Life, and the only way to the Father (John
4:26; 6:35; 14:6; Revelation 22:13). Either Jesus is completely who
he says he is, or he is a liar. Either we accept Jesus as our Savior *and*
our Lord, or we reject him as neither (Luke 14:25–27). Not to decide
is to reject him completely (Acts 4:12).

What have you decided? Have you received Jesus as your Savior
and your Lord?

> Most Gracious God, I thank you for bringing me to a place
> of decision and for giving me the faith that is necessary to
> make that decision. Thank you for the assurance that Jesus
> is my eternal Savior and the Lord of my life.

OCTOBER 15

Luke 10:1–11:13; John 8:21–59

But don't rejoice just because evil spirits obey you; rejoice
because your names are registered as citizens of heaven.
—Luke 10:20

Jesus sends seventy-two disciples ahead of him to all the towns
and villages he plans to visit. He sends them with instructions for
ministry and with authority in his name. They return rejoicing
that even the demons obey them. Jesus reminds them that their joy
must not be on account of their works but because their names are
written in heaven.

How gracious of God to rebuke spiritual pride and set priorities
aright.

We may accomplish much in Jesus's name, but our rejoicing
must not be in what we accomplish; rather we rejoice that we are
citizens of heaven. Anything we accomplish for the Kingdom of
God, is not because of our abilities, but because we have access to
the King who empowers us. We can do nothing of eternal value
apart from him (John 15:5), but in him, there is no limit to what he
might accomplish through us (Ephesians 3:20–21). That our names
are written in heaven is assurance that the Eternal One has saved us
and our citizenship is secure (Philippians 3:20; Hebrews 12:23–24).

Are you a citizen of heaven? Are you living and serving in Christ's
power and under his authority? Do you rejoice in Jesus's power as
you celebrate the glory of God in the victories you experience?

Almighty God, please keep me grounded in the truth that
as your child, a citizen of heaven, I am on this earth for
your use. I rejoice that you have chosen me, saved me, and
empowered me for your good purpose.

OCTOBER 16

Luke 11:14–12:34

Dear friends, don't be afraid of those who want to kill
you. They can only kill the body; they cannot do any
more to you. But I'll tell you whom to fear. Fear God.
—Luke 12:4–5a

Jesus casts out demons and the leaders claim Jesus's power is from the
devil. The crowd presses in; Jesus tells them they live in evil times
and in an evil generation. He rebukes the Pharisees and experts in
religious law. The Pharisees and teachers of the law are offended.
The crowds grow until thousands are milling about. Jesus warns
them to beware of the hypocrisy of the Pharisees and not to fear
them. Jesus promises that anyone who acknowledges him on earth,
he will acknowledge that person in the presence of God's angels.

How gracious of God to minimize the illegitimate things his
people might fear.

We may fear many things in this world, however, there is very
little that we need to fear. Remembering that God is in control of all
things removes our fear (Job 42:2; 2 Chronicles 20:6). God's children
are not victims; nothing happens to you or me that God does not
allow (Job 1). We need not fear what others think of us, or what they
think they can do to us (Isaiah 41:10–14, Romans 8:15–17, 31–39).
Even the power of death has been removed (Hebrews 2:14–15).

What do you fear? Do you fear things more than you fear God?
Do you fear things because they seem bigger than God? Does it
comfort you to remember that nothing is outside the sovereign
control of our God?

God, please cause me to fear you, your name, your amazing
power, and your divine sovereignty more than anything else
in this world.

OCTOBER 17

"It was not because of his sins or his parents' sins," Jesus answered.
"He was born blind so the power of God could be seen in him."
—John 9:3

Jesus heals a man who has been blind from birth. The disciples ask
Jesus whose sin caused the blindness. Jesus tells them the blindness
isn't a consequence of sin, but a means to display God's power.

How gracious of God to give a glimpse of his purpose and plan
from his perspective.

We all have differences that set us apart from the rest of the
world. Unfortunately, sometimes we judge those differences as being
less than perfect or as the product of sin. We wonder if we, or others,
did something worthy of God's punishment. God sees the bigger
picture and assures us that every circumstance of our lives is for
his glory and our eternal good (Psalm 111:2–3; Romans 8:28–29).
Why, like the disciples, do we make negative assumptions about
differences? Wouldn't it be wiser if instead we strove to see God's
glory in the difference?

Will you look for the image of God and the display of his
power in every person? in yourself? in your difference? in your
handicap? in your disability? in your shortcoming? and in your
less-than-perfectness?

> God, I confess, sometimes I get frustrated and wonder why
> you allow difficult things? Then I remember that we live in
> a world that rejected you and is under the curse. I also know
> that you God, are sovereign, and all things have a purpose.
> Father, please open my eyes to see the display of your glory
> and power in all the differences you allow.

OCTOBER 18

Luke 13:22–14:24; John 10

After he has gathered his own flock, he walks ahead
of them, and they follow him because they recognize
his voice. They won't follow a stranger; they will run
from him because they don't recognize his voice.
—John 10:4–5

Jesus provides an illustration of a true shepherd: A true shepherd
enters through the gate. When he calls his sheep, they hear him and
come out to him because they recognize his voice. Jesus explained
that he is the gate for the sheep. Those who come through him will be
saved. He is the good shepherd who lays down his life for the sheep.
He knows his sheep and his sheep know him and follow his voice.

How gracious of God to tune our ears to hear and recognize the
voice of our Good Shepherd.

There are many voices vying for our attention every minute of
every day. There are voices trying to persuade us to do this, buy
that, and go wherever. Voices challenge our point of view and our
foundational moral code. All day long people talk and we listen.

We also listen to the inner voice that tells us we are too fat or too
thin, too weak, too poor, too cowardly, or too foolish. The voices of
our neighbors, children, siblings, parents, bosses, teachers, pastors,
and friends pull us in every direction.

To whom do you listen? Do you know how to recognize Jesus's
voice? Whose voice have you trained your ear to hear? Who are you
following (Isaiah 30:21)?

> God, please help me to hear Jesus's voice over the cacophony
> of voices that distract me and try to orchestrate my life.
> Please tune my ear to clearly hear him and embolden me to
> follow him.

OCTOBER 19

Luke 14:25–17:10; John 11:1–37

So he returned home to his father. And while he was still a long distance away, his father saw him coming. Filled with love and compassion, he ran to his son, embraced him, and kissed him."
—Luke 15:20

Jesus uses illustrations to teach sinners about the joy in heaven when one sinner returns to God. It is like the joy of the shepherd who finds one lost sheep, like the woman who rejoices after she sweeps her entire house to find one lost coin, and like the father who celebrates when the wayward son he has been watching and waiting for returns home.

How gracious of God to value every soul.

We have value simply because we are made in the image of God (Genesis 1:27; 9:6). Whether a person is in the womb or has lived a long life, is an acclaimed celebrity or a virtual unknown, is wealthy or impoverished, we all have God's image in us and that makes us a treasured prize.

Who do you know that needs to hear they are of great worth to you simply because they are who they are? Who do you know that needs to hear they are of great worth to God? Have you thought about your worth to God—you are so precious to God that he sent Jesus, his one and only Son to die for you (John 3:16).

> God, your welcoming and loving arms are the sweetest place I know—they are home to me. Thank you for searching for me, for reaching out to me, and for welcoming me into your kingdom. I love you, Lord, O, how I love you!

OCTOBER 20

Luke 17:11–18:8; John 11:38–57

Jesus responded, "Didn't I tell you that you
will see God's glory if you believe?"
—John 11:40

Jesus hears that Lazarus is sick and deliberately delays his return to Lazarus's home in Bethany. Jesus tells the disciples that Lazarus's sickness will not end in death. Lazarus dies. Jesus and the disciples set out for Bethany. At Lazarus's grave, Jesus tells Lazarus's sister, Martha, to roll the stone away. Martha hesitates; Lazarus has been dead four days—it will stink. Jesus challenges her: Do you want to see the glory of God? Martha obediently rolls the stone away, Jesus calls for Lazarus and Lazarus comes out.

How gracious of God to show his glory.

To see God's glory, we have to believe in and obey Jesus. We must choose to obey even though we do not know what the outcome will be (Isaiah 6:8). We need not worry about how bad something might smell. We need not worry about what God will ask us to do next. If we want to see the glory of God, we must obey in the one thing God is asking us to do today.

Do you want to see the glory of God? Have you forfeited seeing his glory in the past because you were afraid of the circumstances? What is the one thing God is asking you to do today?

God, I confess, there have been times when I failed to obey because I couldn't see beyond what you were asking me to do, or because I was afraid of the fallout, or because I wanted to be in control. God, I repent of that fear; will you help me to fearlessly do the one thing you ask, and trust you with whatever follows.

OCTOBER 21

Matthew 19; Mark 10:1–31; Luke 18:9–30

*I assure you, anyone who doesn't have their kind of
faith will never get into the Kingdom of God.*
—Mark 10:15

Parents want Jesus to touch and bless their children. The disciples
see the children as a bother and turn them away. Jesus rebukes the
disciples and tells them to bring the children close so he can lay
his hands on them and pray for them. Jesus uses the children to
illustrate the type of faith everyone must have if they are to enter
the Kingdom of God.

How gracious of God to embrace children and honor their faith.

We are not to be childish—adults who act like children; but we
are to be childlike—adults who, like children, exhibit complete trust
and faith in God without question. Whether running, laughing,
dancing, sitting, or singing children are comfortable exhibiting age-
appropriate behavior around people who love them. Children simply
trust and love the authorities in their lives until given a reason not
to. Children cling tightly to the people who love them and believe
what they tell them. Unfortunately, as we grow older, we become
skeptical and forget who it is that loves us the most (1 John 4:9–10).

What grown-up biases do you need to abandon in order to
embrace a childlike faith?

> God, I want to enjoy the total abandon of a child sitting at
> your feet in this life. Help me to remember that as much as
> I love you, it cannot compare to how much you love me, and
> therefore I must believe what you command me to believe,
> and cling to you with every fiber of my being. Please remove
> anything that prevents me from living in childlike faith.

OCTOBER 22

Matthew 20; Mark 10:32–52; Luke 18:31–19:27

"Zacchaeus!" he said. "Quick, come down! For
I must be a guest in your home today."
—Luke 19:5b

Zacchaeus, a wealthy tax collector, wants to see Jesus so he runs
ahead of the crowd and climbs a tree. Jesus comes by, looks up, and
calls him by name. Zacchaeus quickly climbs down and takes Jesus
to his house. Zacchaeus shows himself to be a son of Abraham by
generously giving away his wealth and repaying the people he had
overcharged.

How gracious of God to put Jesus in the path of people who
sincerely seek him.

For most of us it is very easy to see Jesus—we can open any
number of translations of the Bible that we have on our bookshelves,
turn on the TV, the radio, or the computer and hear a great sermon
about Jesus, and we can go to church on Sunday. Jesus has never
been difficult to find (John 18:20). However, that does not remove
our responsibility to seek him, nor does it remove our responsibility
to welcome him into our lives when we meet him (Acts 17:22–31).

How far are you willing to go to meet Jesus? How sincerely do
you seek him? Do you look for him on every path you walk? Has he
called you by name? Have you taken him home?

Heavenly Father, I thank you for putting Jesus in my path.
Thank you for opening my heart to respond to Jesus's call
and take him into my home. Please humble me so that I
surrender my pride and yield to the changes you want to
make in my character so that everyone who comes into my
house will see the joy of my salvation.

OCTOBER 23

Matthew 21:1–11; 26:6–13; Mark 11:1–11; 14:3–9;
Luke 19:28–44; John 12:1–36

Jesus replied, "Leave her alone. She did it
in preparation for my burial."
—John 12:7

Jesus is at the home of Mary, Martha, and Lazarus. Martha busily prepares a meal for Jesus and the disciples. Mary takes a jar of expensive perfume and pours it on Jesus's feet. The house fills with the fragrance. Judas complains that the perfume should have been sold and the money given to the poor. Jesus defends Mary explaining that what she does is in preparation for his burial.

How gracious of God to defend Mary on the spot.

Mary worshiped Jesus with abandon. It didn't matter to her who was there, or what anyone else thought. She worshiped in spirit and in truth. God desires that we worship him in spirit and in truth, and that requires worship with abandon (John 4:24). It means that whatever we do, we do for God alone.

However, there is deep heartache when people misjudge our motives, especially in spiritual matters because it is almost impossible to defend ourselves without sounding self-righteous or spiritually proud. Like Mary, we can trust that God sees our hearts and will defend us (Psalm 35; Matthew 25:34–40) in his way and in his time.

Are you afraid of worshiping with abandon because you are afraid of what other people might think? Is anyone else's thoughts more important than what God is thinking?

> God, I am often self-conscious and afraid of being misunderstood or misjudged. I know you will defend me. Please help me to be more like Mary and less like Judas. Please remove my critical spirit and give me a spirit of generosity as I worship you, keeping my eyes focused only on you.

OCTOBER 24

Matthew 21:12–27; Mark 11:12–33;
Luke 19:45–20:8 John 12:37–50

I have come as a light to shine in this dark world, so that all who
put their trust in me will no longer remain in the darkness.
—John 12:46

It is the final week of Jesus's life on earth. Each day he teaches in the
temple and heals the sick, the blind, and the lame. He receives praise
from little children and he stands up to the religious authorities.
Jesus, the light of the world, shines brightly; yet in the midst of
Jesus's miracles most of the people refuse to believe.

How gracious of God to send the Lord Jesus, not to condemn the
world, not to judge the world, but to save the world (John 3:16–21).

The choice is ours whether we want to put our faith in Jesus
for salvation or not. The choice is ours whether we want to be
condemned or justified (Romans 8:1). Nothing prohibits us from
belief except our own blinded eyes and hardened hearts (Psalm
95). Jesus is the light of truth; to reject him is to choose to live
in darkness—blinding our own eyes (Romans 2:5–11). When we
receive the Light we become children of light; rescued from the
dominion of darkness and brought into the kingdom of the Son
(Ephesians 5:8; Colossians 1:13).

Will you reject the darkness and choose to live in light today?

> Almighty God, I know your plan is perfect and your words
> are true. I pray that Jesus will flood my heart with his
> cleansing light so that no darkness remains. Cause me to live
> for you in such a way that I am a beacon that points people
> to you and your saving truth.

OCTOBER 25

Matthew 21:28–22:33; Mark 12:1–27; Luke 20:9–40

Jesus replied, "Your problem is that you don't know the
Scriptures, and you don't know the power of God."
—Matthew 22:29

The Jewish leaders, leading priests, and teachers of the law plan to
arrest and kill Jesus. The Pharisees send their disciples to ask him
questions so they might accuse him of something. The leaders send
secret agents pretending to be honest men to try to trick Jesus into
saying something to get him arrested. The Sadducees try to trip
Jesus with a hypothetical religious situation. Jesus points out their
ignorance of God's Word.

How gracious of God to address real issues, not contrived ones.

Too often we allow ourselves to get drawn into ridiculous
arguments because we fail to see or address the real issue. Too
often we are distracted from the work of God because we allow
cultural issues that have nothing to do with salvation to draw us
away. We must focus on and tap into the power of God which is
revealed in Christ Jesus our Lord, his life, death, and resurrection
(1 Corinthians 2:2).

Have contrived arguments derailed your ability to contend for
the gospel in a way that is not contentious (Jude 1:3)? Are those
contrived issues clouding your testimony of the grace of God in
Christ Jesus?

> God, sometimes I feel like I need to be able to refute every
> argument presented to me. Please humble me to remember
> that your power is seen in me when I simply tell others how
> your saving grace has changed me. Please humble me and
> remind me that your Word speaks clearly for itself, and that
> in itself it is the power to save souls.

OCTOBER 26

Matthew 22:34–23:39; Mark 12:28–44; Luke 20:41–21:4

Jesus replied, "You must love the Lord your God with all
your heart, all your soul, and all your mind." A second is
equally important: "Love your neighbor as yourself."
—Matthew 22:37, 39

The Pharisees bring a fresh question to trap Jesus: Which
commandment is the greatest. Jesus responds that the greatest
commandment is to love God with all your being and the second is
to love your neighbor as yourself. Jesus tells the people not to follow
the Pharisees and the teachers of the law who love to parade around
in their religious clothes, who love to have others bow to them, who
love the seats of honor, and yet shamelessly try to cover up who they
really are with long public prayers. Jesus rebukes the Pharisees and
teachers of the law for their hypocrisy.

How gracious of God to clarify what we must genuinely love:
God first and then our neighbors.

Nowhere does God tell us to love ourselves and yet that is what
the religious leaders love most—the way they practiced their religion
and their high standing in it. Are we any different? Have we ceded
our understanding of love to the world's philosophy that we must
love ourselves before we can love others, even God (Exodus 20:1)?

Who do you love more: yourself, others, or God? Who do you
esteem most highly? How is that priority manifest in your life,
emotions, actions, and your love for the things of God?

> Father, I confess that sometimes I am all about me. Please
> humble me to set my heart on you, and to love you above all
> else so that every expression of my love flows from a heart
> of pure love.

OCTOBER 27

Matthew 24:1–35; Mark 13:1–31; Luke 21:5–33

For false messiahs and false prophets will rise up
and perform miraculous signs and wonders so as to
deceive, if possible, even God's chosen ones.

—Mark 13:22

As Jesus and his disciples leave the temple, the disciples point out the tremendous buildings and massive stones. Jesus tells the disciples that a day is coming when all these things will be completely demolished. The disciples ask when all this will take place and what will be the signs. Jesus tells them there will be a time of false teaching, wars, earthquakes, famines, and great persecution. There will be horrible days ahead and then he will return. Jesus warns them to be on their guard and watch carefully.

How gracious of God to prepare us to watch for Jesus's return.

Thinking about the Lord's return invigorates us even though we do not know when that day will be (Matthew 24:36). There are differing Bible-based theories regarding the persecution that precedes or accompanies the Lord's return, and we must not allow our theories to divide us as Christians (Ephesians 4:1–4). What we do know for sure is that Jesus's return will be public and victorious (Isaiah 62:11). We also know that God's Word is our protection against deception (2 Timothy 2). And, we know that God's people will persevere in faith (Revelation 14:12).

Are you watching? Are you on guard? Are you persevering in faith?

God, I thank you for your true Word, the Bible, which proclaims the gospel of truth that secures my salvation, enables my perseverance, and builds my faith. God, I know that Jesus's return is a day of impending doom for many; please humble me to lovingly testify to your truth today.

OCTOBER 28

Matthew 24:36–25:46; Mark 13:32–37; Luke 21:34–38

So stay awake and be prepared, because you do
not know the day or hour of my return.
—Matthew 25:13

Jesus teaches about the day when he will return. He calls upon
everyone to watch because no one knows the day or the hour, only
the Father. His return will be unexpected on an ordinary day; and
yet his coming will affect every person living on the earth. It is a
day of judgment. It is a day of glory. It is a day of celebration for
those who know Jesus. It is a day of darkness and destruction for
those who do not.

How gracious of God to warn the world of Jesus's return.

All of us have experienced the excitement of waiting for a big
day—a wedding, a military leave, a graduation, a new job, a baby's
birth, or the arrival of a loved one. We know the energy and joy we
feel as the day grows near. We also know the dread of awaiting a day
of sorrow—the pending death of a loved one, the end of a job, the
foreclosure notice, or the day when a child leaves home.

Are you waiting for Jesus? Are you anticipating his return with
great joy and excitement? Are you dreading his return because
you know it will be a day of judgment for many people that you
love (Joel 1:15)? Will you share with them today the reality—the
imminence—of Jesus's return, before it is too late?

Oh, God, I am alert and prepared, but my heart is breaking
over the lost ones I love who have yet to receive you. Please
give me an opportunity to speak truth to them and lead
them to you.

OCTOBER 29

Matthew 26:1–5, 14–30; Mark 14:1–2, 10–26;
Luke 22:1–30; John 13:1–30

Jesus knew that the Father had given him authority over
everything and that he had come from God and would
return to God. Then he began to wash the disciples' feet.
—John 13:3, 5b

It is the night before the cross and Jesus washes the disciples' feet.

How incomprehensibly gracious of God to illustrate the perfect
heart of a servant.

Jesus knows who he is. He knows his authority. He knows he
will soon die a heinous death on a cross. He knows he will live again.
He knows he will be exalted. He knows he came to serve (Mark
10:45). He serves.

Rarely do we desire the dirty jobs, the menial tasks, or the secret
work of serving in the background. Too often we want to be seen
and thanked. We prefer service that is fitting of our station, our
training, our education, and our reputation. But that's not what it
was like for Jesus the Eternal God, the Alpha and the Omega, the
King of kings and Lord of lords, the Savior, the Son of God and Son
of Man. He chose to do the work of a slave and wash the dirty feet
of a dozen grown men. Knowing who he was, Jesus got up to serve
(Philippians 2:6–11).

As a believer, you are a child of the king, you are royalty, you
have received every spiritual blessing, and you are seated with Jesus
in the heavenly realms (Ephesians 1:3–6, 2:6–7). As such, is there
any service beneath you?

O Lord God Almighty, please forgive my haughty attitude.
Father, please humble me to understand that because I am
your child my role is to serve.

OCTOBER 30

Matthew 26:31–35; Mark 14:27–31;
Luke 22:31–38; John 13:31–15:17

But I have pleaded in prayer for you, Simon, that your faith
should not fail. So when you have repented and returned
to me again, strengthen and build up your brothers.
—Luke 22:32

Peter declares he will never desert Jesus. Jesus declares that Peter will
desert him, and deny him, before the rooster crows. Satan sifts Peter.
Jesus prays that Peter's faith will not fail him. Jesus tells Peter that
after he repents and returns to Jesus, he is to strengthen the brothers.

How gracious of God, to reassure his children that failure is not
the end.

You and I will fail Jesus and ourselves (Romans 7:18–25). We will
fail those we lead and those who love us. The people whom we look up to
and whom we have placed on spiritual pedestals will fail. Nevertheless,
failure is not the end of service. Failure is the beginning of repentance,
restoration, and returning to service (Psalm 85). God promises that he
will not give up on us when we fail; he will not abandon us to our failure.
(Romans 8:31–39; 1 Corinthians 1:8–9; Philippians 1:6).

When you fail yourself, the Lord, your family, or your friends
will you, like Peter, repent and return and use your experience to
strengthen other believers?

> God, please keep me from building pedestals, and from
> putting myself or anyone else upon them. Please help me to
> understand that even though I may fail you, my faith will
> not fail because you are the one who holds my faith secure.
> Thank you for the assurance that you use my failures to
> create an authentic humility in me that opens the door for
> more faithful and sincere service.

OCTOBER 31

John 15:18–17:26

My prayer is not for the world, but for those you have
given me, because they belong to you. Holy Father,
keep them and care for them—all those you have given
me—so that they will be united just as we are.
—John 17:9, 11c

In Jesus's final hours, he prays for the disciples and for you and me.
He prays that we will be one just as he and the Father are one. He
prays that we will be in him so that the world will believe God sent
him. He prays that the Father's love will be in us. He prays that we
will not be taken out of the world, but rather kept safe from the Evil
One. He prays that we will be made pure and holy by his words of
truth.

How gracious of God the Son to pray to God the Father on our
behalf.

Jesus interceded for us when he lived on earth, and in heaven his
life continually pleads for our salvation (Hebrews 7:25). Jesus's words
also give us a template of things for which we should be praying for
others. We should pray to be with God in our plans, thoughts, actions,
words, and service. We should pray for God's love to flow through
us and into the hard-to-love people in our lives. We should pray for
safekeeping from the Evil One as we bring God's love into the world.
We should pray for purity and holiness as we study God's Word.

How do your prayers align with Jesus's prayers for you?

Precious Father, I thank you for Jesus who died in my place
and whose life intercedes for me. Help me to love others as
Jesus loved me and to pray for them as Jesus prayed for me.

grace NOVEMBER

NOVEMBER 1

Matthew 26:36–56; Mark 14:32–52;
Luke 22:39–53; John 18:1–24

"Father, if you are willing, please take this cup of suffering
away from me. Yet I want your will, not mine." Then an
angel from heaven appeared and strengthened him.
—Luke 22:42–43

Jesus agonizes in the Garden of Gethsemane. Grief crushes him. Death awaits him. Face down on the ground he prays and asks God to remove the suffering. Yet, he prays for the Father's will above his own. He accepts the cup the Father has prepared; he goes to meet his betrayer.

How gracious of God the Father to meet God the Son with compassion and strength to enable him to complete the task prepared for him.

You and I will suffer; it is the fate of all Christians as we identify with our Savior (Romans 8:17). However, we will never have to bear the spiritual pain Jesus endured when the sinless Son of Man became sin in our place (2 Corinthians 5:21).

When we receive a cup of suffering we must follow Jesus's example: because the Lord Jesus loved and trusted the Father who prepared the cup, he accepted the cup. We can rest assured that our Father who loves us, also perfectly prepares the cup of our suffering. We can trust that he will surely meet us with compassion, comfort, and strength (2 Corinthians 1:3–11; 12:9–10).

Will you submit your will to the Father and receive the cup of suffering that he has personally prepared for you?

> Father, I submit to you and accept the suffering that you have
> prepared for my good and for your glory. Please strengthen
> me in my weaknesses to follow the example of my Savior as
> I walk this path.

NOVEMBER 2

Matthew 26:57–27:10; Mark 14:53–15:1;
Luke 22:54–71; John 18:25–27

At that moment the Lord turned and looked at Peter ...
And Peter left the courtyard, crying bitterly.
—Luke 22:61a, 62

On the testimony of false witnesses, the high priests convict Jesus of blasphemy. They blindfold Jesus, hit, and spit on him. As Peter warms himself by a fire, a servant girl asks if he is with Jesus. Peter quickly denies being with Jesus. Others ask and Peter swears by God that he does not know the man! They lead Jesus past the courtyard. Jesus makes eye contact with Peter. Peter remembers what the Lord said and he leaves the courtyard crying bitterly.

How gracious of God to allow Peter an intimate moment with Jesus in the middle of the night, in the middle of a crowd, in the middle of sin.

What did Jesus convey to Peter in that glance? Was it a look of forgiveness and compassion, or conviction? Was Peter overwhelmed with the reality of his sin, weakness, and betrayal? In a few hours Peter's sin will be laid upon Jesus's shoulders (1 Peter 2:24). Is Jesus reminding Peter that though he has failed, his faith is still intact? What did Jesus see? What did Peter see, hear, and feel?

Is Jesus looking at you: in the middle of the night? in a crowd? in your loneliness? in your sin? in your denial? in your heartache? in your worry? or in your fear? What is he trying to communicate to you? What are you seeing, hearing, and feeling?

> Father, I know that your penetrating look upon me is not condemnation but conviction that leads me to repentance (John 3:17–18; Romans 8:1). Thank you for the forgiveness and redemption that was purchased for me at the cross.

NOVEMBER 3

Matthew 27:11–31; Mark 15:2–20; Luke 23:1–25;
John 18:28–19:16

"You say that I am a king, and you are right," Jesus said. "I was
born for that purpose. And I came to bring truth to the world.
All who love the truth recognize that what I say is true."
—John 18:37b

Pilate knows the truth: that Jesus is under arrest because the religious
leaders are envious of Jesus. He knows that Jesus committed no
crime and doesn't deserve to die. He knows that Jesus is the King
of the Jews. Pilate has a choice: receive the truth that Jesus is King
or reject that truth. Pilate, anxious to please the crowd, chooses to
reject truth.

How gracious of God to give every person an opportunity to
receive Jesus as King.

We will not go to heaven because of the good things we have
done; we will go to heaven because we have received Jesus as King
(Acts 4:12). The Bible says that whoever wants to come to Jesus may
come; Jesus will not turn away anyone who comes to him (John
6:35–37). There are only two choices: Life or Death. To accept Jesus
as King is to live; to reject him is to die (Luke 12:8–10; John 8:24).

As you look back over your life, how has God used your
circumstances to bring you face to face with Jesus? What have you
chosen, will you accept or reject Jesus as King? To hesitate is to reject.

Almighty God, I do believe that Jesus is the truth. I choose
to accept him and submit to him as King of my life. All to
Jesus—my Sovereign, Lord, Savior, and King—I surrender.

NOVEMBER 4

Matthew 27:32–56; Mark 15:21–41;
Luke 23:26–49; John 19:17–37

This report is from an eye witness giving an accurate
account; it is presented so that you also can believe.
—John 19:35

The crucifixion of Jesus commences. Passersby, criminals, teachers of the law, leading priests, soldiers, disciples, and women witness his death.

How gracious of God to accomplish his perfect plan visibly, publicly, and accurately; recording it for all people of all time (Acts 2:22–23).

Jesus lived a perfect life (1 Peter 2:22). He died on the cross as prophesied (Acts 3:18). On the third day he arose from the dead (Luke 24:21). Eyewitnesses forfeited their lives rather than deny what they knew to be true: that Jesus is the Son of God, the Messiah, and the Savior of the World (Acts 7).

Ours is not a blind faith but a faith that is grounded in facts; we are sure of what we hope for and certain of what we do not see (Hebrews 11:1). We are certain of the crucifixion even though we did not see it; others saw and recorded it for us. Our hope is in the resurrected Jesus whom others saw and who one day we will see. Our hope is not wishful thinking; it is the sure foundation of what we know to be true (1 Peter 1:21).

Are your faith and your hope based on this gospel, the truth of the Lord Jesus Christ? If not, why not? Upon what else can you stand?

My God, your Word convinces me that Jesus bore my sin on the cross and that my life is in him. My hope rests in his cleansing blood and righteousness. Thank you for the promise that I will live forever in the presence of Jesus. Praise his holy name!

NOVEMBER 5

Matthew 27:57–28:15; Mark 15:42–16:13;
Luke 23:50–24:12; John 19:38–20:18

The angel spoke to the women. "Don't be afraid!" he said.
"I know you are looking for Jesus, who was crucified.
He isn't here! He has been raised from the dead."
—Matthew 28:5–6a

A new day dawns and some women go to Jesus's tomb to complete the task of preparing his body. Grief fills them. They arrive at the tomb to find the stone rolled aside and an angel tells them Jesus isn't here: Jesus has risen just as he said he would.

How gracious of God to meet his children in their despair, hopelessness, and grief with the joyous news that Jesus, the Christ, has risen from the dead.

There is no greater announcement that we will ever hear than "He is risen!" There is no emptier place on earth than the tomb where Jesus was laid. There is no brighter sunrise than the morning when death's darkness was defeated by the Light of the World (1 Corinthians 15:54–55). The resurrection of Jesus is the solid ground upon which we stand. We have the power of the resurrection—power that defeats every foe—when we have Jesus (Philippians 3:7–14).

The women ran from the tomb to tell the disciples. To whom do you need to run? Is there time to delay the most important announcement they will ever hear?

> God, when despair is knocking at my door, when circumstances overwhelm me, when hopelessness beckons, and waves of grief tackle me please help me to remember that my Savior lives. He has risen from the grave. He has defeated every foe. He lives! He lives in me and therefore, victory is sure.

NOVEMBER 6

Matthew 28:16–20; Mark 16:12–18;
Luke 24:13–49; John 20:19–21:25

Peter asked Jesus, "What about him, Lord?" Jesus
replied, "If I want him to remain alive until I
return, what is that to you? You follow me."
—John 21:21–22

Jesus makes many appearances to many people after his resurrection. On one occasion, Jesus appears to his disciples and cooks breakfast for them. After eating, Jesus walks with Peter and tells Peter that he will live to be an old man and his death will glorify God. Peter turns, sees John following them, and asks Jesus what about John. Jesus asks Peter what that is to him and then commands Peter to follow him.

How gracious of God to draw our focus to what is important: our individual walk with Christ.

It is not terribly unusual when we are asked to do a work for the Lord that our first thought is about someone else. What about her? Where is she serving? Why can't he do it? God has a perfect work prepared for each one of us and our responsibility, like Peter's, is to walk with Jesus and keep our focus on him (Isaiah 30:21; Ephesians 2:10). Keeping one eye on someone else and one eye on Jesus distorts our vision of both, and renders it impossible to walk a straight path with the Lord Jesus.

What has God asked you to do? Will you step out and follow him wherever he leads?

God, I will follow my Jesus wherever he leads. Please give me clarity to see his leading and courage to walk his path. Whether I am alone or in a crowd, please cause me to keep my eyes on Jesus alone so that I don't stumble trying to walk on someone else's path.

NOVEMBER 7

Mark 16:19–20; Luke 24:50–53; Acts 1–2

No, what you see this morning was predicted
centuries ago by the prophet Joel.
—Acts 2:16

Jesus ascends to heaven. The disciples wait in Jerusalem as Jesus instructed, meeting together and praying with other believers. On the day of Pentecost a sound from heaven—like a roaring windstorm—fills the house. Something that looks like flames appears and settles on each of them. The Holy Spirit fills everyone who is present and enables them to speak in other languages. This confuses the onlookers. Peter tells the people that they are witnessing the fulfillment of an ancient prophecy. Three thousand sinners repent and are saved.

How gracious of God to give his people understanding of the Scriptures.

How often do we fail to understand what is happening in the church today because we have a limited understanding of the Old Testament prophets? Joel's prophecy is exactly what we should be telling people: We are in the last days (Joel 1:15; 2:28–32). The Holy Spirit is poured out! Whoever calls on the name of the Lord will be saved (Romans 10:13)!

Have you heard the prophecies? Have you turned from your sin and turned to God? Will you ask God to help you comprehend so that you more fully see and understand what is happening in the world and in the church today? Who do you know that needs to hear that these ancient prophecies are for them and for their children?

Father, I thank you for the outpouring of your Holy Spirit. Thank you for the indwelling Holy Spirit that interprets your Word to me so that I can understand and share your truths. Help me to understand your Scriptures so that I can understand what you are doing in the world today.

NOVEMBER 8

Acts 3–5

But if it is of God, you will not be able to stop them.
You may even find yourselves fighting against God.
—Acts 5:39

Peter and John teach the people about Jesus—the one who was killed but whom God raised back to life. They call everyone to repent, teaching that there is salvation in the name of Jesus alone. The council of Jewish rulers, elders, and teachers of religious law arrest Peter and John and put them in jail. An angel of the Lord opens the gates of the jail and frees them. Against the threat from the council, the apostles obey God and continue to teach. The council orders their flogging. The apostles rejoice that they are worthy to suffer dishonor for the name of Jesus.

How gracious of God to count his people worthy of suffering.

Suffering because of persecution is not typically a goal for most of us, but it is one the Lord Jesus laid out for his disciples and he told them to rejoice when they are persecuted (Matthew 5:10–12). The god of this age has blinded the minds of unbelievers, therefore, we must preach Jesus Christ as Lord and let his light shine in the darkness that surrounds us (2 Corinthians 4:4–6). Therefore, as Jesus's modern day disciples, we can also expect persecution when we preach Jesus; may we be counted worthy of persecution.

How does your message and your life, align with the apostles' preaching? Are you committed to live as powerfully as you preach? Are your words and actions worthy of persecution?

> God, my words are worthless and my preaching is powerless if I don't live faithfully. May I be counted worthy as I lift up the name of the crucified and risen Jesus.

NOVEMBER 9

Acts 6:1–8:1a

And he fell to his knees, shouting, "Lord, don't charge
them with this sin!" And with that, he died.
—Acts 7:60

The leaders arrest Stephen, a man full of faith and the Holy Spirit,
filled with God's grace and power. Stephen presents his defense to
the council. He starts with Abraham and ends with Jesus, the one
whom they killed. The leaders furiously shake their fists. God opens
heaven and Stephen sees Jesus exalted on high. Stephen proclaims
what he sees. The leaders drag him away and stone him.

How gracious of God to give Stephen the power and the grace
to endure to the end.

When we take a stand for Jesus the world will hate us just as
the bloodthirsty hate the upright (Proverbs 29:10; 1 John 3:12).
However, we must not let fear of persecution guide us and we must
not return hate for hate (Matthew 10:28). God commands us to
return good for evil and pray for those who persecute us (Matthew
5:44). Since God commands us to do this, it stands to reason that
he will enable us to endure and to obey, just as he enabled Stephen.

Who is persecuting you? Will you pray for that person? Will
you pray as if you are the only one praying for them? Will you pray
for their salvation? Will you choose today to return good for evil?

Almighty God, you who live in majestic, beautiful glory,
please strengthen me to stand boldly and unwavering for
the truth without shirking in fear over the potential for
persecution. Because I stand forgiven and justified before
you, I beg you to show mercy toward people who have
treated me unjustly and open their eyes to the joy of your
salvation that can be theirs.

NOVEMBER 10

Acts 8:1b–9:43

But the Lord said, "Go and do what I say.
For Saul is my chosen instrument."
—Acts 9:15a

Saul mercilessly tries to destroy the church, going from house to house dragging out believers and throwing them in jail. He sets out for Damascus to arrest believers there. On the way a brilliant light beams down on him and a voice calls out, "Saul! Why are you persecuting me?" Saul falls to the ground. When he gets up, he is blind. He continues to Damascus. In Damascus, the Lord speaks to Ananias, and tells him to go to Saul. Ananias knows Saul's reputation and questions the Lord's instruction. The Lord tells Ananias to go, because the Lord has a plan for Saul.

How gracious of God to call unlikely people into salvation and service for him.

We know who we were before the Lord opened our eyes to see the light of his truth, we may not like to admit it but we were, like Saul, enemies of God (Romans 5:10).

Perhaps we had the privilege of growing up in a godly home and heard about Jesus; so did Saul. Having the facts is not the same thing as knowing the truth. We may like to think that we were always worthy of God's call; but before we responded to that call in faith, we were lost and condemned self-focused, self-promoting souls living in darkness and gratifying the misguided lusts of our own hearts (Ephesians 2:3).

When did you experience the light of truth halting your selfish forward motion and turning you toward God? Will you write out your conversion story today?

God, thank you for stopping me in my tracks, for calling me to personal and saving faith, and for using me to serve you.

NOVEMBER 11

Acts 10:1–12:5

Now here we are, waiting before God to hear
the message the Lord has given you.
—Acts 10:33b

Peter has a vision of a sheet coming from heaven with all sorts of animals, reptiles, and birds. He hears a voice telling him to get up, kill, and eat. Peter is shocked. Peter knows, and strictly follows, the religion and the traditions of Judaism. The vision repeats three times. The voice from heaven speaks to Peter and declares that if God says something is acceptable, don't say it isn't.

How gracious of God to establish right thinking and actions.

When you and I first became Christians we had old ways of thinking and living that needed correction. As we grew in our relationship with God, we began to realize that some things we had previously thought were acceptable to do, watch, read, experience, or think didn't align with God's way of holiness and righteousness (Amos 7:7–8).

Gradually, as we study God's Word, spend time with him in prayer, and fellowship with other believers, he transforms our minds (Romans 12:1–2). As our thinking changes, our behavior changes.

What old things does God want you to remove from your life? What new way of thinking, new action, new habit, or new relationship is God establishing in your life?

> God, I know that the things you want to remove from my life have no value to me now or in eternity, but it is hard to let go of things that I have held onto so tightly for so long. Please help me let go of everything that prevents me from picking up the wonderful things that you have planned for me.

NOVEMBER 12

Acts 12:6–14:20

One day as these men were worshiping the Lord and
fasting, the Holy Spirit said, "Dedicate Barnabas
and Saul for the special work I have for them."
—Acts 13:2

Barnabas and Saul teach in Antioch for a full year and then the Holy
Spirit calls them to a special work. The men of Antioch lay their
hands on Barnabas and Saul and send them on their way.

How gracious of God to unite the Antioch Christians in
obedience to send their pastors, Saul and Barnabas, to the mission
field.

We love our pastors, teachers, Bible study leaders, ministry
directors, and the other shepherds whom God has placed over us.
When God calls them to another place of service it is not always easy
to watch them go. We wonder who will fill their place. Will this new
person have a different vision? Will we like them as much? Will the
transition be difficult? We must let go of the one God calls away,
and we must embrace the one God calls (Hebrews 13:17).

Are you struggling with the idea of letting go? Are you struggling
with the idea of a replacement? Will you ask God to give you eyes
to see his vision and a heart to embrace his plan in whatever way it
might affect you?

Heavenly Father, please cause me to see your mission field,
and your missionaries, as you do. Help me to support the
people you are calling, to send joyfully the ones who are to
go, and to embrace lovingly the ones you bring to me. Please
open my mind and bend my will to go or stay wherever you
want to send or keep me.

NOVEMBER 13

Acts 14:21–28; Galatians 1:1–3:23

Let God's curse fall on anyone, including myself, who
preaches any other message than the one we told you
about. Even if an angel comes from heaven and preaches
any other message, let him be forever cursed.
—Galatians 1:8

Paul and Barnabas preach the good news and make disciples
throughout Galatia (modern Turkey), and then they return to
Antioch. In their absence, false teachers lure the Galatians into
following a false gospel: a mix of grace and law. Paul writes to the
Galatians and reminds them that their salvation is by grace. He
questions why they have returned to the law after experiencing grace.

How gracious of God to inspire Paul to write this letter to clarify
for all time that the way to a right standing with God is by grace
through faith in Jesus Christ.

The enticement to seek a right standing with God through our
own righteousness, or religious activities, is almost irresistible when
we compare ourselves favorably to other people. However, when we
compare ourselves to the righteousness of the Lord Jesus Christ, we
realize that there is nothing we can do to save ourselves. Our only
hope is to run to Jesus for grace and mercy (Romans 9:30–10:4).
The old way is gone: Jesus fulfilled the law. Therefore, we cannot
combine works salvation with grace salvation (Mark 2:22). Either
we accept salvation by grace through faith or we embrace the false
gospel that tempted the Galatians (Ephesians 2:8–9).

Have you believed the message of salvation through Jesus Christ?
Will you confess that the law cannot save you and will you accept
God's plan of salvation through grace?

God, thank you for your precious and glorious grace; grace
that saves sinners like me.

NOVEMBER 14

Acts 15:1–21; Galatians 3:24–6:18

So Christ has really set us free. Now make sure that you stay
free, and don't get tied up again in slavery to the law.
—Galatians 5:1

Paul's beloved Galatians experience freedom from the slavery of
sin when they place their faith in Christ Jesus for salvation. False
teachers lead them back into slavery. Paul writes and reminds them
that they are free! He tells them that if they try to find favor with
God through their actions, even circumcision, they place themselves
under the law again.

How gracious of God to call his people to freedom through faith
in Jesus Christ.

We must remember that though the law was good and perfect,
people are not. The law shows us how far out of alignment we are
from God's perfection. The law compels us to run to Jesus: the one
who lived a perfect life and who died to free us from the powerful
bondage of sin (John 8:32; Romans 6:11–14). Having experienced
justification—being made right with God—we are freed to live in
the power of the Holy Spirit (Romans 3:21–25).

Have you experienced God's acceptance through faith in Jesus
Christ? Are you living in freedom, or do you think you must follow
a pattern that dictates your behavior, what you must believe, that you
must pray a certain way, read a specific translation of the Bible, or
even read your Bible at a certain time of day in order to be acceptable
to God? Has legalism lured you back into bondage?

> God, please help me to live in freedom. Please give me the
> discernment I need to identify false teachers who attempt
> to persuade me to follow after them and their way instead
> of Jesus and the way of grace.

NOVEMBER 15

Acts 15:22–17:15

They were severely beaten, and then they were thrown into prison. Around midnight, Paul and Silas were praying and singing hymns to God and the other prisoners were listening.
—Acts 16:23a, 25

A demon-possessed, fortune-telling slave girl hounds Paul and Silas. They command the demon to leave the girl and it does. Her angry owners grab Paul and Silas and take them to the authorities. City officials order Paul and Silas beaten with wooden rods and jailed. In stocks, Paul and Silas pray and sing to God and other prisoners listen. An earthquake causes the doors to fly open. The chains of every prisoner fall off but no one escapes.

How gracious of God to strengthen and use his people wherever he places them.

We never really know who is watching us or who might be listening to us, but we do know that God has a plan for us even when things seem to be going phenomenally badly (Jeremiah 29:11). Faith doesn't keep us out of harm's way, but it does assure us that wherever we are, God is there. And where God is, so is his strength and power. People will see God's power in us when we rely on him in the most difficult circumstances (2 Corinthians 1:8–11).

How do your words and actions in difficult times reveal the power of God in your life?

Heavenly Father, I confess that when things in my life are not going well I am not always a good witness to the availability of your strength and power. When I am in the dungeon of darkness, or the pit of persecution, please keep me from complaining, and give me a song that reveals to everyone that all of my strength, comfort, power, and hope are in you.

NOVEMBER 16

Acts 17:16–18:3; 1 Thessalonians 1:1–5:11

And they speak of how you are looking forward to the
coming of God's Son from heaven—Jesus, whom God
raised from the dead. He is the one who has rescued
us from the terrors of the coming judgment.
—1 Thessalonians 1:10

Many Thessalonians receive the gospel with joy. They suffer severe
hardship and persecution from their countrymen because they accept
Paul's words as the very words of God. Paul assures them the Lord
has not yet returned, in spite of their intense suffering. Paul tells them
they are not in the dark; they will know when the Lord returns and
when he returns, he will bring judgment upon their persecutors.

How gracious of God to give believers hope in uncertain times.

Our hope is in the fulfilled promise of Christ, and the future
promise of his return with final judgment. Our responsibility as we
anticipate Christ's return is to live holy lives (2 Peter 3:3–12). As
we turn from idols to serve the true and living God, we can expect
persecution (Mark 10:29–30). Yet we know that whatever form our
suffering might present itself in this life it is light and momentary
compared with the glory to come (2 Corinthians 4:16–18). We can
endure whatever God allows, even mistreatment from our fellow
man, because we know that God will judge all people when Jesus
returns; no mistreatment will go unnoticed or unpunished.

How are you living as you await the return of Christ?

God, please make my heart strong, blameless, and holy
as I live each day awaiting Christ's return. Create in me
an overflowing love. And please humble me to receive
persecution with a godly and holy attitude, trusting that it
comes to me sifted through your loving hand.

NOVEMBER 17

Acts 18:4–23; 1 Thessalonians 5:12–28; 2 Thessalonians 1–3

We are thankful that God chose you to be among the first
to experience salvation, a salvation that came through the
Spirit who makes you holy and by your belief in the truth.
—2 Thessalonians 2:13b

Paul writes a second letter to the Thessalonians who are experiencing
even greater persecution. He begins by thanking God for them and
their flourishing faith. He brags about them to other believers. He
prays for them and he tells them to stand firm against those who say
the day of the Lord has already begun. That Day will not precede
two future events: the great rebellion against God and the revealing
of the man of lawlessness.

How gracious of God to comfort his people with truth and praise.

C. S. Lewis said, "I didn't go to religion to make me happy. I
always knew a bottle of Port would do that. If you want a religion
to make you feel really comfortable, I certainly don't recommend
Christianity." This is true, however, in our persecution there is
nothing more comforting to us than the truth of God's character
and Word. God's truth encourages, teaches, and protects us against
wickedness. God's truth enables us to stand firm. His truth reveals
lies and defeats the liar (John 8:44; 1 John 2:18–27). We need
never despair of God's comfort—it is always readily available (2
Corinthians 1:3–7).

How has God comforted and strengthened you with his Word
of truth?

> Father, I know that your Word of Truth will hold me
> secure through whatever persecution arises. I thank you for
> your truth that will never fail to sustain me, comfort me,
> strengthen me, guard me, and make me holy as you are holy.

Acts 18:24–19:20; 1 Corinthians 1–3

For Christ didn't send me to baptize, but to preach the Good
News—and not with clever speeches and high-sounding
ideas, for fear that the cross of Christ would lose its power.
—1 Corinthians 1:17

The Corinthians argue over who is greater: Paul or Apollos? Paul
admonishes them to stop arguing; both Paul and Apollos teach
the true wisdom that comes from God—the only message that
matters—the cross. Paul reminds them that the world's brilliant
philosophers, scholars, and debaters all look foolish—and their
wisdom is nonsense—against Christ who is the mighty power of
God and the wonderful wisdom of God.

How gracious of God to use mere humans to teach his great
truths.

We are often quick to invite people to our church because our
pastor is so wise, or to our Bible study because that's where they'll learn
truth, rather than share with them what we know of Christ. We are
afraid our knowledge just won't stand up under scrutiny. However, like
Paul, all we need to know and give is the cross and Christ crucified.
We do not need clever speeches or high-sounding ideas; we need only
share how the cross of Christ has changed our lives. When we teach
Jesus, the Holy Spirit will empower our words and use our testimony
to change lives (John 14:26; Colossians 1:27–29).

What prevents you from sharing the good news of Jesus with the
people whom God has placed in your sphere of influence?

God, sometimes I forget that my ministry is not a
competition. Please help me to remember that Christians
are all on the same team. Please give me your powerful
wisdom and keep my words focused on Christ crucified,
so that I don't speak empty, powerless, and fruitless words.

NOVEMBER 19

1 Corinthians 4–7

...your sins have been washed away, and you have been set apart for God. You have been made right with God because of what the Lord Jesus Christ and the Spirit of our God have done for you.
—1 Corinthians 6:11b

Paul, a spiritual father to the Corinthians, calls them to model his behavior. He challenges them to live holy and pure lives, mourn over the sin in their church, and discipline sinners. He calls them to live in unity with other Christians, avoid sexual sin, and practice godliness in their relationships whether single or married. He reminds them that they used to be sinners but now their sins are washed away and they are set apart for God because of the work of the Lord Jesus Christ and the Spirit of God.

How gracious of God to save sinners and set them apart for himself.

How is it that as Christians, united with Christ, we can entertain thoughts of uniting ourselves with sinful behavior? How is it that we are quick to tolerate sin rather than lovingly call a fallen believer to account? Have we forgotten that we have been reconciled to a holy God who now calls us to holiness (2 Peter 3:11–14)? Is holiness too much to ask of us? No. It is our destiny (Romans 8:28)

Is there an area of your life where God is calling you to holiness? Will you ask a friend to hold you accountable as you surrender to God?

God, you've washed away my sin. You've drawn me close to you. You've wrapped me up in grace. You saved me, a sinner. Please show me where I am cherishing pride and sin. Please humble me to surrender every area of my life to holiness.

NOVEMBER 20

1 Corinthians 8:1–11:1

Don't think only of your own good. Think of
other Christians and what is best for them.
—1 Corinthians 10:24

Paul tells the Corinthians that their Christian life is like a race, and as they run toward the goal every step must be purposeful. They are to consider the consciences of other Christians, and strive not to offend anyone. They should remember that while everything is allowed, not everything is beneficial for ourselves or for other Christians.

How gracious of God to teach Christians to live disciplined, selfless lives.

As Christians, we are all running the race together; this is not a competition. We all run toward the same goal and we have an obligation to help each other arrive at the goal. Self-focus and self-promotion doesn't help others; self-control does. When we control ourselves, we choose to be faithful, gentle, compassionate, long-suffering, loving, peaceful, and joyful (Galatians 5:19–26). As God moves us beyond self-focus toward self-control he faithfully gives us strength to overcome the temptation to put ourselves first.

As you strive toward the finish line of your race are you careful not to step over, knock down, or push out of their lane others who are also running the race? Will you look around and do your best to assist everyone who is running so that all make it to the finish line?

Father, please teach me how to control myself so that I can focus on helping others. Please cause me to be more aware of the people who are running in the lanes on either side of me, and show me how to encourage them. Help me to accept that this is not a competition and that finishing well does not mean finishing first at someone else's expense.

NOVEMBER 21

1 Corinthians 11:2–13:13

For every time you eat this bread and drink this cup, you
are announcing the Lord's death until he comes again.
—1 Corinthians 11:26

Paul gives the Corinthians instructions for worship; passing on what
he has received. He tells them what Jesus said on the night of his
betrayal, explaining that the bread is Jesus's body, given for them;
they are to eat in remembrance of him. He instructs that the cup is
the new covenant between God and men, sealed by the shedding of
Jesus's blood; they are to drink the cup and remember Jesus every
time they do.

How gracious of God to institute this sacred ordinance,
reminding us of what Jesus did and his promise to come again.

We have a Savior who gave his life for our salvation: dying on a
cross so that we can live. He shed his blood to satisfy the just wrath
of God against our sin, and now he lives exalted in heaven (John 1:1,
14, 29; Romans 5:9–11; Philippians 2:6–11). We have the privilege
of proclaiming his death and celebrating his imminent return every
time we partake of the sacrament of Communion.

What does the Lord's Supper mean to you? How do you prepare
your heart in advance of taking the bread and the cup?

> Heavenly Father, I thank you for this precious reminder
> of the sacrifice of my Savior's life, and his sure and certain
> bodily return as King over the whole earth. Please keep me
> from ever taking Communion with a heart that is less than
> wholly focused on the cross of Christ that won my salvation,
> and his soon return that completes it.

NOVEMBER 22

1 Corinthians 14–15

Since you are so eager to have spiritual gifts, ask God for
those that will be of real help to the whole church.
—1 Corinthians 14:12

Paul encourages the Corinthians to seek spiritual gifts and use them
to build up the body of believers. He instructs them to worship in an
orderly manner so that the whole church receives a word from God.
He teaches that prophesying—speaking the message of God—will
lay bare secret thoughts and bring people to their knees in worship.

How gracious of God to teach us how to use the spiritual gifts
he gives us.

God has given each one of us at least one spiritual gift and
we are responsible to exercise our gift(s) wisely. Just like the
Corinthian church, our goal must be to edify the church, the body
of Christ. Every gift of the Holy Spirit is a tool for enlightening and
strengthening all believers. Our motive and goals as we exercise our
gift(s) must be the benefit of the church—the body of Christ (1
Thessalonians 5:11).

Have you asked God for a spiritual gift? What gift do you desire?
Why? What is your motive in asking for that specific gift?

What spiritual gift(s) has God given you? Are you exercising
your gift(s) to serve the whole church? Will you ask your pastor today
where you might serve for God's glory?

> God, you've given me the gift that is perfect for me, and
> you have placed me in this specific body of believers for
> your purpose. Please help me to use my gifts in love as a
> service to your children. Help me to keep my heart set on
> you as I exercise my gifts so that I am a useful tool to build
> up your church.

NOVEMBER 23

Acts 19:21–20:3; Romans 1; 1 Corinthians 16

This Good News tells us how God makes us right in his sight.
This is accomplished from start to finish by faith. As the
Scriptures say, "It is through faith that a righteous person has life."
—Romans 1:17

Paul prays for an opportunity to visit the Christians in Rome to
encourage them and until then he communicates with them through
a letter. Paul writes about God's good news, the gospel of Jesus
Christ, of which he is not ashamed. Paul knows the gospel is the
power of God to save everyone who believes. It is the gospel that
teaches that believers are made right with God, from start to finish,
by faith.

How gracious of God to grant everyone who believes in the
gospel a right standing in his sight.

We know, by experience and by the Word of God, that there is
absolutely nothing we can do as humans to make ourselves right in
God's sight (Galatians 3:11). We have no righteousness with which
to plead our case before God (Isaiah 64:6). Our righteousness must
come from Christ, imputed to us when we believe in the completed
work of the Lord Jesus Christ on the cross (2 Corinthians 5:16–21).
At that moment, we are reconciled to our holy God and placed in
right standing before him (Philippians 3).

Are you right with God?

Heavenly Father, I thank you for the good news about Christ
Jesus—the power of the gospel that saves sinners like me.
Thank you for the precious gift of salvation through faith
in Christ Jesus that allows me to stand before you, dressed
in his righteousness alone.

NOVEMBER 24

Romans 2–4

We are made right in God's sight when we trust in Jesus
Christ to take away our sins. And we all can be saved in this
same way, no matter who we are or what we have done.
—Romans 3:22

Paul writes to the Roman believers that there is only one means
of salvation, and it is available to all people. Because all people sin
and fall short of God's mark of holiness, no one is in right standing
before God. Right standing cannot be earned because no one can
keep God's good, perfect, and holy law in its entirety. Everyone lives
under the power of sin, therefore, no one seeks God, no one desires
God, and no one fears God.

How gracious of God to show all people a way to be in right
standing before him: by trusting in the Lord Jesus to take away sin.

Because God is just, he must punish all sin. As guilty sinners we
deserve punishment. God sent Jesus, the perfect sacrifice, to endure
that punishment in our place—as our substitute—and thus satisfy
God's just wrath (John 3:16–18). When we accept this sacrifice on
our behalf, God in his grace, mercy, and kindness declares us not
guilty (Romans 2:1, Psalm 14:1–3), and also declares us to be in right
standing before him (Hebrews 10:10, 14).

Do you believe that Jesus paid it all for you? Do you believe
that Jesus endured every bit of the punishment that you deserve?
Do you believe that God has declared you right in his sight because
you believe in Jesus, and not because of anything you have done or
can do?

God, please help me understand more fully the amazing
privilege of being in right standing before you!

NOVEMBER 25

Romans 5:1–8:17

So now there is no condemnation for those
who belong to Christ Jesus.
—Romans 8:1

Because one man sinned, Adam, sin enters the human race. Adam's sin causes death to rule: all people are born under sin, all people sin, and therefore all people die. Everyone stands condemned.

However, one other man, Jesus, brings forgiveness. Through Christ's one act of righteousness, many are made right in God's sight. All who receive God's wonderful gift of righteousness live in triumph over sin and death through the one man, the Lord Jesus Christ.

How gracious of God to provide escape from condemnation.

As our representative, Adam sinned and therefore we inherited his sin. We have a sin nature—our natural bent is to sin—and we stand condemned. In Jesus, also our representative, the penalty for our sin was paid; and his righteousness was imputed to us.

The reality is that we stand condemned because each one of us, like David, knows the reality of the heartache, the hopelessness, and the helplessness of our sinful selves (Psalm 51:1–5). We are sinners and we know it. We know the curse. We can also experience the cure: while we were sinners, God showed his love for us by sending Christ to die for us (Romans 5:8).

Are you living under condemnation or under salvation? The choice is yours.

My gracious and all wise God, how can I thank you for removing me from the realm of condemnation, under which I was born, and placing me in Christ so that I can live in victory? You have moved me from death to life, from darkness to light, from bondage to freedom. I surrender all to you, it is the least thing I can do.

NOVEMBER 26

Romans 8:18–10:21

And I am convinced that nothing can ever separate us from his love … nothing in all creation will ever be able to separate us from the love of God that is revealed in Christ Jesus our Lord.
—Romans 8:38a,39b

Paul tells the Roman Christians to expect suffering as they await the fulfillment of God's promises. Everything on earth groans while it waits. Because Christians are saved, they must wait patiently and confidently. The Holy Spirit helps in the waiting and God works in the waiting by causing everything to work together for the good of those he has called and predestined to glory. No one can condemn believers because Christ died for them and sits at the right hand of God pleading for them. Nothing can separate them from the love of God in Christ Jesus.

How gracious of God to give his children an assuring confidence that nothing can separate them from Christ Jesus.

Like the Roman Christians, we wait. We wait for Christ's return and we experience suffering as we wait. Though we must endure scoffers and unbelievers, we know we will stand firm in truth because God protects us by his power (1 Peter 1:3–7; 2 Peter 3:3–7). We will not fall away because nothing within us, or outside of us, can separate us from the love of God in Christ Jesus.

Are you confident that God is able to keep you from stumbling and present you faultless before his glorious presence (1 Thessalonians 5:23–24, Jude 1:24)? Have you received his great salvation? Will you today?

Almighty God, there is nothing bigger, stronger, or more mighty than you are. I rest in the assurance that you hold me secure in your love and that I will remain with you for eternity.

NOVEMBER 27

Romans 11–14

Don't copy the behavior and customs of this world, but let God
transform you into a new person by changing the way you think.
Then you will know what God wants you to do, and you will
know how good and pleasing and perfect his will really is.
—Romans 12:2

Paul explains God's plan of salvation through Jesus Christ to the
Romans. He assures them that God's salvation is for all people. He
details God's faithfulness. He declares God's majesty in riches, and
wisdom, and knowledge. He challenges them to give themselves to
God as a living and holy sacrifice, to let God use and transform them
because of all God has done for them.

How gracious of God to transform his people and change their
thinking.

We know that no matter how much we try, we can't change
ourselves (Romans 7:15–25). We try to clean up our act, our mouth,
our entertainment, and our bad habits but it is too much work to
keep it up. We know from experience that changes from the outside
in are not much more than temporary good habits. Only as God
transforms us from the inside out, do our thinking, actions, and
desires become natural and therefore sustainable. God transforms us
by changing the way we think as we spend time with him.

Where do you need God's transforming power? In what areas
of your life is God transforming you?

God, I love spending time with you, and learning from you.
Please help me to stand against the culture, the behaviors
and the customs of the world as you transform my thinking.
Help me to become the person that you would have me
be—one who knows and does your perfect will.

NOVEMBER 28

Romans 15–16; 2 Corinthians 1:1–2:4

He comforts us in all our troubles so that we can comfort
others. When others are troubled, we will be able to
give them the same comfort God has given us.
—2 Corinthians 1:4

Paul begins his second letter to the Corinthians praising God, the
Father of the Lord Jesus Christ, the one who comforts him and
comforts all Christians. Paul details his suffering: suffering that
crushed him and completely overwhelmed even to the point of
despair and the expectation of death. As a result of his suffering, Paul
learns not to rely on himself but on God. God's comfort enables Paul
to be an encouragement to others.

How gracious of God to comfort his people; equipping them to
comfort others.

We have heard that God will never give us more than we can
handle, but Paul's experience proves that untrue, as does Job's. We
will suffer (Romans 5:3–5)—and our suffering, like Paul's, may be
more than we can endure on our own—we may even hope for death.
God is always with us in our suffering and he allows it so that we
might learn to rely on him. When God comforts us, and he will, our
suffering is not in vain if we use God's comfort to comfort others.

How is God comforting you in your suffering? Have you asked
others to pray for you? How might you be a tool to bring comfort
to someone else?

God, when my circumstances are overwhelming my comfort
comes as I think of who you are: mighty and majestic,
glorious and merciful, sovereign over the affairs of all
people, full of love and wisdom, sovereign, good, holy, just,
all-powerful, all-knowing, always present, and always doing
what is right. God, you are my comfort.

NOVEMBER 29

2 Corinthians 2:5–6:13

For our present troubles are quite small and won't last very long.
So we don't look at the troubles we can see right now; rather, we
look forward to what we have not yet seen. For the troubles we
see will soon be over, but the joys to come will last forever."
—2 Corinthians 4:17a, 18

Paul knows that physical life, and its accompanying hardships, are
temporary. The body is a weak and perishable vessel but it holds the
glorious power and light of God. The body dies, but the spirit lives. The
spirit eventually puts on an imperishable new body that lives forever
with God. God gives us the Holy Spirit as the guarantee of eternity.

How gracious of God to promise a glorious eternity that enables
us to endure present hardships.

"Life is hard and then you die." We've all heard that before. It
is not easy to live with illness and pain. It is not easy to live without
sight, or hearing, or arms, fingers, legs or toes. It is not easy to live
with heartache, poverty, persecution, and fear. For many of us life is
not easy. For all of us, life is not long (James 4:14; Job 9:25). Life is
too brief to let anything other than the glorious power and light of
God shine through the cracks in these bodies, our temporary vessels.

What troubles overwhelm you in the light of today? How much
smaller do they appear in the light of eternity?

God, please teach me how to focus on the joys of eternity
so that I can manage the troubles of today. Please remind
me that these troubles are indeed light and momentary, and
they are producing an immeasurably great glory that will
last forever.

NOVEMBER 30

2 Corinthians 6:14–10:18

And God will generously provide all you need.
Then you will always have everything you need
and plenty left over to share with others.
—2 Corinthians 9:8

Paul takes up a collection for the Jerusalem church. He wants the believers in Corinth to prepare their gift as they've promised so that no one feels coerced or reluctant to give; each one decides how much to give, and then gives. When God's people give cheerfully, others' needs are met, and God is glorified. Paul teaches them to give out of generosity and gratitude to God for the wonderful gift of Jesus.

How gracious of God to give his people opportunities to help one other.

What a grand cycle—needy believing brothers pray and ask God for help, then God puts it on the hearts of his children to give what they can (Philippians 2:13; Romans 12:8), the recipients are grateful and give thanks for the givers, the givers—grateful to give—pray for the recipients. And on it goes: giving and receiving that deepens affection for one another and brings glory to God's name!

How is God using you to meet others' needs? How is God using others to meet your needs? financially? spiritually? emotionally? or physically? How have your expressed your gratitude to God for your current place in the cycle?

> Father, I know that you could meet every need of your children with a word and yet you have given me the privilege of giving of my time, talent, money, and self to help meet the needs of others. You have given me the privilege of receiving from so many others. You have given me the privilege of praying for others while others pray for me. God, your generosity exceeds my imagination.

grace
DECEMBER

DECEMBER 1

Acts 20:7–12; 2 Corinthians 11–13

But to keep me from getting puffed up, I was given
a thorn in my flesh, a messenger from Satan to
torment me and keep me from getting proud.
—2 Corinthians 12:7b

Paul experiences something remarkable: whether in a vision or in the body, Paul is caught up into paradise where he hears astounding things and receives wonderful revelations from God. Paul also receives a messenger from Satan to torment him and keep him from getting proud. He begs the Lord to take it away; God doesn't.

How gracious of God to allow the things that cause his children to rely on him.

We don't know what Paul saw or heard. Did he see millions who were led to faith because of his faithfulness? Did he hear your voice and mine preaching and reading the words God inspired him to write? Whatever he saw, God gave the experience, and God allowed the thorn.

God allows you and me to experience wonderful things as we accomplish the work he has given us. God also allows weaknesses to prevent pride from overtaking us (Proverbs 11:2; 16:18). If there were no weakness, our pride would rule us (1 John 2:15–17).

What has God allowed you to see or hear that encourages you and keeps you working for his glory? What thorn has God allowed that reminds you that you cannot accomplish anything for him apart from him? How does your weakness enable you to experience God's strength?

Almighty, your grace is sufficient in my weakness because it is there that your power shines. I can do nothing apart from you, but with you, I can do all things. Thank you for wisely allowing the things that keep me humble and relying on you.

DECEMBER 2

Acts 20:13–21:36

"And now I am going to Jerusalem, drawn there irresistibly
by the Holy Spirit, not knowing what awaits me.
—Acts 20:22

Paul meets with the Ephesian elders on his way to Jerusalem.
Hardship and trouble are certain for Paul and yet the Holy Spirit
compels him to go to Jerusalem. He knows he won't see the Ephesians
again, and therefore he takes this opportunity to warn them to be on
guard against false prophets. He entrusts them to God, prays with
them, and with many tears he says goodbye.

How gracious of God to reveal his will to his children.

Oswald Chambers says, "Have you been asking God what he
is going to do? He will never tell you. God does not tell you what
he is going to do; he reveals to you who he is." Despite prophetic
warnings, Paul didn't know what God was going to do in Jerusalem,
he simply knew he was supposed to go there.

Obedience is always a choice, and like Paul, despite the unknown
we must choose obedience. Obedience is possible because God has
revealed himself to us as a faithful and loving God (Deuteronomy
7:9; Psalm 25:10).

How has God revealed himself to you? Will you take a moment
and list God's attributes? Does your list compel you to go wherever
God sends you, no matter the hardship that might await you?

> God, I confess that sometimes I place the comforts of my life
> above serving you and your people. I forget how wonderful,
> majestic, powerful, and glorious you are. I forget that there
> is nothing more worthy than spending my life serving you
> and your people. Help me to keep my priorities aligned with
> yours so that I humbly yield to your Holy Spirit's leading.

DECEMBER 3

Acts 21:37–23:35

"Brothers and esteemed fathers," Paul said,
"listen to me as I offer my defense."
—Acts 22:1

A riot breaks out in Jerusalem and the Romans rescue Paul. Paul asks for an opportunity to speak to the people and begins his defense with the truth that he is a Jew educated in Jerusalem. He confesses that he was a persecutor of Christians. He tells them about his conversion. When Paul tells the crowd that Jesus sent him to the Gentiles, the people call for his life.

How gracious of God to give his people a platform and a testimony to share.

Every one of us has a testimony. The story of our conversion may not be as dramatic as Paul's, but we should all have a story of how the Lord Jesus Christ changed us (2 Corinthians 3:15–18).

Every one of us has a platform. It may not be in front of crowds of people, but it is in front of someone who needs to hear what God has done in your life. When God saved you, the miraculous happened, and people need to hear about miracles (John 4:28–30).

Are you prepared to share your conversion experience? Can you tell the story of how God moved you from the realm of darkness into light (Colossians 1:13)? Will you pause today and write it out so that you are ready whenever God gives you the opportunity? Will you look for opportunities to share the ways in which God works in your life?

> Lord, please teach me how to tell my story so that the spotlight shines brilliantly on you. Please help me to remember that there is no reason to be nervous or afraid; because it is not about me, it is always about you.

DECEMBER 4

Acts 24–26

And King Agrippa knows about these things. I speak
frankly, for I am sure these events are all familiar
to him, for they were not done in a corner!
—Acts 26:26

Paul arrives in Caesarea to stand trial before Felix, the Governor. For two years, Paul speaks to Felix about faith in Christ Jesus. Porcius Festus becomes Governor. Festus wants to return Paul to Jerusalem but Paul appeals to Caesar. King Agrippa, who is well versed in Jewish customs, interrogates Paul. After listening to Paul, Agrippa questions Paul's attempt to make him a Christian so quickly.

How gracious of God to place his people exactly where he wants them.

We don't know if Agrippa ever received Jesus as his Savior. We do know that God placed Paul before Agrippa, and can place his people wherever he wants—before kings, presidents, governors, teachers, principals, and supervisors—whenever he wants.

We also know that while God works privately in each individual heart he does not work in a vacuum; as the heavens declare the glory of God so must God's people, wherever they find themselves (Psalm 19:1; 32; 51:10; Proverbs 21:1).

Before whom has God placed you? Are you prepared to stand before people in authority? Are you prepared to speak of the glory of God? What is your preparation plan?

> God, wherever, and to whomever you would have me give my testimony, please help me to stand firm and strong for you. Help me to prepare wisely, to look at my life closely, to know you as well as I possibly can, and to speak clearly whether I am speaking to a child or a king, so that your kingdom is advanced and a lost soul is led to your glorious salvation.

DECEMBER 5

Acts 27

Then he took some bread, gave thanks to God before them all,
and broke off a piece and ate it. Then everyone was encouraged.
—Acts 27:35–36

Under the custody of an army officer, Paul sails toward Rome. A
storm blows in that lasts for days. An angel of the Lord appears
to Paul and tells him that he will stand before Caesar, and that
everyone on board will survive the storm. When Paul tells the men
there will be a shipwreck, some try to abandon the ship, but Paul
insists everyone remain. Paul begs them to eat. When the ship
breaks, Paul orders everyone to jump overboard. Everyone survives.

How gracious of God to use believers in the lives of unbelievers.
We know that all 276 souls on that ship survived the shipwreck.
We don't know how many were saved spiritually. We do know
that their salvation, whether physical or spiritual, was accomplished
because they listened to a believer who had listened to God.

When we are encouraged by God we must use his words to
encourage others (2 Corinthians 1:3–7). We may not know for sure
that we will survive the disasters that come upon us, but we do
know that we will survive for eternity—everyone does—the only
question is where: heaven or hell? The only way to heaven is to grab
onto Jesus (John 14:6).

What are you holding on to for dear life? Jesus? or a piece of
debris? Only Jesus will bring you safely to heaven. Anything else
will deposit you in hell.

> Father, I am clinging to the gospel: the truth that Jesus is
> the only way of salvation. Please help me to speak the truth
> of the gospel clearly, lovingly, compassionately, and boldly
> to drowning unbelievers.

DECEMBER 6

Acts 28; Ephesians 1–2

When we arrived in Rome, Paul was permitted to have his own private lodging, though he was guarded by a soldier.
—Acts 28:16

Paul arrives in Rome: a prisoner guarded by a Roman soldier. For two years, people come to listen to him. Despite his imprisonment, he welcomes every visitor, proclaims the Kingdom of God, and teaches about the Lord Jesus Christ. During these years, Paul dictates letters to the Ephesians and Colossians, to his friend Philemon, and to the Philippians.

How gracious of God to give every person the perfect opportunity to hear the gospel.

We might wonder what kind of relationship Paul had with the Roman soldiers assigned to guard him every day while he was a prisoner of Rome. Paul had a captive audience, literally and figuratively. It is easy to imagine that there were long conversations that lasted well into the wee hours of the night. It is easy to imagine that these soldiers surrendered their lives to Christ Jesus.

How do you welcome people forced to spend time with you? in your hospital room? in the nursing home? in your classroom? in your kitchen? in your bedroom? in the playroom? in your carpool? in your Bible study? in your Sunday School class? in your office? or in the cafeteria? Do you welcome every opportunity to share with everyone your glorious God (1 Peter 3:15–16)?

God, I know that your truth will be proclaimed to all people, and I thank you for the opportunities you've given me to be a voice. Please humble me and cause me to be wise with my words and to be a loving witness to your saving grace whenever there's an audience. Help me to always represent you well no matter who might be listening.

DECEMBER 7

Ephesians 3:1–5:14

And this is the secret plan; The Gentiles have an equal share with
the Jews in all the riches inherited by God's children. Both groups
have believed the Good News, and both are part of the same body
and enjoy together the promise of blessings through Christ Jesus.
—Ephesians 3:6

Imprisoned in Rome, Paul writes to the church in Ephesus. Paul
praises God who has blessed him and all Christians with every
spiritual blessing in the heavenly realms because they belong to
Christ. He praises God for the wonderful kindness he has poured
out on them. Paul tells the Ephesians that God's secret plan, to bring
everything together under the authority of Christ, is now revealed.
Paul prays for them constantly. He wants them to realize the rich
and glorious inheritance God has given to his people.

How gracious of God to pour his blessings on everyone who
comes to him in faith.

We are the wealthiest people on earth. We lack nothing. In
Christ Jesus, God has given us everything we need to live holy and
righteous lives (Philippians 4:13). God's great power is for us; the
same mighty power that raised Christ from the dead and seated
him in the place of honor at God's right hand (Ephesians 1:18–21).

Are you living in spiritual poverty? in fear? in shame? in guilt?
in falsehood? or in lust? Do you lack understanding? Why? Will you
choose instead to live in the glorious wealth of your new nature in
God's almighty power?

> O God, thank you for reminding me that I am not a pauper,
> I am a child of the King! Please teach me how to step out of
> spiritual poverty, and what it means to live in the richness
> of your power and grace.

DECEMBER 8

Ephesians 5:15–6:23; Colossians 1:1–23

> He made peace with everything in heaven and on
> earth by means of his blood on the cross. This includes
> you who were once so far away from God.
> —Colossians 1:20b, 21a

Paul's letter to the Colossian believers tells them how he prays for them. He prays that they will be filled with joy. He thanks God for rescuing them from the one who rules the kingdom of darkness, and bringing them into the Kingdom of the Son. He reminds them that they have seen the visible image of the invisible God—Christ Jesus—the one who existed before God made anything at all, who is supreme over all creation, and who reconciles them as friends through his death on the cross in his own human body.

How gracious of God to reconcile sinners—his enemies—to himself as his friend.

Every one of us was at one time an enemy of God, separated by sin. We lived in darkness and sin (Ephesians 2:1–10). It is only through Christ Jesus's blood, shed on the cross in his human body, that we are reconciled to our holy God, and able to stand holy and blameless before him (2 Corinthians 5:11–21).

On the Day of Judgment, in what will you trust to enable you to stand before Almighty God?

Gracious God, it is an awesome thought that I, a sinner to the core, can be your friend. It overwhelms me that I, the one who denied you by actions and words, am reconciled to you. Who is a God like you who loves your enemies and reconciles them as your friend? You are my God! You are my glorious, gracious, loving God who saved me by grace through faith in Christ Jesus. To you be glory forever.

DECEMBER 9

Colossians 1:24–4:18

You were dead because of your sins and because your
sinful nature was not yet cut away. Then God made you
alive with Christ, He forgave all our sins. He canceled
the record that contained the charges against us. He took
it and destroyed it by nailing it to Christ's cross.
—Colossians 2:13

Paul explains the reality of salvation to the Colossians: That moment
when truth is received and trust is placed in the mighty power of
God who raised Christ from the dead. God makes them alive with
Christ, and in that moment of belief, because they are alive with
Christ, they are free of condemnation.

How gracious of God to explain clearly the glory of salvation
to his children.

We don't need to wonder what salvation means; God tells us that
it means we will live forever with Jesus in heaven (John 3:16). We
won't bear his just wrath (1 Thessalonians 5:9). We are born again
in newness of life (John 3:3). We are declared in right standing with
God (Romans 3:23–25). Our sin—past, present, and future—is
cancelled, and no one can condemn us (Romans 8:1). We know that
God holds us secure and we cannot lose our salvation because it was
accomplished at the cross and Calvary can't be undone (Jude 1:24).

Are you living in the wealth of life that God has given you in
Christ Jesus? Are you standing in freedom knowing evil has been
defeated? Are you living in the kingdom of light?

> Oh God, I stand amazed at the depth of the riches of your
> love for me. Please help me to grasp all that is mine in Christ
> Jesus so that I might live in the abundance of my new life
> and forgiveness.

DECEMBER 10

Philippians 1:1–2:11; Philemon 1

And I am sure that God, who began the good work within
you, will continue his work until it is finally finished
on that day when Christ Jesus comes back again.
—Philippians 1:6

Paul, a prisoner in Rome because of Christ, writes to the Philippians.
Paul knows that God is in control and will eventually deliver Paul by
freedom or by death. Paul encourages the Philippians to live worthy
of the gospel in the face of their own persecution. Paul assures them
that God continually works in them and will complete the work he
began.

How gracious of God to complete the work he begins in every
one of his children.

When we believe in the Lord Jesus and receive salvation, we are
immediately sanctified: set apart for God's use (1 Corinthians 6:11).
However, sanctification is also a process that God accomplishes over
time as God works in us to make us holy (John 17:17; Hebrews 12:14).
As we cooperate with God's Holy Spirit within us, he continues to
work out the sinfulness that is a part of our person and character
(Romans 12:1–2). God will complete the task. We are destined for
holiness (Romans 8:28–30).

What is God working out of you? What is he working into you?
How are you working with God in this process of sanctification?

> Father, you know me better than I know myself. You know
> what needs to go, what needs to be refined, what must be
> scraped off, what must be cut out, and what needs to be
> polished. You know what hinders me. You know what causes
> me to stumble. Please do what needs done to make me into
> the spiritually mature person that you intend I become.

DECEMBER 11

Philippians 2:12–4:23

For God is working in you, giving you the desire to
obey him and the power to do what pleases him.
—Philippians 2:13

Paul tells the Philippians they must work out their salvation: put into action God's saving work in their lives and obey God with deep reverence and fear. Paul admonishes them to stay away from complaining and arguing and to live innocent and clean lives. He tells them to press on toward the goal of becoming all that Jesus saved them for and wants them to be, and to hold tightly to the word of life.

How gracious of God to give his people the desire—and the power—to work out their salvation.

We know the reality of the sinful nature of our own hearts and we know that we are not worthy of the great salvation that God has given us as a gift of his grace (Romans 5:8; Ephesians 2:4–10). We can never earn our salvation, however, once salvation is ours we must live out what God has put in us; we must live worthy of the gospel. God's power within us enables our work for him; not earning our salvation, but proving it (Ephesians 3:20; James 2:14–26).

Having received the free gift of salvation, how are you living it out? Do your choices reflect the desires that God has put within you?

> Gracious God, as my response to your gift of salvation, I ask you to please fill my heart with a desire to obey you. Reveal my selfish thinking, motives, and actions so that I can humbly repent of them. Please help me to live in gratitude, ever mindful that everything I have, including the power to obey, is a work of your grace.

DECEMBER 12

James 1–3

Whenever trouble comes your way, let it be an opportunity
for joy. For when your faith is tested, your endurance has a
chance to grow. When your endurance is fully developed,
you will be strong in character and ready for anything.
—James 1:2b–3, 4b

The Lord Jesus's half-brother, James, writes to all Christians encouraging them to put their faith into practice. He tells them that every circumstance of life is an opportunity to live by faith whether in trouble, poverty, wealth, tests, temptations, or relationships. James commands Christians to live out their faith through good deeds.

How gracious of God to use the circumstances of life to test faith.

All of us have experienced the reality that God tests our faith; faith that isn't tested can't be trusted (Hebrews 11:17–19). God tests our faith so we can understand how strong or weak our faith is (2 Corinthians 13:5–6). Tests also reveal in what or whom we have placed our faith (Revelation 2:10). Faith placed in anything other than God will ultimately fail.

Does it bring you joy—deep-seated pleasure—to know that God considers your faith worthy of tests? What will God's tests reveal?

Does it delight you to know that God wants to grow your endurance and your character by testing your faith? Does it comfort you to know that God is revealing weaknesses to strengthen your character so that you are ready for whatever lies ahead?

God, I confess that I don't enjoy the times of testing, but I do thank you for the testing because it means you care enough about me to mature my faith. There is great joy and comfort in knowing that you are strengthening and preparing me for whatever the future holds.

1 Timothy 1–2; James 4–5

For there is only one God and one Mediator who can reconcile God and people. He is the man Christ Jesus.
—1 Timothy 2:5

Paul's letter of encouragement to Timothy reminds Timothy that he, Paul, was once an ignorant unbeliever upon whom God had mercy, and now uses as a prime example of his great patience with sinners. Paul instructs Timothy to cling tightly to his faith in Christ, keep his conscience clear, and fight well in the Lord's battles. He urges Timothy to pray for all people, pleading for God's mercy upon them, for God wants everyone saved and to understand the truth.

How gracious of God to provide reconciliation to sinners through Jesus Christ.

It often appears that false teachers and false doctrine are winning the day. We see the seeds of false teaching—disunity, arguing, and disobedient rebellion—taking root in our homes, our neighborhoods, and our churches. We pray, but like Timothy, we get discouraged and need reminded that God has provided a way to reconcile lost sinners to himself: the truth of the gospel. Because of the work of Christ Jesus, no one is beyond salvation (Romans 5:10; Colossians 1:19–20). We must continue to pray fervently, cling tightly to the truth, and root out every deception (2 Corinthians 5:18–19).

Have you been reconciled with God through the sacrifice of Jesus? With whom will you share the truth of reconciliation?

God, I forget how repulsive I appeared to you before Christ saved me. Like Paul, I am overwhelmed with gratitude for the saving blood of Jesus, provided free to me, but at such a great cost to you. Please help me to pray ceaselessly as I cling tightly to this truth.

DECEMBER 14

1 Timothy 3:1–6:10

An elder must not be a new Christian, because he
might be proud of being chosen so soon, and the
Devil will use that pride to make him fall.
—1Timothy 3:6

Paul advises Timothy on the governing of the community church. Paul gives instructions regarding the selection of elders—those who manage the affairs of the church. Paul also gives guidelines for selecting deacons. Paul desires that Timothy understand the way people must conduct themselves in God's household. Paul warns against people who pretend to be religious yet spend their time arguing over godless ideas. He exhorts Timothy to spend time in training himself for spiritual fitness and to keep a close watch on himself and his teaching.

How gracious of God to outline specific qualifications for leadership positions.

When we take on a leadership position we paint a bull's-eye on our backs. The enemy will do his best to expose our hidden sins, capitalize on our weaknesses, and dishonor us (1 Peter 5:8). As leaders, we must not assist the enemy by placing new believers in positions that will make them vulnerable to the Devil's onslaught. It makes sense that following God's guidelines protects the church, the leadership, and the members.

Are you taking specific steps to mature your faith so that God can use you as a leader in your church? Will you pray for protection over the private and public lives and over the decisions of the leadership in your church?

> God, please protect me from taking on responsibilities that
> I am not yet ready for or envying the leaders who serve
> in those positions. Thank you for reminding me that my
> responsibility today is to live a godly life that is worthy of
> my calling and that represents you well.

DECEMBER 15

1 Timothy 6:11–21; 2 Timothy 1; Titus 1–3

But as for you, promote the kind of living
that reflects right teaching.
—Titus 2:1

Paul encourages the young pastor, Titus, to sternly rebuke people who rebel against right teaching deceiving other people. Paul tells Titus to teach older men to exercise self-control and to be worthy of respect. He tells Titus to teach older women to live in a way that is appropriate for someone serving the Lord, so that they can teach the younger women. Paul exhorts Titus to encourage the young men and be an example to them. Paul reinforces the truth to Titus that believers must live in this evil world with self-control, right conduct, and devotion to God.

How gracious of God to provide right teaching and expect right living.

We expose ourselves to all kinds of teaching and the choices of our lives reflect what we have learned. As we spend time in God's Word, applying what we read and hear, God transforms our actions by changing the way we think (Romans 12:1–2; Philippians 4:9). When our thoughts align with God's Word, so will our lives.

Are you receiving right teaching? How do you know? Are you in a Bible-teaching church? Does your Bible study class actually study the Bible? Are you applying what you learn? How does your life reflect what you are learning?

God, I want to live the way you would have me live, not adhering to a legalistic or Pharisaical set of rules, but living in your righteousness. I want to live beautifully different from the world so that I make a beautiful difference for you. Please give me a hunger for your Word so that as I study it my life is transformed to reflect right teaching.

DECEMBER 16

2 Timothy 2:1–4:18

All Scripture is inspired by God and is useful to teach us
what is true and to make us realize what is wrong in our
lives. It straightens us out and teaches to do what is right.
—2 Timothy 3:16

Paul writes to his beloved Timothy and tells him to be strong with
the special favor God gives in Christ Jesus. Paul commands Timothy
not to be ashamed of the gospel he preaches. He tells Timothy to
study the Scriptures so Timothy can explain correctly the word
of truth: the same truth Timothy received as a child, the same
Scriptures that led him to faith in Christ Jesus, the same gospel for
which Paul is imprisoned.

How gracious of God to give his people the enduring Holy
Scriptures.

The Scriptures are God's revelation of himself to the world.
It is God's story from beginning to end even though he used the
personalities, cultures, lives, and histories of over forty human
authors to write it (2 Peter 1:20–21). The Bible tells one story, the
story of the redemption of humankind. It is the living, breathing
word of God and will accomplish the purpose for which God intends
every time it is read or heard (Isaiah 55:11). It will endure forever
(Matthew 5:18).

Do you struggle with the relevance or usefulness of the Bible in
today's culture? Are you allowing it to teach you what is true? As you
study, do you see areas where you are out of alignment, areas that
need straightening, areas that need the light of truth?

God, I thank you for your Word, the tool of my refinement.
Teach me to handle your truth aright, so that I am fully
equipped to do what you would have me do.

DECEMBER 17

2 Timothy 4:19–22; Hebrews 1:1–4:13

Through the suffering of Jesus, God made him a perfect
leader, one fit to bring them into their salvation.
—Hebrews 2:10b

The writer to the Hebrews presents the supremacy of Jesus. Jesus:
greater than the angels, (for he is the eternal Son) sits at the right
hand of the Father. Jesus: greater than Moses, (for he is the faithful
Son) commands the entire household of God. Jesus: superior to
the priests, (for he is the sinless Son) holds his priesthood eternally.
In taking on flesh, Jesus becomes like us so that he can die, defeat
death, and lead his brothers and sisters in a victory procession.

How gracious of God to provide the supreme Savior: the Lord
Jesus Christ.

Jesus is our savior because of who he is and what he did. He lived
a perfectly righteous life on earth (2 Corinthians 5:21; 1 Peter 2:22).
Jesus was not made perfect from imperfection. We are saved because
Jesus left the glory of heaven, took on human flesh, lived a perfect
life, died on the cross, and rose to new life (Philippians 2:6–11).
Today he lives, exalted in heaven (Acts 2:33). Jesus is the only one
who can lead us in salvation (Acts 4:14).

When you think of your salvation, do you stop at the thought
that it is free to you? Have you pondered the cost to Jesus? When
you think of all Jesus did for you, does the grace of God amaze you?

Almighty God, the thought of the suffering that Jesus
endured for me brings me to my knees. The reality that
the Eternal Son left heaven to lead sinners—of whom I
am worst—in salvation overwhelms me. I give you my all,
because he gave his all; anything less is insulting.

DECEMBER 18

Hebrews 4:14–7:28

So let us come boldly to the throne of our gracious
God. There we will receive his mercy, and we
will find grace to help us when we need it.
—Hebrews 4:16

The writer of Hebrews teaches believers that their Great High
Priest, the Lord Jesus Christ, the Son of God is a High Priest who
understands their weakness for he faced all of the same temptations
and yet did not sin. While on earth, Jesus pleaded for deliverance
from death, but accepted the will of the Father. He learned obedience
through his suffering and is qualified as the perfect High Priest; the
source of eternal salvation for all who obey him.

How gracious of God to open the way for believers to come
directly into his presence.

We know that in the centuries before the cross, the high priest
had to atone for his own sin before he could represent human beings
in their dealings with God (Leviticus 16:6, 11). Only then could he
enter the Most Holy Place, which was separated from the rest of the
temple by a curtain (Exodus 26:33–34). Jesus, our Great High Priest
had no sin for which to atone because he was eternally without sin,
the only perfect sacrifice (John 1:29). When Jesus died, the curtain
was torn allowing access to God (Matthew 27:51). Now, we have
the privilege and responsibility to come boldly, because of Christ's
sacrifice, before the throne of God at any time.

How often do you avail yourself of the amazing gift of access to
God, the Creator of the universe? Will you boldly go today?

God, I am awed, humbled, and thankful for this glorious
gift and privilege! That I have access to you—the God of
creation—it is almost too wonderful to comprehend!

DECEMBER 19

Hebrews 8–10

> For by that one offering he perfected forever
> all those whom he is making holy.
> —Hebrews 10: 14

After accomplishing the work of salvation, Jesus sits down in the place of highest honor in heaven. He guarantees a better covenant with God based on better promises. The old covenant is now obsolete. Jesus mediates the new covenant between God and people so that all who are invited can accept and receive the eternal inheritance God promises. Christ died to set them free from the penalty of the sins they had committed. They are made holy by the sacrifice of the body of Jesus Christ once for all time.

How gracious of God to give believers a perfect standing before him.

We know the bias toward sin that is within us (Romans 7:14–25). We know that we suffer guilt and shame over our actions. However, we can rest in the truth that when we accept the work of Christ on our behalf we are declared right with God and are clothed in Jesus righteousness, even while God continues the work of making us holy (Romans 3:22; Ephesians 4:24, 6:14; Philippians 1:6, 11).

How does God's promise that you have been perfected cause you to think about your salvation? Though you stand before God in Christ's righteousness, what unrighteous things is God removing from your life as he continues to make you holy?

God, I thank you that your Word and your Spirit testify to me that I am yours, and will be forever, because I have been perfected by the blood of Christ. Please break my heart over the sins in my life that break yours. Cause me to be a person who desires holiness in all things.

DECEMBER 20

Hebrews 11–12

Therefore, since we are surrounded by such a huge crowd of
witnesses to the life of faith, let us strip off every weight that slows
us down, especially the sin that so easily hinders our progress.
—Hebrews 12:1a,b

By faith Abel, Enoch, Noah, Abraham, Sarah, Isaac, Jacob, Joseph,
Moses' parents, Moses, the people of Israel, Rahab, and many others live
their lives fully trusting God's promise. They never abandon their faith;
they choose to believe God. These faithful ones die without receiving all
that God promised; they only see from a distance. God's evaluation of
them and their faith is that the world is not worthy of them.

How gracious of God to encourage present believers through
the lives of past believers.

Living for God is not easy today, but then again, has it ever been?
Is life any different today than five thousand years ago? Believers
have always been different, and will always be different from the
world, and they will be persecuted because of that (John 15:19; 1
Thessalonians 3:3–4; 1 Peter 4:12).

As we read this list of faithful believers, we may wonder if our
faith will endure persecution. God promises us that our true faith
will endure (John 10:27–30; Philippians 1:6). Amazingly, you and
I will be the examples of faith for future generations.

Who has God used to encourage your faith? How is he using
you to encourage someone else? What confidence does this give you
in the face of suffering?

> Heavenly Father, please convict my heart of the sin that
> hinders me so that I can cast it off. I want to run the race
> in a way that honors those who have gone before me and
> encourages the next generation as they follow you.

DECEMBER 21

Hebrews 13; 1 Peter 1:1–2:3

And now, may the God of peace, who brought again
from the dead our Lord Jesus, equip you with all you
need for doing his will. May he produce in you, through
the power of Jesus Christ, all that is pleasing to him.
—Hebrews 13:20–21a

The writer to the Hebrews exhorts Christians to love each other, to show hospitality to strangers, and to remember those in prison. He tells them to be faithful and honor one another in marriage. He commands them to be satisfied with what they have because God will never fail them. He warns them to stay away from strange and new ideas about Christ Jesus. He exhorts them to obey their spiritual leaders joyfully and he asks for their prayers.

How gracious of God to equip his people to live holy and productive lives.

This passage tells us that we are equipped to do what we are commanded to do: to love the Lord with all our hearts, souls, bodies, and minds (Matthew 22:37–38), to believe on the Lord Jesus Christ (1 John 3:23), and to serve others (Galatians 5:13). For believers, as we let go of sin, we experience the power that is the deity of the Lord Jesus Christ. Holding on to sin prevents us from experiencing the equipping and power of God.

To what is God calling you? Do you believe that God has already equipped you to accomplish whatever he is calling you to do?

God, I confess there are times when I live in fear because I fail to trust you. Please teach me to live in the assurance of your power and your equipping. I know this as knowledge; please help me to know it as experience.

DECEMBER 22

1 Peter 2:4–5:11

For you are a chosen people. You are a kingdom of
priests, God's holy nation, his very own possession. This
is so you can show others the goodness of God, for he
called you out of darkness into his wonderful light.
—1 Peter 2:9b

Peter, writing from Rome, tells Christians that they are not like
unbelievers: they are God's chosen possession. Peter tells them to
keep away from evil desires that fight against their souls, to live
carefully and visibly honorable among their unbelieving neighbors,
to show respect for everyone, to love their Christian brothers and
sisters, to accept authority, and to fear God. Peter warns them to be
on guard against the Devil who prowls around like a roaring lion,
looking for a victim to devour.

How gracious of God to call his chosen ones out of darkness and
into his wonderful light.

We have all experienced the darkness of deceit and disobedience,
destruction and disappointment (Psalm 107:10–16). It is a thick,
overwhelming, and all-consuming darkness. However, it isn't an
impenetrable darkness (John 1:4–5). God's goodness, shining
through his glorious Word and through the lives of his children,
brings light into the darkness.

How is God using your life to shine his goodness into someone
else's darkness? What would God have you do today to show his
goodness to someone at work? at school? in the nursing home? in the
barracks? at the park? in the neighborhood? or at church?

God, I know the only way I can shine your goodness is to
stop trying to shine my own. Please help me to stop living
for myself and rather live the life that you have called me to
live, so that many people will see your goodness!

DECEMBER 23

1 Peter 5:12–14; 2 Peter 1–3

> Above all, you must understand that no prophecy in
> Scripture ever came from the prophets themselves or
> because they wanted to prophesy. It was the Holy Spirit
> who moved the prophets to speak from God.
> —2 Peter 1:20–21

The Lord shows Peter that Peter is soon to die. Peter wants believers to remember that he never made up clever stories: he saw Jesus with his own eyes and heard God's voice. His confidence is in the message of the prophets who, moved by the Holy Spirit, spoke from God. Peter exhorts believers to pay close attention to the prophets' message of the Lord's return. False teachers will laugh at what they don't understand and scoffers will taunt, but the Lord has a purpose in his delay.

How gracious of God to give his enduring Word for all people of all time.

As we listen to teachers and preachers, we must be vigilant regarding the truth and pray for discernment. God's Word tells us there will be false prophets that will lead many astray by their evil teaching and shameful immorality (1 Timothy 4:1–5). The motivation of these false teachers is greed and yet they will try to cover it with lies. Woe to us if we become an easy target for deception because we are not sufficiently saturated in God's Word.

What do you read most: the Scriptures written by God's prophets and apostles, or books about the Scriptures written by ordinary men? Why? At what cost?

> Almighty God, I ask you to give me wisdom through your
> Holy Spirit as I read your Word. I ask for guidance to choose
> wise commentaries and for discernment to know when I am
> reading a lie.

DECEMBER 24

1 John 1:1–4:6

These people left our churches because they never really
belonged with us; otherwise they would have stayed with us.
When they left us, it proved that they do not belong with us.
—1 John 2:19

The Apostle John writes about the truths that he has seen and heard.
His testimony is in Jesus, who is eternal life. He writes to people
whose sins are forgiven, who are mature because they know Christ,
who have won their battle with Satan, who know the Father, and
who are strong with God's Word living in their hearts. He calls
them to live faithfully to what they have been taught; to continue
living in fellowship with the Son and with the Father, and in that
fellowship to enjoy God's promised eternal life. He tells them how
to know they belong to God: they will live obediently and they will
love other Christians.

How gracious of God to lead his children in the truth.

When someone who has lived publicly as a Christian denounces
the faith, it causes us to question our own faith. If others can we lose
their faith, can we lose ours? Have we been deceived? God's Word
tells us the truth: true believers stick. Anyone who can walk away
was never really a believer. This passage gives us confidence that God
who called us will hold us until the very end (Philippians 1:6, Jude
1:24, John 10:4, 9, 14, 27–30).

Have you received Jesus as your Savior? Are you confident in his
ability to hold you?

> God, I believe that you are the one in whom truth dwells;
> that there is no darkness in you. I believe that your Holy
> Spirit living in me is the sufficient guarantee of my eternal
> inheritance.

DECEMBER 25

1 John 4:7–5:21; 2 John 1; 3 John 1

God showed how much he loved us by sending his only Son
into the world so that we might have eternal life through him.
—1 John 4:9

John writes to assure believers that they belong to God. Previously
John contrasted obedience and disobedience, in this passage he
contrasts love and hate: love comes from God. Anyone who loves is
born of God and knows God. But anyone who does not love does
not know God—for God is love. It is not that we loved God, but
that he loved us and sent his Son as a sacrifice to take away our sins.
Therefore, if we love each other, God lives in us, and his love has
been brought to full expression through us.

How gracious of God to love the world so much that he sent his
one and only Son so that whoever believes in him will have eternal
life (John 3:16).

The baby in the manger and the man on the cross are the same
man: Jesus (Matthew 13:54–56). He is the one who existed from the
beginning (John 1:1). He is eternal life (John 17:3). To believe in the
Son is to accept that Jesus humbled himself, took on humanity and
subjected himself to death on a cross for your sin: this is eternal life
(Romans 6:23; Philippians 2:6–11).

Have you received God's gift of love? Will you, today, enter into
an assurance of eternal salvation through the sacrifice of Jesus on
your behalf?

Glorious God of Love and Mercy: thank you for the gift
of Jesus, the baby in the manger, my Savior on the cross.
Thank you for the gift of eternal life through Jesus, my
Lord and my King.

DECEMBER 26

> I must write ... urging you to defend the truth
> of the Good News. God gave this unchanging
> truth once for all time to his holy people.
> —Jude 1:3b, c

Jude urges believers to contend for the faith against false teachers who claim authority from their dreams and infiltrate the ranks of believers. Though not unexpected, their arrival causes division. Jude commands those who are called to live in the love of God the Father and the care of Jesus Christ to remember what the apostles of our Lord Jesus Christ told them: that in the last times there would be scoffers; and now they are here. However, believers are to continue building their lives on the foundation of their holy faith.

How gracious of God to give to his people a foundation of unchanging truth.

We believe that the gospel that Jude taught is the same gospel that saves today (Romans 1:16–17). There is no salvation apart from Jesus Christ, the eternal Word (John 1:1; Acts 4:12). The glorious truth is that the Bible is God's Word and it presents the same gospel: salvation by grace through faith in Jesus Christ (Luke 16:16–17; Ephesians 2:8). Our responsibility, as Jude said, is to contend for the gospel without being contentious.

Are you living your life on the foundation of the Bible? Are you prepared to lovingly, and amiably, share with anyone who asks the unchanging truth of God?

> Father, I love your Word, your gospel, the faith that you have created in me, and I love the great salvation that is mine through Christ Jesus. Help me to contend for the gospel whenever an opportunity arises, and keep me from becoming contentious in my zeal to protect and uphold your True Word.

DECEMBER 27

Revelation 3–6

Go back to what you heard and believed at first;
hold to it firmly and turn to me again.
—Revelation 3:3a

John sees the glorious and victorious risen Christ, the King of kings and Lord of lords in a vision of destruction and judgment, of salvation and restoration. John hears Jesus's messages for the churches: both commendation and warning. John records the vision and messages. Jesus calls the churches to return to him, to stand firm, to repent, and to hold tightly to the truth.

How gracious of God to extend the gift of repentance, and the choice of life or death, victory or defeat, until Christ returns.

There is always an opportunity to repent until time runs out; unfortunately, we don't know when that will be (1 Peter 3:7–9). There is no guarantee of tomorrow. There is no promise we will survive today. The Lord could return at any moment; we know his return will not be expected (Matthew 24:36–41). To delay making a decision to receive Jesus as Savior is to fight against Jesus—the one who is the ultimate Victor (Isaiah 63:1–3).

What have you chosen? Life or death? Victory or defeat?

> Almighty God, I thank you for choosing me and extending to me the gift of repentance and salvation. I know that my victory is in Jesus. I know that in him I can overcome the daily sins that distract me and keep me from living victoriously. Please reveal to me the sin that is winning in my heart today, and the unconfessed sin of my past, so that I can lay it before you for cleansing. May my life reflect the victory that is mine through Christ Jesus my gracious Savior and my victorious King.

DECEMBER 28

> After this I saw a vast crowd, too great to count, from
> every nation and tribe and people and language, standing
> in front of the throne and before the Lamb.
> —Revelation 7:9

John sees a vision of God's throne surrounded by angels and elders and a vast crowd clothed in white celebrating the salvation of God that comes through Jesus! John experiences a vision of worship and adoration of God. He sees the martyred souls of believers clothed in the righteousness of their Savior. He sees the Lord Jesus Christ, their Shepherd, living among them.

How gracious of God to include people of every race, ethnicity, age, culture, language, skin color, gender, and all other distinctions into his family.

We know that whoever wants to be a disciple of Jesus may do so (Mark 8:34–38). Salvation is a gift of grace but it comes with a great cost: the cost of dying to our own selfish ambitions and submitting in wholehearted obedience to Jesus (Luke 14:27; Ephesians 2:8–10). There is nothing outside of our hearts that prevents us from coming to Jesus and being adopted into the family of God (Hebrews 4:6–8; Galatians 4:4–7).

Who needs to hear your testimony of how God brought you, an unworthy sinner into his family as his child? For whom do you need to pray? To whom could you introduce Jesus today?

God, when I look at who I was apart from you, it amazes me that you chose me and saved me. Because I know how unworthy I am, far be it from me to think of excluding anyone from hearing the good news of salvation through Jesus Christ my Lord. Please remove any prejudice that resides in me, and help me to see everyone as you do: sinners in need of a Savior.

DECEMBER 29

"Fear God," he shouted. "Give glory to him. For the time
has come when he will sit as judge. Worship him who made
heaven and earth, the sea, and all the springs of water."
—Revelation 14:7

John's vision continues: he sees Jesus, the Lamb, standing on Mount
Zion. He sees a great choir singing new songs before the throne
of God. He sees angels flying through the heavens carrying the
everlasting gospel to the world. He hears the angels proclaiming to
the people to worship God. He sees the destruction of those who
refuse to worship God.

How gracious of God to give the choice to all humankind to
worship or reject God.

God won't force anyone to choose him or to worship him;
however, everyone will be held accountable for their choice and
both choices have consequences. God will judge both believers and
unbelievers. Believers will be judged for the works done while in
the body for which they will receive rewards (2 Timothy 4:8; 2
Corinthians 5:10). Unbelievers will be judged for their sin, for which
they will be condemned to eternal destruction (2 Thessalonians 1:5–
10). Either Christ Jesus carried our sin on the cross, or we bear it alone
before God at the judgment (1 Peter 2:24). Every person must choose
and what we choose will dictate how we live, eternally worshiping
God or eternally separated from him in horrifying darkness.

Are you prepared to face God at the judgment seat?

> O God, how I long for the day when I will sing before
> your presence in worship and adoration! Thank you for the
> promise that there is no condemnation for me as I stand in
> Christ Jesus, that my sins were judged at the cross, and I
> stand justified before your throne.

DECEMBER 30

Revelation 15–18

*Take note: I will come as unexpectedly as a thief! Blessed
are all who are watching for me, who keep their robes ready
so they will not need to walk naked and ashamed.*
—Revelation 16:15

John sees God's tabernacle opened wide and filled with God's glory
and power! He sees terrible destruction poured out upon the earth
and unbelievers at the end of time. In the midst of John's vision, Jesus
gives a warning and a promise: his return is unexpected, therefore,
believers must be vigilant and ready!

How gracious of God to both promise and warn that Jesus will
come again!

We don't know when the day or hour will be, but we do know
that Christ will return and when he does he will come with judgment
(1 Thessalonians 5:1–11). It is a warning to heed, for when Christ
returns everything will be laid bare (2 Peter 3:10). Unbelievers
will stand naked before God with nothing to cover their sin and
shame (Revelation 3:18). Believers, however, clothed in Christ's
righteousness will bear no shame because he bore it in our place on
the cross (Isaiah 61:10; Romans 10:11; 1 Peter 2:6).

Have you taken note? Do you expect Jesus to return any day? Are
you watching? Have you received the robe of Jesus's righteousness
in which to stand? Or will you be naked, with every sin exposed?

> Heavenly Father, I am living in expectation! I am the child
> who is continually peering through the window and looking
> out the door in anticipation of my Savior's return. My robe
> is ready, I am covered by the blood of Jesus; I stand in his
> righteousness alone!

DECEMBER 31

Revelation 19–22

And the one sitting on the throne said, "Look, I am making all things new!" And then he said to me, "Write this down, for what I tell you is trustworthy and true." And he also said, "It is finished! I am the Alpha and the Omega—the Beginning and the End."
—Revelation 21:5, 6a

John's vision ends with the glorious reality of a new heaven and a new earth. The Devil is cast into the lake of fire for all eternity. The dead arise to stand before the Great White Throne of judgment. Unbelievers are cast into the lake of fire. Believers, the church—those whose names are written in the Book of Life—will live with God for all eternity.

How gracious of God to accomplish his perfect plan to redeem all humanity and the earth.

When God speaks it, it is accomplished (Genesis 1:3). Even though we have not yet experienced this reality in history, it is finished in eternity. Death dies. Life reigns.

Jesus is coming soon, will you be with him? Have you washed your filthy robe of sin in the cleansing blood of the Lamb? Have you come to the Living Water to quench your thirst for righteousness? Have you come to the Bread of Life to satisfy the hunger of your soul? Have you come to the Light of the World to illuminate your spirit and mind?

Will you come!

Oh God, I will see your face! Your name is written on my forehead! Your light shines on me and I will reign with you forever and forever. What a glorious day that will be. What a glorious God you are! Your word is true. Your grace saves. Your love endures forever. Amen and Amen.

Printed in the United States
By Bookmasters